"*Grand Central Question* is a very informed and well-written tour of important worldview topics. The book's unique strength resides in its fruitful interaction with Islam. I highly recommend it."

J. P. Moreland, distinguished professor of philosophy, Talbot School of Theology, Biola University, and author of *Love Your God with All Your Mind*

"Everyone in the world knows something is wrong and in need of fixing. Abdu Murray's stirring account of his conversion from Islam to Christianity, and his earnest engagement with people of other worldviews, will help you quickly identify the pressing questions each worldview is attempting to answer and see how Christ is the one true answer."

Jeff Myers, president, Summit Ministries

"An attorney by training, Abdu Murray keenly recognizes, as Jesus' own ministry unveiled, that often there is a deeper question and motive behind a question, and 'until the heart is open, the ears remain closed.' He soberly reminds us that truth is costly—and sometimes it costs us dearly, as Abdu's own journey reveals. Here you will find a wise and gentle voice who truly understands the doubter and skeptic. Abdu has wrestled with the claims of truth made by many worldviews and shows how the gospel is utterly unique and beautiful. I enthusiastically recommend his work."

Ravi Zacharias, author and speaker

"Outstanding! My friend Abdu Murray, an attorney and former Muslim, uses his razor-sharp intellect to analyze the big questions addressed by various worldviews—and explains why Christianity offers the most satisfying answers. Written with compassion and keen insight, this book will both equip Christians and bring clarity to the spiritually curious."

Lee Strobel, professor of Christian thought, Houston Baptist University, and author of *The Case for Christ*

"I have long awaited a book such as this, which gives a sensitive but critical hearing to the major world and life views and which then also engages them in the light of the gospel. This is a very good book, and although there are others of this genre, it is quite unique, as it shows the skill of a well-honed mind—one which demonstrates both compassion and critical thinking, and one which, above all, leads us to compare and contrast competing answers to essential questions. Abdu is uniquely qualified to offer this critique, with his background in law, his history with Islam, and his experience as a father, a husband and an honest seeker. This book will help many, and I highly recommend it, especially for those who need good reasons for any belief."

Stuart McAllister, regional director of the Americas, Ravi Zacharias International Ministries

"*Grand Central Question* is fantastic! I am so impressed at both the personal experience and depth of study that Abdu brings to the table. He takes the biggest life questions and provides insightful, provocative answers. I am thrilled and honored to endorse a book that will equip and challenge so many people."

Sean McDowell, speaker, educator and author of *Is God Just a Human Invention?*

"I like this book for two major reasons. In these pages, Abdu examines the major worldviews fairly and provides a fresh approach to showing how the Christian gospel best answers worldview questions pertaining to value, purpose, suffering and the greatness of God. Moreover, Abdu is a former practicing Muslim and attorney who has successfully field-tested in public forums the ideas presented in this book. So, readers are receiving content that is as sound and practical as it is interesting. An enjoyable read!"

Michael R. Licona, associate professor of theology, Houston Baptist University

"Abdu Murray's *Grand Central Question* is a practical, powerful guide to the explanatory value of the Christian faith, both intellectually and practically. This book contains helpful personal illustrations, very telling quotations, and real-life dialogues with Muslims, atheists and advocates of other worldviews that will make us wiser in proclaiming and defending the gospel of Christ."

Paul Copan, professor and Pledger Family Chair of Philosophy and Ethics, Palm Beach Atlantic University

"Applying several fundamental questions, Murray works his way through a number of philosophical and religious stances in an effort to ascertain the best basis for how we believe and behave. What grounds the atheist's good behavior? Should pain have a purpose, and should grief be accompanied by hope, or are both simply meaningless struggles? Does holding that reality is only an illusion make life hurt any less? Still, Murray is at his best when examining Islam, a belief system which he embraced for most of his life. Citing the Qur'an frequently, he shows how contemporary Muslim responses differ from what the Qur'an itself teaches. The overall affect is that of a volume that clearly shows that Christianity is well grounded, unlike other systems."

Gary R. Habermas, Distinguished Research Professor and chair, Department of Philosophy, Liberty University

"If comfort is more important to you than truth, you're going to be made uncomfortable by *Grand Central Question*. No matter what you believe about God, former Muslim Abdu Murray will show you convincingly that the answers to everyone's deepest questions lead right to the foot of Christ's cross. Thankfully, ultimate comfort is free to all those who will follow the truth where it leads!"

Frank Turek, coauthor of *I Don't Have Enough Faith to Be an Atheist*

GRAND
CENTRAL
QUESTION

Answering the Critical Concerns of the Major Worldviews

ABDU H. MURRAY
FOREWORD BY JOSH McDOWELL

IVP Books

An imprint of InterVarsity Press
Downers Grove, Illinois

InterVarsity Press
P.O. Box 1400, Downers Grove, IL 60515-1426
World Wide Web: www.ivpress.com
Email: email@ivpress.com

InterVarsity Press® is the book-publishing division of InterVarsity Christian Fellowship/USA®, a movement of students and faculty active on campus at hundreds of universities, colleges and schools of nursing in the United States of America, and a member movement of the International Fellowship of Evangelical Students. For information about local and regional activities, write Public Relations Dept., InterVarsity Christian Fellowship/USA, 6400 Schroeder Rd., P.O. Box 7895, Madison, WI 53707-7895, or visit the IVCF website at www.intervarsity.org.

Scripture quotations, unless otherwise noted, are from The Holy Bible, English Standard Version, *copyright © 2001 by Crossway Bibles, a division of Good News Publishers. Used by permission. All rights reserved.*

Unless otherwise noted, all Qu'ran quotations are taken from Abdullah Yusuf Ali, The Holy Qur'an: Translation and Commentary *(Damascus: Ouloom AlQuran, 1934).*

While all stories in this book are true, some names and identifying information in this book have been changed to protect the privacy of the individuals involved.

Design: Cindy Kiple
Interior design: Beth Hagenberg
Images: crushed white paper: © dbabbage/iStockphoto
       trains: © Leontura/iStockphoto

ISBN 978-0-8308-3665-9 (print)
ISBN 978-0-8308-9621-9 (digital)

Printed in the United States of America ♾

Library of Congress Cataloging-in-Publication Data

Murray, Abdu.
  Grand central question : answering the critical concerns of the major
worldviews / Abdu H. Murray.
    pages cm
  Includes bibliographical references.
  ISBN 978-0-8308-3665-9 (pbk. : alk. paper)
  1. Christianity and other religions. 2. Religions. I. Title.
  BR127.M87 2014
  261.2—dc23

                                                                2014003605

| P | 18 | 17 | 16 | 15 | 14 | 13 | 12 | 11 | 10 | 9 | 8 | 7 | 6 | | |
| Y | 29 | 28 | 27 | 26 | 25 | 24 | 23 | 22 | 21 | 20 | 19 | 18 | 17 | 16 |

For all those who labor for answers that
touch the heart and stir the mind.

CONTENTS

FOREWORD

If you care about the truth, this book is for you. I say that regardless of whether you're a Christian or a non-Christian.

Here's why I'm so confident about that. For more than fifty years, I've been talking to people all over the world about ultimate truth. I've spoken to big audiences at packed arenas; I've lectured at meetings of political and business leaders; and I've spoken to waiters, cab drivers and hotel staff members. No matter how different people are and no matter what their walk of life or profession, they all have questions about ultimate truth. The nuances in those questions can be as different as the people asking, but the substance of those questions is similar.

People are looking for answers to the deepest questions in life. Some think that they have found the answers in a particular worldview or religion, but many are still looking. Maybe their worldview gives them answers to only some of their questions. Maybe it doesn't even get that far. The point is, they are looking. This book, *Grand Central Question*, is meant both for the people looking for those answers and for those who want to know how to provide the answers lovingly and intelligently.

When sincere seekers ask for answers to challenging questions, many Christians are left without much to say. It's frustrating that Christians have the most important things to say about the most important questions in life, yet they're often silent because they're timid, frustrated or overly cautious about engaging with someone about difficult issues. Some Christians might be timid because they think they don't know how to answer tough questions or how to articulate the answers persuasively. They might be frustrated because they feel they don't know enough about a questioner's background or worldview to be able to talk to him. And some Christians might be so afraid of offending someone by saying that Jesus is the only way to God that they never actually say anything.

But people deserve to be told Jesus' message in a persuasive way. In *Grand Central Question*, Abdu has provided us with a way to get around those barriers to sharing the truth. This book aims at both the heart and the mind when it presents biblically centered answers to the fundamental questions we've all had.

That's how I know that this book is for you. If you're a Christian, *Grand Central Question* will give you the confidence, understanding and method to be able to offer profound answers to significant questions. If you're not a Christian, and you want to know if the gospel has anything to offer that will not only satisfy your intellectual quest but also be relevant to your life, you'll find these answers clearly articulated in *Grand Central Question*.

I recommend this book to you because of the way Abdu has blended questions of the mind with issues of the heart. He has done his homework, and he's pulled no punches in comparing the major worldviews with the answers provided by the gospel of Jesus Christ. But he's done so with winsomeness and understanding. You see, Abdu wasn't raised in the church. He spent most of his life as a Muslim. In his effort to spread the message of Islam, he tested the claims that other worldviews made, including atheism, Eastern religions, Islam and Christianity. He put them all to the test, and at the end of the day, he found that the Christian faith stood up to the challenges. He found that the gospel didn't just give emotional answers. And he found that it didn't just provide intellectual answers. He found that it was worth believing because the intellectual answers it provided to the toughest questions were emotionally satisfying.

Abdu's experience as a lawyer and his knowledge of real-life observation have allowed him to do two things in writing *Grand Central Question*. First, he has kept the perspective of what it's like to be a non-Christian investigating Christianity and dealing with Christians. That's no small thing. If you're a Christian, your witness for Christ is made better when you know what the person you are talking with is going through or is thinking about. Abdu presents the material in this book in a way that puts you in the mindset of the truth seeker so you can present the gospel with credibility. If you're not a Christian, you'll find that Abdu has taken the time to understand what you think about Christians and Christianity as you explore what it has to offer. He knows what it's like to ask the hard questions. He knows what it's like to not necessarily be thrilled when you find these answers, because sometimes the truth hurts. And Abdu knows what it is like to take the plunge and embrace the truth despite the pain. He knows it's worth it.

Second, Abdu's experience and research, both in dealing with followers of every worldview and from his background as a former Muslim, allow him to get right to the heart of the answers different groups are looking for and how the gospel can give those answers. By getting to the core issues, *Grand Central Question* gives us answers that speak to people of many different worldviews without requiring us to have a doctorate in comparative religions to do so. Abdu has cut right to the issues that secular humanists care about. He has examined the heart of what pantheists think is ultimately important. He has fairly and compassionately demonstrated what Muslims strive for in trying to submit to God. Abdu has validated their searches, and he has validated their questions. But he offers the gospel's answers as the best and, in fact, the only answers to those questions.

I highly recommend that you read this book from start to finish. Don't skip the prologue. If you miss what Abdu says there, you'll miss something critical to understanding how everyone struggles with the questions that matter most and how the truth can get lost in the struggle. But once you've read the prologue, you can jump to any major part of the book. If you want to try to understand Muslims, jump to part 3. If you are trying to understand what pantheists are concerned with and how the gospel addresses that concern, dive into part 2. And if secular humanist issues concern you, by all means, start at part 1.

But I urge you to read the entire book, and here's why: If a worldview is true, it should answer all of life's fundamental and central questions coherently. By the time you turn the last page of this book, you'll see how Abdu has shown that the gospel is the worldview that does that.

It's rare to read a book that blends uncompromising conviction with compassion and understanding. When there's too much emphasis on conviction, the truth may sound obnoxious and repulsive. But if there's too much emphasis on compassion, we wind up saying nothing because we're afraid to hurt feelings. In the pages of this book, Abdu has balanced conviction and compassion because he has the right attitude. He addresses ideas while respecting people. That's how I know this book is for you.

If you are a Christian and you want to learn how to share your faith confidently, this book is for you. If you're not a Christian, but you've been looking for the answers that will stimulate your mind and inspire your heart, this book is for you too.

Josh McDowell
Author and speaker

WHAT TRUTH COSTS—WHAT TRUTH IS WORTH

His illness was grave, a heart condition as I recall, and he was facing a risky medical procedure. He had been in the hospital for several days before I was invited to visit him. Probably in his midfifties, he was alone in the United States as he waited for his children to arrive from the Middle East. He was no longer married, either because his wife had passed away or because they were divorced. But regardless, he was alone.

And afraid.

A woman who had heard me speak about Islam and my journey from Islam to Christ invited me to visit the man and share the gospel with him. She served as a Christian chaplain at the hospital and had stopped in to ask the man if he needed any spiritual support. He told her that he was a Muslim, and they struck up a conversation about their respective faiths and their opinions about Jesus. As their conversation progressed, his questions became increasingly difficult to answer, and the fact that English was his second language didn't help. Having heard me talk about the evidence for the Christian faith and how it factored so heavily in my own conversion from Islam, she thought of me and asked the man if I could visit him to address his questions. He agreed, and she called me straightaway.

Before I knew it, I was riding up an elevator smelling of disinfectant to share Christ with a man I had never met. As the elevator doors opened on his floor, I expected to face many of the same challenges I myself had put to Christians who shared the gospel with me. Little did I realize that the usual intellectual and theological questions that Muslims lodge against the gospel would not be the main topic of our discussion. Instead, I would be reminded of something far more profound.

The harsh lights of his hospital room greeted us as my wife and I walked in at the chaplain's invitation. She smiled and made our introductions. Despite his illness, the several tubes sticking out of him and the always-embarrassing hospital gown, the Muslim man exhibited quintessential Arab hospitality as he sat up to greet us, grasping my hand, saying "Marhaba"—hello in Arabic. I sat down next to his bed, and we made small talk. Soon, however, the conversation turned to the main reason for my visit. "So," he began, "I understand that you used to be Muslim and may be able to answer some of my questions about Christianity."

"Well, I guess we'll find out," I responded. "What questions do you have?"

And with that, he began. To be sure, he provided many of the usual questions Muslims ask about Jesus, the Bible and the gospel. Isn't the Trinity polytheistic? Hasn't the Bible been corrupted over time? How could God become a man and die a humiliating death on a cross? They were all objections I used to lodge against Christianity ad infinitum. Taking the questions at face value, I began to address them one by one.

I provided philosophical, theological, historical and scriptural answers to his questions, and he was a bit more open to them than most Muslims—but only a bit. As he offered up the usual rejoinders, I answered them. But still he was coolly resistant, stony even. In fact, with every answer, he became stonier and stonier. Frankly I was getting discouraged and somewhat frustrated, so I paused and turned things toward a different topic: his family.

His children were all he really had left. Having heard that their father was ill, his sons and daughters were making arrangements to fly to the States to see him. And when talk turned to his children, the first crack in his stony veneer appeared. His lip quivered just a bit, ever so slightly, but it was there. "Your children mean a lot to you, don't they?" I asked.

"They are all I have in this life," he answered in his heavy accent. "Without them, I may die in this country alone."

"Do you believe that God is with you? That he cares about you and wants you to know him?"

"I believe that he is everywhere. But I'm not sure that I can ever know him," he said. "God is too great for mere humans to know." That is a belief many Muslims have, which is why this dear man was afraid that without his children he would die alone. It was so sad, yet so profound. I let his disclosure hover in the room a moment as I prayed for guidance about the next thing to say. And then it occurred to me.

I gathered up whatever boldness I was capable of and began the part of our conversation that really mattered. "We've been talking for some time now about the answers to your questions about the gospel. But can I ask you a personal question?"

"Please. Go ahead," he answered, sounding more confident than his eyes suggested.

I swallowed hard and asked the question I feared might derail the discussion for good. "What would happen if you did become a Christian? What would your kids think or do?"

His eyes lowered as a slight sigh left his lungs. "They would disown me. It is unforgivable and a shame for me to become Christian."

I knew that fear all too well. I had to face the possibility of such losses when I was wrestling with (and even against) the answers that Christianity offered to my toughest questions. "I know what it's like to have to face that kind of rejection. I also know that the possibility of losing the people you love the most is a powerful reason to close your ears to the answers the gospel provides."

The historical evidence, the philosophical and theological arguments—none of them—broke through the man's stony veneer like the words I had just spoken. A tear escaped his eyes and rolled down his cheek. "Thank you," he said, surprising me. "Thank you for understanding that I might lose everything if I even consider what you are saying."

Though our conversation did not last much longer, the tenor changed dramatically from that moment on. After realizing that it was not the gospel itself that he had difficulty with, but the possible consequences of accepting it, he began to ask me follow-up questions instead of just lobbing rejoinders.

And then a minor miracle happened. Some Muslims will not even touch a Bible, fearing that it is an unclean corruption that pollutes them. But this Muslim man, having realized where his real difficulty lay, asked to keep the Arabic Bible I had in my hand. I gave it to him, put my hand on his shoulder and said, "Allah Ma'ak, Amu," which means "God be with you, uncle." (Arabs call male elders, even strangers, "uncle" as a sign of respect.)

THE TROUBLE WITH TRUTH

As my wife and I walked into the hallway, I was reminded of the sober reality that truth has a cost. That cost may vary from person to person and from circumstance to circumstance, but there is no doubt that truth is costly.

My conversation with the Muslim man in the hospital punctuates this point in an important way. It shows us that while we often say that we love truth or that truth is important, we seldom actually mean what we say. Some years ago, I read a line from Judith Viorst's play *Love and Shrimp* that humorously highlights our dance with and around the truth.

> I made him swear he'd always tell me nothing but the truth
> I promised him I never would resent it
> No matter how unbearable, how harsh, how cruel
> How come he thought I meant it?[1]

While whimsical, these words remind us how duplicitously we can act when it comes to truth. We can offer platitudes to imply we want the truth, no matter what it may mean, but we seldom act accordingly.

The famed thinker and writer C. S. Lewis was an atheist who eventually bowed his knee to Christ after being confronted with the credibility of the gospel. In his own words, Lewis was "the most dejected and reluctant convert in all England" when he finally gave his life to Jesus.[2] In the opening pages of his classic work *Mere Christianity*, Lewis makes an insightful comment about the tension between our pursuit of truth and our desire for comfort: "If you look for truth, you may find comfort in the end: if you look for comfort, you will not get either comfort or truth—only soft soap and wishful thinking to begin with and, in the end, despair."[3]

We know this deep within ourselves, do we not? We tend to take the path of least resistance. But when we do, we find that although that path provided the least resistance, we found plenty of resistance at the destination. Yet, time and again, we opt for comfort over truth. The tendency to sacrifice truth for comfort seems practically hardwired into our psyches. In saying this, I need look no further than my own past to see how often I sacrificed truth on the altar of my own comfort. As a Muslim, I did not want to admit that the gospel was true, that Jesus is who the Bible claims he is, because doing so would cost me dearly.

The cost of truth is quite plain and easy to grasp as a concept. It is the emotional barrier or personal bias that prevents a person from sincerely considering whether his worldview might be false and another worldview might be true. Though the concept is quite easy to understand, the consequences are quite easy to overlook. Lest we chalk our resistance to truth up to just pride or stubbornness, I suggest we look at history to see examples of just how high the cost of truth is.

Consider the most famous trial in history: Jesus of Nazareth standing before Pontius Pilate, the Roman governor of Judea. Jesus had been brought before Pilate on charges of blasphemy and of making himself a king over and above Caesar. Ironically, it was not Jesus who was really on trial, but Pilate. The Roman governor was face to face with the very One who claimed to be Truth Incarnate, "the way, and the truth, and the life" (John 14:6). And Pilate's reaction to the truth was being put to the test.

> Therefore Pilate said to Him, "So You are a king?" Jesus answered, "You say *correctly* that I am a king. For this I have been born, and for this I have come into the world, to testify to the truth. Everyone who is of the truth hears My voice."
> Pilate said to Him, "What is truth?" And when he had said this, he went out. (John 18:37-38 NASB)

Pilate asked the most important question he could have asked in light of Jesus' statement equating his voice with truth. Pilate, the pagan Roman politician, had asked the Author of truth—Truth Incarnate—to describe truth for him. But he squandered the opportunity. He did not want an answer. He merely asked the question as a sarcastic, rhetorical device, having become fed up with the whole process. Pilate asked the right question but with the wrong motive. And it was because of the cost of truth.

The Gospel of Matthew provides further detail about how powerful the cost of truth was in this encounter. Matthew records that the night before Pilate's encounter with Jesus, his wife had a dream about Jesus. It so disturbed her that she went to her husband the day of the trial to warn him (Matthew 27:19). But Pilate did not listen. He feared that the crowd might flare out of control if he did not hand Jesus over to be crucified (vv. 23-24). Pilate was concerned not with Jesus' innocence or the truth of his claims; he was concerned only with the consequences of his decision to condemn or not condemn Jesus, regardless of the truth of the matter. He was too preoccupied with the cost of truth to see reality as it was. Is it not the irony of ironies that Pilate stood before someone claiming to be Truth Incarnate—who had just told him that if one recognizes truth, one recognizes his very voice—and yet Pilate failed to consider the matter sincerely because the consequences terrified him?

AN EQUAL OPPORTUNITY DISCOURAGER

Though Pilate's response to truth was dismal, we shouldn't rush to deem ourselves to be superior, lest we judge hypocritically. I certainly have no room to do so. I can recall my own situation, having been a proud Muslim my whole life only to be confronted with the evidence for the gospel, yet wanting so desperately to deny it. My mind had accepted the overwhelming evidence establishing Jesus' claims to be God's Son and the Savior of the world through the cross. But I allowed that truth to be eclipsed by the looming losses I might suffer if I chose a life for Christ. Identity, close relationships, community, even safety—all were at risk if I followed Jesus. And the cost was just too much to bear, leading me to years of indecision and despair.

So many have shared their painful stories of rejection when they turned from their worldview to the gospel. Jewish friends who have embraced Jesus as the Messiah share how their families and communities cast them out, how their parents shouted with tears in their eyes, "You've betrayed us!" or "You're killing Judaism!" In his book *New Birth or Rebirth? Jesus Talks with Krishna*, Ravi Zacharias recounts the true story of Subramaniam, a man born into the highest caste of orthodox Hindu priests, and how his family and community threatened his life when he chose to follow Christ.[4] Interesting, is it not, that even Hindus, who hold to a religion that claims to be tolerant and inclusive, can suddenly become incredibly intolerant and exclusive when one of their own gives his life to Christ?

And Zacharias, himself a native-born Indian Christian from a Hindu Brahmin heritage, goes on to observe that "when a westerner is attracted to Eastern spirituality, the East claims credit for having had the answers all along. But should an easterner be attracted to Christianity, it is seen in the East as a betrayal of one's culture. Ask any Christian from India and you will find that to be true."[5] Indeed, the cost of truth stirs up our duplicity quite powerfully.

Lest we think that the cost of truth impairs the judgments and perceptions of only the religiously minded, let us consider some frank statements from leading academic atheists that show how emotional barriers and biases factor into their rejection of God. Thomas Nagel, professor of philosophy at New York University, one of America's leading institutions, candidly wrote,

> I want atheism to be true. And I'm made uneasy by the fact that some of the most intelligent and well-informed people I know are religious believers. It isn't that I don't believe in God and naturally hope that I'm right in my beliefs, *it's that I hope there is no God. I don't want there to be a God.* I don't want the universe to be like that."[6]

Doesn't the cost of truth bubble over in that statement, practically startling us? Nagel candidly admits that he is *uneasy* because intelligent people are religious. He strongly implies that if there is a God, he will lose his hope. He doesn't *want* God to exist. But if he rejects God because of purely evidential reasons, why the *unease,* why the loss of hope? Nagel admits that his atheism is not merely about intellectual conclusions, but about emotional desires.

Aldous Huxley is even more candid in exposing that his personal biases—even more than the evidence—influenced his rejection of God. In *Ends and Means*, he writes,

> I wanted to believe the Darwinian idea. I chose to believe it not because I think there was enormous evidence for it, nor because I believed it had the full authority to give interpretation to my origins, but I chose to believe it because it delivered me from trying to find meaning and freed me to my own erotic passions.[7]

There it is again. Huxley, an intelligent and erudite thinker, did not embrace evolution because of the evidence. Nor did he reject God for the lack of it. Rather, he wanted to rid himself of the burden of trying to find meaning. He wanted no sexual restrictions. In other words, he did not want to pay the cost associated with belief in God. For Huxley, disbelief was not a matter of the mind, but a matter of the heart and will.

From those who come from religious backgrounds and communities to lofty academics and social commentators to those in positions of power, truth's consequences can be a powerful motivating factor in allegiance to a worldview. We cling to our worldview and reject the possibility that another opposing worldview might be true, because so much about us is at stake in the debate. As journalist Upton Sinclair writes, "It is difficult to get a man to understand something, when his salary depends upon his not understanding it."[8]

COUNTING THE COST

But why must we even bother to expose the cost in the first place? Why not leave one another to our personal biases and prejudices?

For Christians, the answer is simple. Jesus is Christians' supreme example, and he challenged nearly everyone he met to confront their own biases and barriers. In fact, Jesus' powerful admonitions were not reserved for those who were unwilling to follow him. No, he was an equal opportunity exposer of biases, leveling his critiques (especially) at his own followers. As his following increased greatly, Jesus asked the multitude of new disciples to consider whether they were really interested in embracing the truth he was offering, in light of the great cost that would come with it (Luke 14:27-33).

It's interesting that Jesus challenged the crowd of people who chose to follow him to reconsider in light of what they would have to lose. Leaders who are primarily interested in self-glorification constantly think of ways to increase their following and are constantly worried about causing people to abandon them. A call to give the matter further reflection is just the kind of thing that might deflate a crowd's enthusiasm and leave a leader standing alone. But Jesus was not interested in popularity. He was interested in the futures of all those he came in contact with, and he wanted them to think hard about what it would mean to follow him.

Likewise, we should not shrink from the sometimes unpleasant job of exposing barriers to truth. In fact, Jesus shows us that doing so is not harsh, but loving. Consider his encounter with a rich young man. The man asks Jesus, "Good Teacher, what must I do to inherit eternal life?" (Mark 10:17). With a view toward addressing the man's hidden assumptions, Jesus first answers him with a question: "Why do you call me good? No one is good except God alone" (v. 18). He asks this, forcing the rich man to consider the implications of his question.

And then, to expose the man's hidden motivation in asking the question, Jesus references six important commandments from Exodus and Deuteronomy that the man likely knew well (v. 19). Taking the bait, the man shoots back a self-confident answer, "Teacher, all these I have kept from my youth" (v. 20). And with that response, he unwittingly lays bare an important truth that he has to come to grips with in order to truly follow Jesus. He knows that he has obeyed the commandments of how to act toward humanity and that he is able to proudly proclaim that fact to Jesus and all those around him. But still there is an underlying need to ask Jesus what more is expected of him.

There are two things at war within that rich man: the desire to justify himself and the subconscious knowledge that he can never really do so. Because the man's desire to justify himself before God stands in the way of embracing that truth, Jesus seizes the opportunity to expose the man's cost:

> And Jesus looking at him, *loved him*, and said to him, "You lack one thing: go, sell all that you have and give to the poor, and you will have treasure in heaven; and come, follow me." Disheartened by the saying, he went away sorrowful, for he had great possessions. (Mark 10:21-22, emphasis mine)

Tellingly, the rich young man, who has kept the law from his youth, does not disagree with Jesus. Rather, he is saddened and walks away grieving. Why? Because Jesus exposes something sensitive and subconscious: the man's underlying desire to justify himself. The man knows that his self-righteousness is not enough, so he walks away sad, unwilling at that point to let it all go for the sake of truth. Jesus tenderly yet firmly taught the young man—and teaches us today—the not-to-be-overlooked maxim "Until the heart is open, the ears remain closed."

But there is something subtle yet profound in the encounter that must not escape our notice. Mark records that just as he was beginning to expose the man's cost, Jesus "loved him" (Mark 10:21). It was after feeling this love that Jesus addressed the man's personal barriers. Jesus shows us that it is not harsh or patronizing to expose another's barriers. It is an act of love. It is, perhaps, one of the most loving things we can do for another so that emotion-laden rebellion can give way to sincere investigation.

BRINGING THE COST TO THE SURFACE

But how do we bring to the surface the subconscious and powerful cost of truth so that it can be addressed and, once addressed, be put behind us so that we can address the tough intellectual questions? Allow me to suggest three ways.

1. Socrates and scribes—answering questions with questions. First, we need to be upfront about the cost of truth when we discuss matters of deeply held beliefs. Some years ago, I was invited to participate in an interfaith dialogue at a university with a sizable Muslim student body. A Christian group invited me to speak opposite a Muslim scholar who had been invited by the school's Muslim student association. The topic we were to address was somewhat unconventional for such engagements: "How Can a Loving, All Powerful God Exist in a World of Suffering? A Christian and Muslim Response."

During the talk, I offered philosophical, theological and scriptural reasons for my belief that the existence of an all-powerful, all-loving God is not incompatible with the reality of suffering and evil. Specifically, I argued that in the gospel we not only have a theoretical answer to the problem of evil, but we actually have God entering into the human condition to deal with evil as a matter of history. The point, I argued, is that the gospel provides the best answer to suffering.

The event was geared to get Christian and Muslim students to sit next to each other and interact on the material presented. But sadly, like many such meetings, Muslims and Christians kept to their own sides of the room. During the event, I saw a Muslim student sitting with his friends, and I knew, just from seeing his reactions to me and the scowl on his face, that he would be the first student to interact with me after we finished our remarks. Sure enough, as soon as my counterpart and I closed our remarks, the student stood up and all but ran to the front of the room to confront me.

In a loud voice, he began his questioning. "I heard you appeal to logic and reason during your talk," he said. "But how can you believe such nonsense like the Trinity?" The volume and zeal in his voice had their desired effect. A crowd gathered around us to see who could best whom. I wanted to address the student's question, if for no other reason than that the Trinity is a stumbling block for most Muslims who consider the gospel, but I was not interested in a verbal slugfest. So I gently responded by offering a question of my own. "The Trinity is an important topic, but can I ask you a question first? Do you want to consider my answer, or do you want to stump me in front of everyone? Do you want a conversation or a fight? I'm interested in the first one, not the second. If you want a spirited discussion, great. Otherwise, I'm not interested."

His tone changed as he responded, "No, I want a conversation. I want to hear your reasons for believing in the Trinity." And with that, we had an actual conversation. It was a spirited conversation to be sure, but it was a real conversation, and those who stood by listened intently.

I am an attorney by training, so the best way I can think to expose someone's underlying biases and barriers is to ask questions. In case you are leery of following the voice of a lawyer, you can take solace in the fact that we have great examples of world-changing thinkers who have done exactly what I suggest. The great philosopher and teacher Socrates was famous for answering a question with a question. In fact, professors at institutes of higher learning all over the world employ the Socratic method by answering questions with questions. Though initially frustrating to students (I flash back to my Constitutional Law class), this method gets them to realize the underlying assumptions they bring to the topic.

And if Socrates is not enough of an authority to show us the value of this principle, let's consider Jesus. He answered the rich man's question ("What must I do to inherit eternal life?") with a question ("Why do you call me good?"). Jesus did this throughout his earthly ministry. (A particularly masterful example is Jesus' confrontation with the scribes recorded in Luke 20:1-8.) In every encounter, Jesus exposed the motives behind the questions. In doing so, he teaches us another valuable maxim: addressing the question's content is not as urgent as addressing the question's intent.

2. *A careful ear listens for the cost.* Asking questions is good only if we listen to the answers. Strange, is it not, that we need to be reminded of so obvious a truism? But most of us can recall times when we asked someone for the time, only to realize moments after being told the answer that we still didn't know what time it was. Careful listening, as important as it is, has become something of a lost art.

We must also be careful to listen to others' explanations of their circumstances and their worldviews, not just their answers to our questions. I think of an incident involving the satirical storyteller Quentin Crisp. He was in Northern Ireland when the strife between Catholics and Protestants was quite intense. During a performance there, he stated that he was an atheist. A woman in the audience immediately stood up and asked him, "But is it the God of the Catholics or the Protestants you don't believe in?" She obviously hadn't listened carefully to Crisp, revealing more about her personal biases than Crisp's—and getting more laughs than Crisp did in the process.

Careful listening not only keeps us from making fools of ourselves, but also helps us to understand the costs others face in considering the gospel. About a year after I had become a Christian, I received a phone call at my home. As soon as I said hello, I heard a woman's heavy Middle Eastern accent. "Mr. Murray? I heard that you converted from Islam to Christianity. How could you do that?"

Other than the quite natural reaction of asking her who she was and how she got my home phone number, my inclination was to launch into an argument about the Bible's veracity and Christian doctrine—which I did. I laid on her a dissertation about the philosophical, theological and historical proofs for Christianity, citing theologians from Augustine to Zwingli. When I finished my response, I sat back in silence and let my diatribe sink in, thinking she would be utterly impressed with the sheer volume of my arguments. But then she responded with a simple follow-up question. "That's all very nice, but I want to know how you could become a Christian knowing what you would lose."

I felt like I had taken a long walk off a short pier. I had failed to listen to the woman's question, and instead of addressing her primary issue, I had spent time trying to impress her with information she wasn't asking about or ready for. I could have easily understood where she was coming from by simply asking her what she meant when she asked, "How could you do that?" (This is yet another reason why asking questions is so important.) But I forged ahead with an answer to the question I *thought* she was asking. The lesson I learned that day was simple yet powerful: careful listening is integral to understanding another's place on the journey toward truth.

Often the cost a person faces is not as obviously or easily admitted as it was when I spoke to the woman on the phone or talked with the student at the university. The hiddenness of the cost, or a person's unwillingness to reveal it, may make it difficult to see. Careful listening is key in such situations, because a person's cost often bubbles up to the surface during conversations—sometimes obviously, sometimes subtly.

A Christian cannot pretend that the cost of truth does not apply to her. Indeed, it applies in many ways. Christians have often engaged with each other in debates about nonessential doctrines and have gotten emotionally worked up or even offended at one another in the process. Why? Because everyone—yes, everyone—has an emotional attachment to their view, no matter how trivial. Some attachments are more easily severed than others. But they are still there. This is as true for Christians as it is for anyone else.

For a Christian to admit that she, too, faces consequences in considering the possibility that the gospel is not true is nothing more (and nothing less) than credibly engaging in conversation. And to do so is not to say that we hold onto our faith tenuously. Far from it. Rather, we show that we are confident enough to shine the light of evidence and reason on our beliefs. And that light shines brightest when it is powered by sincerity.

3. Truth has a cost, but why should I pay? Another very important question rises from the reality that truth has a cost. Why should we pay it? What makes truth worth taking such enormous risks? In the pages that follow, we'll examine the central questions that the major non-Christian worldviews seek to answer. Those worldviews exist—and people give their allegiances to them—because they think the answers to those questions are worth it. In the chapters to follow, I intend to sustain the thesis that the gospel not only validates those questions, but also offers better answers than any other worldview. It is these answers that show why the gospel is worth paying the price. And it is to them that we now turn.

1

GRAND CENTRAL QUESTIONS

QUESTIONS ETCHED IN BRONZE

My wife and I recently traveled to New York City to celebrate our wedding anniversary. Within a couple of days, we had taken what seemed like a walk through the entire island of Manhattan. But there was one site we had yet to see—the September 11 memorial at Ground Zero. Although we had gone to New York to celebrate, this part of our trip commanded our solemn silence.

There, in the very place where the North and South Towers of the World Trade Center had crumbled before the world's disbelieving eyes more than ten years before, were two square pools, enormously wide and thirty feet deep. Water cascaded into the pools on all sides from a great height, yet with a strange gentleness. From there, the water drained into deeper, yet smaller pools, the bottoms of which we could not see. Surrounding both pools were bronze parapets, roughly waist high. Etched in the bronze are the names of those who died in the September 11, 2001, attacks and the 1993 World Trade Center bombing.

As we paused to read the names, we were struck by the display's two unique features. First, the names are not arranged alphabetically. Rather, they are arranged by "meaningful adjacencies."[1] The names of victims who worked together, who were related or who died together were listed near each other. The names of first responders and rescue workers who served, lived and died together were also in close proximity. The meaningful adjacencies conveyed just that—a sense of meaning to the names and a relational context that a mere alphabetical listing could not provide. The memorial subtly tells the stories of people and the significance of their everyday lives in addition to how they tried to help each other amid the chaos. It speaks of relationships, not just of one event.

The memorial's second striking feature was not as obvious. Among the meaningful adjacencies, we saw several names of women etched in the bronze along with the inscription "and her unborn child." Yes, the unnamed unborn were listed among those who lost their lives in the tragedy. The loss of those unborn lives was just as meaningful.

One cannot linger in a place like the 9/11 Memorial without pondering serious questions. What was going through the minds of those who were facing death? What accounts for evil in the heart of humanity, and what accounts for the heroism of those who tried to save lives at the expense of their own? What accounts for human suffering? Does religion or religious belief necessarily entail violence? Where is God when tragedy strikes?

And seeing the effort to list the names of those who died in meaningful ways and the recognition of the unborn people as meaningful brought up further questions: Do people have objective value? What determines their value? Is there something intrinsically valuable about a person even if he hasn't had the chance to contribute to society or the well-being of others?

Every major worldview claims to provide answers to such questions. But what do I mean by "worldview"? I like James Sire's definition of a worldview as "a commitment, a fundamental orientation of the heart, that can be expressed as a story or a set of presuppositions . . . that we hold . . . about the basic constitution of reality, and that provides the foundation on which we live and have our being."[2] Generally speaking, there are three main worldviews: naturalism (including atheism), pantheism and theism. Major views and world religions come under the umbrella of these worldviews.

From atheism to Hinduism to Islam to Christianity, there is no major view that has not struggled to provide answers to the questions that haunt us when we view memorials or are alone with nothing but our thoughts. In fact, for any system of belief to qualify as a worldview—or a way in which we view the world—the system has to be comprehensive. It has to address all facets of life's main questions, from the broad ideas to the minute details. If a belief system fails to address all the central questions of life, it fails to be a view of the world, because it leaves significant aspects of our existence unaddressed.

Any worldview worth believing should also be internally consistent as it answers these questions. In other words, a worldview's answers to one set of questions (say, answers to questions about human origins) should not contradict its answers to another set of questions (say, answers to questions about meaning and purpose). If it provides fundamentally contradictory answers, there simply is no way to have any confidence in any of those answers. If a worldview fails to provide cohesive answers—answers that directly address a particular question while consistently cohering to the answers it gives to other questions—it fails what is called the "coherence test for truth."[3] And if it fails that test, it should lose in the competition for our allegiance.

QUIETING A CACOPHONY OF QUESTIONS

Questions about ultimate reality are not in short supply. Doubtless, we can easily think of dozens of such questions. Indeed, the list can go on ad infinitum. If somehow all the different questions running through the minds of every person on the Earth could be spoken out loud, the noise would be deafening.

But perhaps we can quiet the cacophony and filter out the main questions that are the umbrellas under which all others fall. Ravi Zacharias has categorized the fundamental questions in terms of (1) origin, (2) meaning, (3) morality and (4) destiny.[4] I will modify these categories slightly and suggest that the four fundamental questions can be phrased in the following way:

1. What explains existence? Or, is there a God?

2. Is there an objective purpose and value to human existence?

3. What accounts for the human condition?

4. Is there a better life or a salvation from our present state?

I call these the four fundamental questions.

The first fundamental question—about the origins of the human species (and even existence itself)—is perhaps the most fundamental. *How did we get here?* simply must be a question that nearly every single person, regardless of his or her belief system, has asked. How we answer this fundamental question informs how we answer all others. For example, if we believe that we are here merely as the result of a mindless accident or by a quirk of blind evolutionary processes that could not have had any particular result in mind, our view about how (or even whether) humanity has an objective purpose or value will be far different than if we conclude that a transcendent being created us on purpose. And our explanation for the existence of pain and suffering in the world will be influenced by whether we affirm or deny (or have no beliefs about) the existence of a divine being.

Of course, should we answer that there is a divine being who created everything, we would not necessarily have to believe that pain and suffering have explanations other than chance. Deists believe that a nonphysical, transcendent god exists, but once that god finished creation, it took its hands off the wheel and let mindless forces, blind chance and intentional evil run their course in the universe. It seems that if such a god were to exist, we might justifiably be angry that this god of infinite power has no interest in using that power to improve the human condition.

What this all means is that what we think about our origins greatly influences what we think about everything else.

The second fundamental question—of objective purpose—is intimately connected to the question of our origin. Perhaps the question *Why are we here?* is just as ubiquitous as *How did we get here?* Everyone strives to find his or her place in this world, to find out what he or she is "meant" to do and what his or her contribution to humanity should be. But the question is not just about what our individual lives mean. It is more about the meaning of human existence *in and of itself.*

Many of us struggle our entire lives to figure this out, which suggests that many of us believe that there are objective, knowable answers that are worth pursuing. But some of us believe that there are only subjective answers—answers that depend on the opinions of the person asking the question. And still others of us believe that there is no ultimate purpose, despite the illusion (or our delusion) that there is.

Directly related to (if not completely subsumed by) the question of purpose is the issue of objective morality: whether there are objective virtues and evils, or rights and wrongs, independent of human opinion. Indeed, objective human purpose and value necessarily entail objective morality. If objective purpose implies an "ought" to human existence or what human existence "should" mean, then objective morality is the set of rules or intuitions by which we fulfill that purpose. At the risk of appearing reductionistic, I posit that morality can be viewed as the means by which we fulfill objective purpose and immorality as the means by which we violate objective purpose. It follows, then, that if we ask what humanity's ultimate purpose is, we must also ask whether objective moral values and duties exist.

The third fundamental question, which is about the human condition, cries out for explanation. What I mean by the human condition is simply the state of affairs that humans find themselves in. This world is filled with seeming polar opposites of experience. There is much pain, suffering, evil and injustice. Yet comfort, pleasure, goodness and justice exist at the same time. Why is that so? Why do we experience such a spectrum? Interestingly, we dwell most often on the question of why there is pain, suffering or evil.

The so-called problem of evil or problem of pain is addressed in university philosophy departments, in factory lunchrooms and at memorial sites around the world. I have often found it fascinating that we, as a species, dwell on the problem of pain—we ask ourselves how God could exist in a world of suffering and pain. But we give hardly a moment's thought to the question of how pleasure or fulfillment can exist in a world such as this. In any event, every worldview tries to provide an answer to the human condition; every worldview tries to explain why there is suffering and evil in the world.

This brings us to the fourth of the fundamental questions: is there a better life or a salvation from our present state? We strive to find a way to improve the human condition or even to escape from it. In some worldviews, the end of sorrow, pain and suffering is found in an afterlife, a state of existence where there is only bliss and harmony. According to others, there is no afterlife, and so the only solution to the human condition is to engineer a better world through individual and collective human effort and achievement right here on Earth.

A CACOPHONY OF ANSWERS

If the cacophony of questions seems disorienting, the cacophony of answers may seem even more so. It should surprise no one that perhaps thousands of different philosophies and religions have risen through the years. To address them all here would not be productive or even possible. It has been quipped that in America alone, there are three hundred million different "religions"—one for every American. While that is an amusing exaggeration, it highlights the very real fact that humanity is always tweaking, always making finer and finer worldview distinctions, especially in the individualistic culture of contemporary Western society. This makes it necessary to tune our receivers to decipher the main answers to the fundamental questions.

Every worldview that would compete for our attention simply must provide coherent answers to these fundamental questions. And many try. But not every worldview places equal emphasis on all four. Some—in fact, most—place greater emphasis on answering one of the fundamental questions—the Grand Central Question, the question that each worldview claims to answer better than any other. A worldview's answer to its Grand Central Question defines it, and how it answers the Grand Central Question tells us whether it can answer the other fundamental questions in a cohesive way.

And while there are so many different views and religious systems, they fall under the umbrellas of what we'll call the major worldviews: naturalistic atheism, pantheism and theism. While we will look at pantheism broadly, we'll examine naturalistic atheism through the lens of its most influential form: secular humanism. We will look at theism through the lens of one of the fastest-growing and most influential forms: Islam. As we look at these views, we will examine how each answers its Grand Central Question and how the gospel—the central message of Jesus of Nazareth—answers that same question.

SECULAR HUMANISM

"Secular humanism" aptly describes what amounts to an atheistic or at least nontheistic worldview. The title is very descriptive because it tells us much of what we need to know about what the worldview espouses. Simply put, secular humanism is the view that humanity is intrinsically valuable, but in a nontheistic way. The *humanism* in secular humanism refers to the objective meaning and value of human beings. It is the affirmation of human dignity and value. The *secular* in secular humanism refers to the idea that human dignity and value can be realized without reference to any higher power or transcendent being.

Yet those who ascribe to this view, who may even be card-carrying members of various humanist societies, are not as homogenous in their beliefs as one might think. Secular humanists include atheists, to be sure. But we also find true agnostics, "spiritual" people and even theistic evolutionists among their ranks. In fact, a great number of modern Jews—whose culture gave us much of what the Middle East and the West believes about God—are agnostics or avowed atheists and consider themselves to be secular humanists. I have also encountered spiritual agnostics, those who do not necessarily believe in a personal god yet believe in the power of the human spirit, who considered themselves secular humanists.[5]

Despite the spectrum of secular humanists, we can readily see secular humanism's Grand Central Question. As the moniker suggests—and as I hope to sustain in the coming pages—secular humanism aspires to answer the fundamental question of purpose: what is humanity's purpose, and do we have intrinsic value?[6] Its answer is that humanity does, in fact, have value and purpose—but without God. We will test that answer, compare it to how the gospel answers the fundamental question of objective purpose, and see which satisfies the mind's need for rationality and the heart's need for existential satisfaction.

PANTHEISM

Pantheism is an umbrella worldview that covers a wide variety of religious or spiritual expressions. Pantheism, simply put, is the view that "all is one and all is God." Indeed, that is the meaning of the Greek roots that form the word. *Pan* is a part of speech that denotes "all" or "everything," and *theos* denotes "god" or "divinity."

Thus pantheism means "all is God." For most pantheists, everything that is God is connected such that God is all there is. The distinctions between the divine and nondivine and between individual persons or things are largely considered to be illusions.

Pantheism's most prevalent forms are Hinduism, Buddhism[7] and their Western counterparts, which include New Age beliefs, Scientology and the so-called New Spirituality (the popular views of media gurus like Eckhart Tolle, Deepak Chopra and even Oprah Winfrey). Nearly every pantheistic religion or view espouses some form of reincarnation and a cyclical view of death and birth.

Hinduism and Buddhism dogmatically affirm *samsara*, the idea that all life undergoes a cycle of death and rebirth. They also posit that karma affects us from life to life, determining our station in each successive life until we reach enlightenment. Karma from our past and present lives determines how much suffering we endure in the next. It also determines how far we are from ultimate enlightenment. The goal of existence is to achieve that enlightenment, called *moksha* (release), so that we can be free of the painful cycle of death and rebirth. For the Hindu, moksha entails attainment of unity with the Brahman, the impersonal absolute spiritual reality. While some Buddhists share that view, the strict Buddhist (usually of the Theravada school) believes that the escape from pain and suffering comes from realizing that they are mere illusions. This results in the Buddhist version of moksha, which is a state of nothingness.

While subtly different in form and substance from Hinduism and Buddhism, pantheism's Western daughters, like Scientology and the New Age movement, share the idea of reincarnation and the evolution of the self until our divine identity is realized and we are enlightened. In that state, we can master reality, change it as we see fit and alleviate pain and suffering. The New Spirituality is practically obsessed with wellness and health, and teaches that through a mastery of the mind and a realization of inner divinity, we can be truly well—body, mind and soul.

From these doctrines and ideas emerge pantheism's Grand Central Question, which is about the human condition. To be sure, pantheistic views try to answer questions about origins and destiny, but they are fundamentally concerned with how we escape this world of pain (or at least the illusion of a world of pain) and attain bliss. The human condition—why we are in the state that we are in—and its solution are central to pantheistic thinking.

ISLAM

Islam is the religion of my birth and the religious view that I followed for much of my life. Today, an estimated 1.5 billion people—nearly one-sixth of the world population—claim to follow Islam to some degree. Islam is a staunchly monotheistic religion. Monotheism, called *Tawhid* by Muslims, is a key doctrine of Islam. Tawhid is not just the idea that there is only one God, but also that the one God is indivisible and does not exist as a "godhead." Tawhid is fundamentally distinct from Christian trinitarian monotheism, which holds that there is only one God who exists as three distinct personhoods sharing the same, single divine nature. For Muslims, doctrines like the Trinity and the incarnation of God in Christ are anathema, because they diminish God's greatness by suggesting that which is unthinkable. To even conceive of God as existing in a differentiated state or as a being who dwells in bodily form with his creation is to conceive of a less-than-perfect God, a God who is not great. This is why Islam's foundational writings spend a great deal of time denying Christian doctrines, saying they denigrate God.

And so Islam's Grand Central Question deals with God's existence and specifically with the greatness and majesty of his existence. The idea of God's greatness is so important that Islam codifies the dogma in a word: *Takbir*. The Takbir in Arabic is "Allahu Akbar," which literally means "God is greater." Muslims all over the world, whether they are committed Muslims or Muslims in name only, are often heard to say "Allahu Akbar" as part of their daily lives. The idea that Allahu Akbar—God is greater—soaks the very fabric of Islam today. As Tawhid is the root of all other Muslim doctrines, Takbir, the vaulting of God's greatness, is the root of Tawhid.

From this we see Islam's Grand Central Question quite clearly: how should we respond to God's greatness? The history of Islamic theology is laced with answers to this question. It is fascinating that many of those answers come in the form of denials—specifically denials of Christian monotheism. In the chapters to come, we will compare and examine Islam's theology of God's greatness with the Christian view on this issue so that we can see which worldview provides a view of God's greatness robust enough to quench the mind's need for consistency and the heart's need for communion with the Ultimate.

THE CHRISTIAN GOSPEL

Christianity also addresses the four fundamental questions. But unlike secular humanism, pantheism and Islam, Christianity does not focus on one Grand Central Question. Rather, the gospel gives us a central narrative. This narrative is that the triune God purposefully created humanity to be in relationship with him, but humanity rejected that relationship and thus rejected its very purpose. But God redeems humanity through his incarnate Son, Jesus, restoring the relationship and thus restoring our purpose. From this central narrative spring the gospel's answers to all the Grand Central Questions.

The gospel, when properly understood and fully expressed, seeks to answer those questions in ways that appeal to the rational and emotional aspects of humanity. Whereas secular humanism seeks to provide an answer to the question of human purpose in a way that satisfies reason, the gospel offers a rational answer that also provides a sense of existential fulfillment. Where pantheism offers a means to escape from the human condition by relying heavily on mysticism, the gospel faces the human condition by undergirding spirituality with realism, evidence and God's compassion. And while Islam expresses its ideas of God's greatness in pure reverence and obedience, the gospel highlights God's greatness by espousing a consistent theology that is supported by history and philosophy.

We must acknowledge, however, that Christians have not always expressed the gospel in ways that satisfy the mind and the heart. I would venture to guess that if atheists were to describe their impression of contemporary expressions of Christianity, they would use the word *emotional*. With Christian book titles that overuse the words *you* and *your* and smack of self-help ideas, it is difficult to disagree. Fluffy, feel-good sermons that never mention Jesus' cross do not help matters.

It appears that the contemporary church, while meaning well, has become obsessed with "relevance." That is not solely the church's fault. Popular Western culture has misdefined a relevant message to mean one that is "useful in my life," or, even worse, as one that addresses "my current emotional state." To remain relevant in that way, the church has sacrificed the intellectual aspect of the gospel for the sake of the experiential.

But there is a danger in the opposite approach. Christian apologists (me included) struggle with the temptation to focus too heavily on answers that appeal only to the mind. We can completely denude the gospel of its existential power and profundity by trying to outsmart challengers to the faith or just win debates. The late Francis Schaeffer was intensely focused on using the right balance of argumentation and grace. "You are not trying to win an argument or to knock someone down," he said. "You are seeking to win a person, a person made in the image of God. This is not about your winning; it is not about your ego. If that is your approach, all you will do is arouse their pride and make it more difficult for them to hear what you have to say."[8]

To be sure, there are those who need intellectually rigorous answers to the Grand Central Question that matters most to them. And there are those whose intellectual issues pale in comparison to their emotional roadblocks. Meaningful answers to our deepest questions must come from a balanced search that seeks to satisfy our emotions and our intellect in person-specific ways. How we view the questioner—not just the question—is critical.

THE DIFFERENCES MAKE ALL THE DIFFERENCE

Why examine these various worldviews and their Grand Central Questions? Why care what their respective answers are and how the gospel's answers compare? It is not merely an academic exercise or a matter of mere philosophical or theological curiosity. True, if we take this investigation seriously, we may have to dwell on our differences and not just our similarities, which causes us to run the risk of challenging the politically correct version of pluralism that holds sway in the West. But we cannot sacrifice an honest assessment of our differences on the politically correct altar of tolerance.

For one thing, saying that all worldviews are basically the same does not compliment them; it insults them. To tell a Muslim that his or her views about God are the same as a Christian's is to ignore Islam's deeply held doctrine that God is a monad. To tell a Buddhist that his or her beliefs are identical to a Hindu's is to denigrate the fact that Buddha founded his religion in rejection of some Hindu doctrines.

Indeed, celebrating superficial similarities and downplaying underlying fundamental differences in our worldviews is dangerous. Jesus tells us the parable of two men who built separate houses. One built his house on a foundation of rock. The other built his house, likely similar in appearance, on sand. Though that house was superficially similar to the house built on rock, when the storms came, the house built on sand crashed down (Matthew 7:24-27). In the same way, while some of our worldviews may have superficial similarities (and even that is debatable), the differences in our worldviews determine how we view the world around us, how we view each other, how we act and ultimately where we will spend eternity. As has been said often, our differences make a difference.

But a commonality will undergird our exploration of worldview differences in the pages to come. The commonality is found in the questions themselves. Every worldview shares the fundamental questions, and I believe that Christianity tries to answer each of the Grand Central Questions. And so we can proceed from that common ground. All of us, regardless of our beliefs, can affirm the questions and the sincere questioner's quest. Having studied these major worldviews for some years and having debated their adherents in public and private settings, I am convinced that the gospel is unique in that its central claim—that God has purposed to redeem humanity from its iniquity—provides answers to all the Grand Central Questions without focusing on just one of them.

As I read the Scriptures, I understand that Jesus validates the non-Christian's struggle to find answers to the Grand Central Questions. But he does not stop at mere validation of the questioner or the questions. He cares enough to challenge the intellect and the emotions. And in doing so, I am convinced that he provides answers that satisfy both.

Part One

SECULAR HUMANISM

OR THE GOSPEL

Which Provides Us with Intrinsic Value and Objective Purpose?

SECULAR HUMANISM—THE SECULAR SEARCH

Whether we agree or disagree with its substance as a philosophy, it cannot be disputed that secular humanism is an aptly named worldview. Its name accurately captures and communicates its essence and what it seeks to affirm. Its influential (and curiously numerous) manifestos and creed-like statements tell us that secular humanism affirms, as objectively true, that humanity has dignity, value and purpose. These affirmations, in and of themselves, are neither controversial nor unique. It is not difficult to find someone, regardless of their religious or nonreligious persuasion, who believes that human beings are imbued with these qualities.

What makes secular humanism interesting, however, is the way it couples its affirmation of human dignity and purpose with its affirmation that these things can exist without God. To be clear, both atheists and theists commonly misunderstand the issue here. The issue is not whether *belief* in God's existence is necessary to value humans and act morally. The issue is whether God's existence is necessary to do so objectively.

Theists claim that God must exist for objective human value, purpose and morality to exist. Secular humanists argue that these things objectively exist, even if God does not. As Paul Kurtz, the author of *Humanist Manifesto 2000*, declares, "The underlying ethical principle of Planetary Humanism is the need to respect the dignity and worth of all persons in the world community."[1] And so, the Grand Central Question that secular humanism must answer is this: how does humanity have inherent dignity, purpose and moral value?

To fairly assess whether secular humanism has succeeded in its quest to rationally and emotionally ground its position, we must delve deeper into secular humanism's development and the language that its leading thinkers use to convey their answers to secular humanism's Grand Central Question.

DISTINCTIONS THAT MAKE A WORLD OF DIFFERENCE

Subtleties of language can make quite a difference in whether we understand the true version of an idea or we are examining just a caricature of the real thing. Because words can have dual or even multiple meanings, we must be careful to define our terms. Words like *secular*, *secularism* and even *humanism* are context-dependent. And so as we begin to unpack what secular humanism has to say to us, we need to understand the sometimes subtle difference between *secular*, *secularism* and *secularization*.

Secular is merely a word, not a worldview per se. It is just an adjective to describe certain kinds of concepts. Something is secular if it is neutral as to different religious or nonreligious beliefs. Something is secular if it is devoid of any religious or supernatural considerations while at the same time not being hostile to them or favoring antireligious ideas. For example, the government of the United States is secular in the sense that it is not set up to favor one religious tradition over another or to mandate any religious beliefs at all. Indeed, the First Amendment of the United States Constitution prohibits the establishment of a state religion while at the same time preventing the government from interfering in the religious expressions of Americans, whatever their beliefs might be. In America, the public school system is meant to be neutral toward religious ideas—meaning that it should neither favor any religious idea nor be hostile to it. The federal government cannot mandate that people observe Christian holidays, nor can it prevent them from doing so. In that sense, the American government is secular.

Contrast this with governments that are specifically and intentionally based on religious beliefs and laws. Examples include Saudi Arabia, Afghanistan, Pakistan, Iran and others where the Sharia—the Islamic legal code—forms the law of the land. In some such countries, the state requires women—regardless of whether they are Muslims—to wear head coverings because Islamic law requires it. In Saudi Arabia, it is illegal to build a church anywhere in the country, because Saudi Arabian leaders believe that Islamic law forbids the propagation of Christianity. This is the very opposite of a secular government and, by contrast, shows us what a secular government actually is.

Thus a secularist can be someone who favors and seeks to promote religiously neutral governments and public institutions over and against those that are religiously nonneutral. In this sense, one could be both a secularist and a religious person. Consider how the British Humanist Association defines a secularist:

> "Secularists" believe that laws and public institutions (for example, the education system) should be neutral as between alternative religions and beliefs. Almost all humanists are secularists, but religious believers may also take a secularist position which calls for freedom of belief, including the right to change belief and not to believe. Secularists seek to ensure that persons and organisations are neither privileged nor disadvantaged by virtue of their religion or lack of it. They believe secular laws—those that apply to all citizens—should be the product of a democratic process, and should not be deter-

mined, or unduly influenced, by religious leaders or religious texts. The word "secularism" was once used to describe a non-religious worldview generally but this meaning is now very old fashioned.[2]

While this definition of a secularist allows for both religious and nonreligious people within its ambit, there is another form of secularism that is important to understand, and it is quite distinct from the religiously neutral form discussed so far. That distinction makes a world of difference. This different form of secularism seeks to keep religion and religious expressions private—completely out of the public square. It seeks to change societal and cultural constraints so that they are devoid of religious beliefs and expressions. This form of secularism thus would be more accurately termed "secularizationism," because it posits the belief that the state (or at least society) should suppress religious expression that currently exists in the public square.

Consider France, for instance. In 2004, the French legislature enacted a law prohibiting its citizens from wearing "symbols or clothing denoting religious affiliation" in public schools and colleges.[3] That this law was enacted specifically to promote secularism is evident from its title, which tells us that it is a law enacted "En application du principe de laïcité," or "Under the principles of secularism."[4] The short law states in its entirety, "In schools, colleges, and public schools, the wearing of signs or dress by which pupils overtly manifest a religious affiliation is prohibited."[5] Its rationale is that prominent displays of religious symbols in schools would stir up controversy and possibly foster discrimination. To quell such controversy and strife, the government of France determined to curtail religious expressions in public and solidify a decidedly secular state.

Note carefully that the law did not just prohibit the espousal of religion by the public institution, but by the people the institution serves. This law does not say to the people that the government or public institutions are religiously neutral and unbiased toward a particular religion. Rather, it sends the clear message that religious expressions in public schools are somehow bad and naturally lead to strife. This strongly implies that religion itself is bad. While the French government would not stop private worship and religious devotion, it stops their public expression. This legislatively imposed suppression of religion is not really secularism. It is secularization—the shift toward promoting and imposing nonreligious values on a culture.

France's version of secularization is relatively tame in comparison to others. The more drastic examples of secularization are found in countries like the former Soviet Union, China and North Korea. Indeed, the Soviet Union, which sprang up from the soil of Russian suffering that was seeded by Marxism and watered by the leadership of Lenin and Stalin, purposefully sought to expunge the very idea of God from the Russian consciousness as a matter of policy. Communist China, cultivated by the antireligious ideas of Mao Zedong, similarly sought the expulsion of religious ideas, especially Christianity. Indeed, in 1966 Chairman Mao declared that Christianity was dead and buried in China, never to rise again.[6] And in North Korea, religious liberties are nonexistent. The only aspect of public life allowed to resemble something religious is the government-enforced deification of its all-too-human (and now quite dead) former leader Kim Jong Il.

Somewhere between the idea of secularism and secularizationism lies the worldview of secular humanism. To be sure, not all secular humanists want to stamp out private or public religious expression. I am confident that there are many secular humanists who would uphold and even give their lives to defend the First Amendment to the United States Constitution, which vouchsafes the basic human freedom to believe.

Nevertheless, secular humanists reject religious ideas as having any importance in life and human endeavors and try to convince others to reject belief in the supernatural as well. This leans more toward a secularist—as opposed to a secularizationist—view. It is understandable that a secular humanist would try to convince others that his worldview is correct. After all, he thinks his view is true and wants others to believe what is true. But there has arisen a strident movement among secular humanists that not only espouses an affirmation of nonreligious or atheistic ideas, but also champions hostility toward religion, religious ideas and the people who ascribe to them. This is the shape secular humanism is taking and where it is headed as a movement. Thus today's secular humanism leans more toward secularizationism than mere secularism. And it is this secular humanism that we will engage with the Grand Central Question of human dignity and purpose.

We need look no further than the wildly popular New Atheists, whose books that rail against religion and religious believers have sold multiple millions of copies. Men like Richard Dawkins, Daniel Dennett, Sam Harris and the late Christopher Hitchens have filled many a page denigrating religious ideas as absurd and labeling those who hold to them as deluded and even evil. These influential secular humanists are interested not only in trying to show the rational superiority of atheism, but they are also most definitely interested in stamping religion out of the human experience. At the March 24, 2012, Reason Rally—a gathering of up to ten thousand atheists and agnostics on the National Mall in Washington, D.C.— Dawkins exhorted his nonreligious devotees to mock theists and their beliefs publicly:

> So when I meet somebody who claims to be religious, my first impulse is: "I don't believe you. I don't believe you until you tell me do you really believe—for example, if they say they are Catholic—do you really believe that when a priest blesses a wafer it turns into the body of Christ? Are you seri-

ously telling me you believe that? Are you seriously saying that wine turns into blood?" Mock them! Ridicule them! In public! Don't fall for the convention that we're all too polite to talk about religion. Religion is not off the table. Religion is not off limits.

Religion makes specific claims about the universe which need to be substantiated and need to be challenged and, if necessary, need to be ridiculed with contempt.[7]

Dawkins has not just admonished the nonreligious to mock the religious. He goes so far as to equate religious education of children with child abuse.[8] And, of course, if this is true, if teaching children religious beliefs is abusive, then the government would have to step in to stop such actions.

Likewise, Sam Harris, the author of the bestseller *The End of Faith: Religion, Terror and the Future of Reason*, said, "The link between belief and behavior raises the stakes considerably. Some propositions are so dangerous that it may be ethical to kill people for believing them. This may seem an extraordinary claim, but it merely enunciates an ordinary fact about the world in which we live."[9]

Harris's characterization of his statement as an "extraordinary claim" does not go far enough. It is a shocking claim. Now, Harris's claim is in the context of his statement that the West is in a war of ideas with radical Muslims who carry out their beliefs in the form of violence. But he prides himself on striving to be precise with his language. So when he says that some propositions are so dangerous that it may be ethical to kill people *for believing* (as opposed to acting on) them, I take him at face value. And, indeed, his book is generally about religious belief, and its implications are not limited to radical Islam, so it is quite fair to interpret Harris broadly. Dawkins's and Harris's statements show that secular humanism is beginning to rally behind the banner of secularizationism, not merely secularism.

UNPACKING SECULAR HUMANISM

Though the decidedly hostile opinions of Dawkins, Harris and their ranks are influential, happily they are not held by all secular humanists. The public platform that Dawkins, Harris and others command entices the use of dramatic rhetoric. The anonymity of the Internet allows for the same (and even less civil) discourse on these ideas.[10] But personal interactions sometimes give secular humanists a different, less aggressive face. True, they may be hostile to religion or even certain religious people, but in the main, they are people like everyone else; they hold certain beliefs, hope those beliefs are true and try to get others to agree with them. It is this more common attitude—of disagreement without being disagreeable—that has made Dawkins's call for the mockery of religious believers cause even his fellow atheists to bristle. They have had to defend Dawkins's comments as "taken out of context," have apologized for them or have denounced them outright.

DIGGING AT THE ROOTS OF HUMANISM'S SECULARITY

The increasing influence of secularizationists like Dawkins and Harris is shaping how secular humanism answers its Grand Central Question of human value and dignity. But to see the broader spectrum, we must look at the words of influential secular humanist thinkers and writers. Certainly there is nothing wrong with looking to Dawkins's and Harris's statements to understand secular humanism. After all, they have sold millions of books and have the cachet to rally thousands together and incite their cheers. So it is fair to say that they speak for a large portion of secular humanists when they call religion "child abuse" and so dangerous that believers should be killed just for their beliefs. But because these are not the only voices in the movement, other secular humanist writings, not nearly so incendiary, can help us get a fuller picture.

Though the moniker "secular humanism" sounds ultramodern, as if the view were born sometime in the trendy 1990s, it actually has a (relatively) lengthy past. Of course, there have been atheists since the dawn of humanity. But what is now called secular humanism took root as an organized movement and worldview with the European Enlightenment of the late seventeenth to the eighteenth centuries. Popular belief is that the Enlightenment movement was born in reaction to the medievalism of the "Dark Ages" that were mired in superstition and religious domination. According to secular humanists, "Secularism and humanism were eclipsed in Europe during the Dark Ages, when religious piety eroded humankind's confidence in its own powers to solve human problems."[11] That's debatable, of course, because many Christian thinkers of that time, such as René Descartes and John Locke, to name but two, encouraged the use of reason to understand the world as created by God, an ultimately rational being.

Still, some leaders in the Enlightenment movement aimed to free humanity from supposed social prejudice and scientific error. They thought that a pursuit of truth, untouched by prejudice and religious dogma, would result in human freedom and advancement. Thus, it was no surprise that such Enlightenment thinkers opposed religious dogma and institutions, particularly Christianity, viewing them as the main propagators of intellectual error and social prejudice.[12] Men like Voltaire and David Hume were champions of skepticism, the idea that everything—even our most cherished beliefs—should be challenged and examined. Indeed, as one French philosopher said, "All things must be examined, debated, investigated, without exception and without regard for anyone's feelings."[13]

Early on, the Enlightenment emphasized empiricism, the idea that all things worth believing have to be rationally based and testable. Men like John Locke (though himself a Christian theist) championed Enlightenment empiricism, the idea that reason is a valuable determiner of what is true.[14] Later, the famous Scottish thinker David Hume took empiricism a step further, claiming that only ideas that could be empirically tested or quantified are worth pursing or believing. Specifically, Hume declared,

> It seems to me, that the only objects of the abstract science or of demonstration are quantity and number, and that all attempts to extend this more perfect species of knowledge beyond these bounds are mere sophistry and illusion.
>
> When we run over libraries, persuaded of the principles, what havoc must we make? If we take in our hands any volume; of divinity or school of metaphysics for instance; let us ask, Does it contain any abstract reasoning concerning quantity or number? No. Does it contain any experimental reasoning concerning matter of fact and existence? No. Commit it then to the flame: for it can contain nothing but sophistry and illusion.[15]

But this is utterly self-defeating, isn't it? Hume's statement that all propositions that are not "quantifiable" or that cannot be empirically verified must be committed to the flame itself cannot be empirically verified. Thus, according to Hume, we should commit his very own statement to the flames.

The self-defeating nature of Hume's position highlights an important point. Some ideas lend themselves to being tested through quantifiable and experimental means, but some do not. Yet both kinds of ideas can be equally true. Some ideas touch on the physical—and we have science to test them. Some ideas touch on the metaphysical—and we have philosophy, psychology, the arts, theology and experience to test them. To cast off entire academic and professional disciplines is to be rather close-minded.

Yet Hume's brand of empiricism seems to have hung on in popular works and even among scholarly scientists. We need only look to Sam Harris once again to see the efforts being taken to try to ground metaphysical ideas like morality in the physical realm. In his book *The Moral Landscape: How Science Can Determine Human*

Values, Harris tries to combat the problem atheist philosophers have encountered in trying to ground objective moral values without relying on God's existence. In an effort to do away with the thorny philosophical challenge secular humanism faces when it comes to morality, Harris posits that there are scientifically measurable phenomena that reveal the objective nature of morality.[16] But science, by definition, assesses only the physical world. Morality, by definition, is nonphysical or metaphysical. Using the former to ground the latter is bound to result in a category mistake.[17]

Indeed, the very existence of the effort to test the foundations of morality scientifically shows that Humean empiricism is alive and well among leading secular humanists. This commitment to empiricism among scientists has caused many to repeat Hume's mistake of arguing that the only way to know truth is through the scientific method of repeated experimentation and drawing conclusions from the data.

In his recent book *The Grand Design*, Stephen Hawking, the famous theoretical physicist from Cambridge, opens with the statement "Philosophy is dead" to make his point that hard sciences, like physics and mathematics, are the only real methods for determining truth. Interestingly, Hawking spills quite a bit of ink in the pages of his book philosophically defending his position that there is no grand design to the universe.[18]

Hawking has been called the smartest man alive. Hume was brilliant in his own right, having been admitted to Edinburgh University at just twelve years old. Yet both Hawking and Hume saw off the very limbs on which they sit in relying solely on science as the supreme arbiter of truth.

Such a view is not scientific—it is *scientism*. It is based on an unjustified, metaphysical commitment to the idea that science is the only way in which humans can know truth. It is scientism that motivates secular humanism's attempt to oust religious inquiry from among the possible ways we determine truth. As Michael Polanyi has put it,

Intellectual assent to the reduction of the world to its atomic elements acting blindly in terms of equilibrations of forces, an assent that has gradually come to prevail since the birth of modern science, has made any sort of teleological view of the cosmos seem unscientific and wool gathering to us. And it is this assent, more than any other one intellectual factor, that has set science and religion (in all but its most frothy forms) in opposition to each other in the contemporary mind.[19]

To be fair, secular humanists "recognize the need to balance scientific and technological advances with cultural explorations in art, music, and literature."[20] Even so, secular humanism remains committed to naturalism. And naturalism, simply put, is the view that all of reality is found in, and only in, the natural world. There is no reality beyond what can be experienced in the natural realm or what can be perceived by natural means. This applies not only to the natural world outside each human being, but also to human beings themselves. As *Humanist Manifesto II* declares, "As far as we know, the total personality is a function of the biological organism transacting in a social and cultural context. There is no credible evidence that life survives the death of the body."[21] In other words, we are our bodies. We are complex chemical machines interacting in social contexts. And once the machine stops working, its existence is ended.

With this in view, we can begin to assess how secular humanism tries to answer its Grand Central Question regarding the basis for human value and purpose. Sire summarizes secular humanism as "the overall attitude that human beings are of special value; their aspirations, their thoughts, their yearnings are significant. There is as well an emphasis on the value of the individual person."[22] From the strictly naturalistic form of humanism, it becomes evident that secular humanism is the broad view that humanity has intrinsic value that is worth recognizing, encouraging and defending quite apart from God's existence.

We need only look to the very words of secular humanists them-selves to see that they affirm the intrinsic value, meaning and purpose of humanity while rejecting the supernatural and God's existence. The influential British Humanist Association (BHA) defines a secular humanist this way:

> "Humanist" is used today to mean those who seek to live good lives without religious or superstitious beliefs. A humanist may embrace all or most of the other approaches introduced here, and in addition humanists believe that moral values follow on from human nature and experience in some way. Humanists base their moral principles on reason (which leads them to reject the idea of any supernatural agency), on shared human values and respect for others. They believe that people should work together to improve the quality of life for all and make it more equitable. Humanism is a full philosophy, "life stance" or worldview, rather than being about one aspect of religion, knowledge, or politics.[23]

That definition is laden with implications and assumptions about the objective value and purpose of humanity. The BHA affirms that a secular humanist seeks to live a "good life" and believes that "moral values follow from human nature." Human reason and "shared human values" are the basis for moral principles. People should work together to "improve the quality of life for all." Underlying every one of those statements is the assumption that humanity has objective meaning, value and purpose. Otherwise why should we work to improve the quality of life for all?

In a section of its website titled "What Do We Want?" the BHA makes it clear that the secular humanist movement seeks to uphold the dignity of human life, but without God: "We want a world where everyone lives cooperatively on the basis of shared human values, respect for human rights, and concern for future generations. We want non-religious people to be confident in living ethical and fulfilling lives on the basis of reason and humanity."[24]

Again, here the BHA admonishes us to live according to shared human values, to "respect" human rights, to ensure that people can have "fulfilling lives." According to the *Humanist Manifesto II*, humanity has objective meaning in and of itself, based on a shared human experience. It says, "We affirm that moral values derive their source from human experience. Ethics is autonomous and situational, needing no theological or ideological sanction. Ethics stems from human need and interest. To deny this distorts the whole basis of life. *Human life has meaning because we create and develop our futures.*"[25]

Secular humanists seem to have quite a lofty view of humanity: we are the sole determiners of meaning. In an earthly sense, doesn't that elevate us to the rank of a (nonsupernatural) "supreme being"? Not long ago, an encounter with a committed secular humanist highlighted (quite ironically) just how highly secular humanists think of themselves. We were sitting across a table from each other, discussing religion, when I asked him, "What is your main hang-up with Christians?"

He gave it a moment's reflection and said, "Christians are arrogant. They think they have the only way and that everyone else is wrong and going to hell."

"Arrogance?" I asked. "Really? That's a main hang-up you have?"

"Among others," he replied.

"That's an interesting critique coming from a secular humanist."

"How so?" he asked.

"Well, you'd agree with the Secular Humanist Manifesto III, which says that humans have the ability and responsibility to 'lead ethical lives of personal fulfillment that aspire to the greater good of humanity,'[26] right?" (Yes, I had that statement memorized.)

"Yeah, so?"

"Well, you believe that *you* have those abilities. *You* can lead an ethical life for the greatest good of humanity. That wonderful ability is inherent in *you*, right?"

"Yeah . . ." he said with anticipation.

"The gospel tells me that I am a sinner, you are a sinner and my children are sinners. It tells me that I cannot save myself and that I need someone who is not me to save me from myself. I believe in Jesus as savior; you believe in you. Now tell me again, who's arrogant?"

While secular humanism seeks to affirm human value without invoking God, to do so it has to elevate humanity to being the object of salvation and the savior itself. As Tom Flynn says, "Because no transcendent power will save us, secular humanists maintain that humans must take responsibility for themselves."[27] But if history teaches us anything, it is that humanity is a dismal savior at best.

Yet some would go so far as to argue that the rise of secular humanism is the very thing that has birthed a new sense of valuing of human dignity that does not require allegiance to religious ideas. These secularists would argue that belief in an afterlife cheapens what we do in this life and trivializes our actions to mere attempts to earn a reward later. They would further argue that, in contrast to religious devotion to God as a means of reward for ourselves (a charge, we'll see later, that cannot be leveled at the gospel), secular humanists believe that true meaning and fulfillment come from acting in ways conducive to human flourishing, because humanity is an end in itself without the need for a transcendent being to invest us with dignity. Charles Taylor summarizes modern secular humanism this way:

> I would like to claim that the coming of modern secularity in my sense has been coterminous with the rise of a society in which for the first time in history a purely self-sufficient humanism came to be a widely available option. I mean by this a humanism accepting no final goals beyond human flourishing, nor any allegiance to anything else beyond this flourishing. Of no previous society was this true.[28]

That is a high (and dangerous) view of our abilities indeed.

LOOKING FOR THE FOUNDATION

Thus there can really be no doubt that the central tenet of secular humanism—the tenet that underlies and informs every other—is that humanity has inherent dignity, purpose and moral value. But what is missing from every one of the statements quoted above by secular humanists in their widely published and endorsed documents? It certainly isn't the affirmation that humanity has objective value and purpose. Rather, it is the affirmation's justification that is lacking. In other words, it is not the *what* that is missing, it is the *why*.

To be fair, while manifestos and declarations can tell us the what, they are not necessarily the right places to find extensive arguments about the why. Secular humanists have long struggled to find and articulate a justification for how they can believe that humanity has objective purpose and dignity without a transcendent being as the root of value and purpose. From theistic morality to Aristotle's metaphysics and Plato's ethical questions to today's ethicists and philosophers, the search for what grounds human morality and purpose has persisted.

The centuries have shown that theists affirm the same *what* as secular humanists (that humans have value, dignity and purpose), but we have a far different *why*. In the past few years, with the increasing popularity of atheistic writings, secular humanists have endeavored to offer naturalistic justification for objective morality and human value. What we must consider now is whether secular humanism has any foundation that can justify its very name.

SAYING NOTHING AS LOUD AS WE CAN

As I think about the common affirmation secular humanists and theists have—that humanity has inherent dignity and purpose—I cannot help but recall an incident from my childhood. On a late summer afternoon when I was eleven years old, my younger brother, my cousin and I went to a local pizza shop. We were standing just outside the shop's windows, enjoying our freshly made slices, when I looked into the shop and saw something that jarred me. One of the employees, a young man no more than eighteen years old, was staring at me with his right hand raised in a vulgar gesture.

For some reason—maybe because I was so shocked—I opened the shop's door and asked him if he meant that gesture for me, though he obviously did. "That's right, camel jockey," he answered with a condescending smirk. "What're you gonna do about it?"

My initial shock over the rude gesture was instantly replaced by my shock at the ethnic slur. Without knowing the slightest thing about me and without even a modicum of concern over the fact that I was eleven years old, the pizza shop employee was perfectly willing to try to rob me of my dignity. He insulted me not because of any actions I had taken or any words I had spoken. No, he denigrated me solely because of my ethnicity. A part of my identity. A part of my humanness.

Race, ethnicity and gender are immutable human characteristics. When we are judged based on something about us that we cannot change—and that need not be changed—our very right to exist is called into question. In other words, racism and ethnic prejudices cause both theists and secular humanists to bristle with indignation precisely because they are an affront to our shared affirmation that humans are essentially, intrinsically valuable.

Christians and secular humanists dare not forsake this point of solidarity, lest we risk losing it and letting the evil and the ugliness we commonly abhor drive a wedge of disagreement where none need be. But we can't gloss over profound disagreements just for solidarity's sake. Yes, both atheistic secular humanists and Christians can agree *that* ugly prejudices are wrong and must be stopped because they do violence to human value, dignity and purpose. But we cannot agree about *why* they are wrong, because we do not agree about the source of human dignity.

Why are race, ethnicity and gender inviolable? Why is it wrong to discriminate against people based on these characteristics? The answer seems obvious, but let us give it a moment's thought. One could argue that discrimination is nonrational, perhaps even irrational, because discriminating based on race or gender in certain situations may not benefit humanity as a whole. But there is something more to it than that, isn't there? Beyond the cost-benefit analysis, there is something inherently moral in affirming that race and ethnicity are valuable. And there is something immoral about denigrating another for their race, gender or ethnicity. To treat someone disparately because she is black is unfair, in part because she had no control over being born black. But this cannot be the final analysis, can it? If it were, the statement itself has a racist element to it. It's as if being black is an unfortunate circumstance that the person had no choice in. And, poor soul, she would have chosen otherwise had she been given the choice.

No, racial, ethnic and gender discrimination are not immoral because race, ethnicity and gender are uncontrollable circumstances, but because they are sacred circumstances. Race, gender and ethnicity have inherent, objective value across humankind. In other words, they are sacred, and the sacred ought not be violated. The quest for both secular humanists and theists is to find the foundation for that sacredness and the value of humanity. This struggle is not just for philosophy professors. As we'll soon see, whether our worldview can justify the foundation for its answer to this Grand Central Question has implications and practical outworkings that may shock us.

The struggle to find objective purpose and meaning is inextricably intertwined with the question of our origins. Take the observations of Stephen Jay Gould, the late evolutionary biologist and paleontologist of Harvard University. Gould admitted that if humanity had no purposeful origin, there is no objective purpose to our existence:

> The human species has inhabited this planet for only 250,000 years or so—roughly .0015 percent of the history of life, the last inch of the cosmic mile. The world fared perfectly well without us for all but the last moment of earthly time—and this fact makes our appearance look more like an accidental afterthought than the culmination of a prefigured plan. . . .
>
> We are here because one odd group of fishes had a peculiar fin anatomy that could transform into legs for terrestrial creatures; because comets struck the earth and wiped out dinosaurs, thereby giving mammals a chance not otherwise available (so thank your lucky stars in a literal sense); because the earth never froze entirely during an ice age; because a small and tenuous species, arising in Africa a quarter of a million years ago, has managed, so far, to survive by hook and by crook. *We may yearn for a "higher" answer—but none exists.*

> *This explanation, though superficially troubling, if not terrifying,
> is ultimately liberating and exhilarating. We cannot read the
> meaning of life passively in the facts of nature. We must construct
> these answers ourselves—from our own wisdom and ethical
> sense. There is no other way.*[1]

If there is no God who created us, then Gould was right. He conceded that if we believe we were created as a matter of natural accident, then there is no higher answer, no objective meaning to life. He declared that we must construct these answers ourselves. Thus there is only the purpose and ethics we—the subject—create ourselves. Purpose is, by definition, subjective and dependent on the vagaries of our own wisdom and ethical sense.

Let us indulge in going beyond the face value of Gould's statements. Admittedly, this involves a bit of conjecture, but Gould's words reveal an existential undercurrent that comes from embracing a naturalistic worldview. As Stephen Crane puts it,

A man said to the Universe,
sir, I exist!
Nevertheless, replied the universe,
that fact has not created in me
the slightest feeling of obligation.[2]

How stoic Gould seems as he squarely looks into the yawning chasm of purposelessness and creates purpose and value by the sheer force of human will. But his words betray him as he admits something quite telling. A world without objective purpose beyond mere preference *is* terrifying. But Gould does not want to be terrified, so he proclaims this troubling fact to be liberating. He alleviates his terror by creating subjective meaning and value where neither exists objectively. This is what is supposedly liberating: we are the ultimate creators and arbiters of morality and value. Gould wants us somehow to feel exhilarated by this, despite the fact that centuries of human history have shown how little we actually value human life and how bad we are at agreeing on moral principles.

Perhaps unintentionally, Gould captures the ethos and pathos of secular humanism's struggle to support the ethical roof it has built over its head. What Gould has admitted—and why we start with him—is that secular humanists live in a state of cognitive dissonance. They want to affirm purpose, value and morality as objectively real, but they are confounded by the logic of their view that tells them they are merely convenient fictions.

THE VALUE OF PURPOSE

When we assert that humans have objective value and purpose, what are we talking about? What both secular humanists and theists want to affirm is that humans have *intrinsic* value as opposed to *extrinsic* value. Let us take extrinsic value first. Something has extrinsic value—value outside of its very nature—if its purpose is to achieve a desired end that is more fundamentally valuable than the thing itself. Take tools, for example. A tool has extrinsic value because it helps us accomplish certain tasks or build things that are more valuable than the tool itself. Money is another good example. It has extrinsic value because it helps us attain other ends, such as food, clothing, shelter or power, that mean more to us than the money we give up to acquire them. And even the things we give our money for, such as food, clothing and shelter, have only extrinsic value because they are means to a greater end—a more comfortable life.

Intrinsic value is much different. Something has intrinsic value not because it is a means to an end, but because it is an end in and of itself. In and of themselves, tools and currency are just collections of wood, metal and paper. They have no intrinsic value. If humans are to have intrinsic value, they cannot be merely tools for some other purpose. Humans must be the purpose themselves. This is not to say that something with intrinsic value cannot also serve an external purpose. For example, human beings can have intrinsic value even though God might use them for his purposes. Even that example does not belie humanity's intrinsic value, because God's purposes are meant to result in humanity's ultimate good.

In this way, to say that something has either extrinsic or intrinsic value is to say something important about the nature of its purpose. If something has only extrinsic value, then its purpose is merely subjective. A hammer is valuable to a carpenter for the purpose of making a living, but is not at all valuable to a software engineer for that purpose. But if something has intrinsic value, then its value is not a matter of opinion or circumstance. It is always just as valuable in every circumstance. And its purpose would not be merely a matter of subjective opinion, but of objective reality.

Sometimes seeing the distinction between extrinsic value and intrinsic value is difficult, but we need to make the effort, especially when the differences are subtle. If we fail to understand the differences, then we can fall into the trap of confusing the ends with the means. We can confuse the tool for the goal, and vice versa. This has happened all too frequently in human history, when we have sometimes confused people as the means to an end instead of being an end in and of themselves.

ACCIDENTALLY ON PURPOSE

Gould's comments have highlighted the rub for secular humanists: does secular humanism offer any grounding for its assertion that humanity as a whole and each human in particular have intrinsic value in an objective sense without God? James Sire explains the subjectivity of value and morality that logically follows from secular humanism, showing Gould's terror of a world without God to be quite understandable:

> We exist. Period. Our maker has no sense of value, no sense of obligation. We alone make values. Are our values valuable? By what standard? Only our own. Whose own? Each person's

own. Each of us is king and bishop of our own realm, but our realm is pointland. For the moment we meet another person, we meet another king and bishop. There is no way to arbitrate between two free value makers. There is no king to whom both give obeisance. There are values, but no Value. Society is only a bunch of windowless monads, a collection of points, not an organic body obeying a superior, all-encompassing form that arbitrates the values of its separate arms, legs, warts and wrinkles. Society is not a body at all. It is only a bunch.[3]

Without God, everyone is his or her own king or queen. At first, this may seem ennobling, even liberating, as Gould would say. But when we have displaced God as the authoritative Value Giver, we have stepped through the portal to a purely subjective realm. After all, what right does one king have to tell another king that his values are wrong? For that matter, how can one queen tell another queen what her intrinsic value is or even that she has intrinsic value at all, if they have equal authority? One king can say that society is better off without allowing Down syndrome–affected babies to live, while another winces at the thought. But the liberty that comes from making everyone a master is insidious because pure subjectivity makes us all slaves. *That* is terrifying.

Scientists like Lawrence Krauss are seeing the dilemma quite well, though they might mask it with talk about self-fabricated "purpose." In his book *A Universe from Nothing: Why There Is Something Rather Than Nothing*, Krauss tries to make the case that the universe actually did spring from nothing, but not because nothing is literally "not anything," but because it is actually "something," like a quantum vacuum.[4] He plays with words and definitions to get around the obviously inviolable maxim *ex nihilo, nihilo fit*—out of nothing, nothing comes. The punch line for Krauss is that ours is an existence without purpose. And, by implication, ours is an existence without objective, intrinsic value.

And so in a *Los Angeles Times* article Krauss asks us to consider a "universe without purpose."[5] He tells us that the "illusion of purpose and design" is pervasive and that science has to "confront" it.[6] It's interesting that Krauss thinks it's science's obligation to confront the illusion of purpose and design. Why can't science's obligation be to determine whether there *is* purpose and design? For Krauss, purpose is illusory not because the facts dictate it, but because it simply must be so.

He goes on to tell us that evolutionary science has supposedly shown us that this illusion can come about without a "governing plan."[7] What does this all mean for human purpose and intrinsic value according to Krauss? He acknowledges that we have an innate need to believe in objective purpose, but that we must get past it:

> As a cosmologist, a scientist who studies the origin and evolution of the universe, I am painfully aware that our illusions nonetheless reflect a deep human need to assume that the existence of the Earth, of life and of the universe and the laws that govern it require something more profound. For many, to live in a universe that may have no purpose, and no creator, is unthinkable.
>
> But science has taught us to think the unthinkable.[8]

One has to wonder what is so "painful" about Krauss's awareness of the human need for something more profound than the mere accidental creation of the universe. Perhaps he has evolved beyond such a pedestrian need and finds it painful to tolerate while he educates it out of us. But I digress. Krauss goes on to tell us the unthinkable things that science has supposedly led us to think:

> Does all of this prove that our universe and the laws that govern it arose spontaneously without divine guidance or purpose? No, but it means it is possible.
>
> And that possibility need not imply that our own lives are devoid of meaning. Instead of divine purpose, *the meaning in*

our lives can arise from what we make of ourselves, from our relationships and our institutions, from the achievements of the human mind.[9]

There is no ultimate meaning to anything, Krauss tells us. But rest assured, we can simply conjure up meaning and intrinsic value because, well, we say so. Somehow this is supposed to be as satisfying as Gould finds it exhilarating. But like Gould before him, Krauss unwittingly highlights the cognitive dissonance with which many secular humanists live. They find attractive the view that we have intrinsic value and dignity, yet they believe that we have no objective purpose. The tension between those two beliefs is difficult to exist in, and it is painfully broken when the nihilism that logically follows from atheism gets the upper hand. Krauss says that on a cosmic scale "we're just a bit of pollution" and that "if you got rid of us, and all the stars and all the galaxies and all the planets and all the aliens and everybody, then the universe would be largely the same. We're completely irrelevant."[10]

Is that liberating? How is that possibly in line with a belief in humanity's intrinsic value? But on atheism, how is Krauss wrong? If the source of humanity is "nothing," then why think that its goal is something—or anything—of significance? What does significance even mean? What Krauss, Gould and others really seem to be saying is that the only real value is the value of determining values for ourselves, without a transcendent authority telling us what to do. In other words, unfettered liberty is both the greatest and only value. We must jettison anything that gets in its way.

This is double talk and utterly circular, of course. We cannot reject the idea of purpose and then punctuate the nothingness with a made-up purpose and give it a positive-sounding name like "liberty." As David Bentley Hart observes,

> We trust, that is to say, that there is no substantial criterion by
> which to judge our choices that stands higher than the un-

questioned good of free choice itself, and that therefore all judgment, divine no less than human, is in some sense an infringement upon our freedom. This is our primal ideology. In the most unadorned terms possible, the ethos of modernity is—to be perfectly precise—nihilism.[11]

The evolutionary process as proposed by Darwin offers us no grounding for the objective purpose or intrinsic value that secular humanists seek to affirm. Indeed, it does quite the opposite. In the tautology that is natural selection's "survival of the fittest" and random genetic mutation, the superior species dominate the inferior ones. We humans are the current master race, but our empire may be supplanted someday should cataclysms and mutations cause our downfall or extinction. But such a coup would not be purposeful or tragic. It would be a purely mindless happenstance. Richard Dawkins makes this quite clear:

> If the universe were just electrons and selfish genes, meaningless tragedies . . . are exactly what we should expect, along with equally meaningless good fortune. Such a universe would be neither evil nor good in intention. . . . The universe we observe has precisely the properties we should expect if there is, at bottom, no design, no purpose, no evil and no good, nothing but blind pitiless indifference.[12]

Indeed, Dawkins is being too gentle in his description of the atheist's view of the universe as having "blind pitiless indifference." Indifference is too emotive a word, because it suggests that the universe could pay attention to us but chooses to ignore us. In an atheistic view, the universe is utterly mindless. It cannot be indifferent to us, because it would have what philosopher Michael Ruse calls "mindful inattention." But, according to Dawkins and the secular humanists, the universe has no mind to be inattentive with, just as a crayon cannot possibly be inattentive. The reality, according to Dawkins, Krauss and atheism in general, is that we are utterly alone with no one to value us on a grand scale.

Lest we misunderstand Dawkins and think that he allows the slightest room for intrinsic value or objective purpose for humanity (or any living creature), consider what he calls "purpose": "Human beings are simply machines for propagating DNA, and the propagation of DNA is a self-sustaining process. It is every living object's sole reason for living."[13]

Does that sound anything like the kind of purpose or intrinsic value each one of us innately desires to find? Is that really our sole reason for being? Put another, perhaps more pointed, way, when we look at our children, is it the case that they are merely the continuation of our genetic material? Do we hug and kiss bags of genetic material goodnight so that we can raise well-adjusted DNA carriers? It goes against our intuitions, and frankly it defies our sense that objective purpose is a reality and objective moral values exist.

Within themselves, most secular humanists, whether steeped in philosophy and science or unconcerned with either, would not accept it as true that humanity has no purpose other than to multiply. That would put humanity on a par with the influenza virus. Most secular humanists would not agree with that. But if there is no Creator, how is it wrong?

The cognitive dissonance, indeed the self-contradiction, inherent in secular humanism is made even plainer when we consider Dawkins's view of human purpose (to transmit DNA) and the New Atheists' moralizing against the church's view on homosexuality. The New Atheists all have branded conservative Christians as hate-filled bigots for wanting to preserve God's purpose for human sexuality. But Dawkins believes that our "sole reason for being" is to pass on genetic material, which implies that homosexual attraction violates that purpose:

> We can no more help ourselves feeling pity when we see a weeping unfortunate (who is unrelated and unable to recip-

rocate) than we can help ourselves feeling lust for a member
of the opposite sex (who may be infertile or otherwise unable
to reproduce). Both are misfirings, Darwinian mistakes:
blessed, precious mistakes.[14]

Does the contradiction not leap out at us? It is quite obvious that
if lust for someone of the opposite sex who cannot reproduce is
pitiable as an evolutionary misfiring or mistake, then so is homosexual attraction, because sexual consummation of that attraction
cannot possibly lead to reproduction. And evolutionarily, it should
eventually be selected out.

What warrant do we have for perpetuating a genetic mistake?
And why should rights and legal protections attach to genetic
mistakes that should be weeded out by natural selection? But
more to the point is this: if the sole purpose of humanity is to
transmit DNA into the next generation, as Dawkins says, then
homosexuality, which has no chance of doing that, is the very
violation of human purpose and is "unevolutionary." Essentially,
for Dawkins's view to be consistent, homosexual expressions are
cardinal sins because they violate the "sole" purpose we have. Yet
according to Dawkins, Christians—who believe in the inherent
sacredness of every person and their sexuality—are bigoted. One
can't help but think of pots and kettles.

The upshot is that many secular humanists admit that there is
no real purpose to humanity in an objective sense, but then get
angry when one set of subjective ideas about purpose conflict with
another set of subjective ideas about purpose. They admit that there
is no objective human purpose, but they write books and give
speeches as if there really is.

Theists have long claimed that atheists, including secular humanists, have no foundation for the inherent value of humanity that
secular humanists hold dear. In response, secular humanists affirm
their continued belief in intrinsic human value and purpose. Consider

the response of mathematical logician Raymond Smullyan, who says,

> I have always been extremely puzzled by those who have claimed that if there is no God, then life is meaningless. Is there the slightest shred of evidence that secular humanists find life less meaningful than do religious believers? I am not claiming that there is no God, nor am I claiming that there is one. All I am claiming is that life is extremely meaningful to most of those who live it—God or no God![15]

Smullyan's statement actually undermines the idea that human life has objective meaning and intrinsic value. He declares that life is meaningful "to most" who live it. It's not meaningful in and of itself; it's meaningful *to* the ones who live it. But they are the subjects of their lives, making the meaning that they give their lives subjective, not objective—by definition.

Smullyan is trying to make the point that life has objective meaning without God, but his very words betray him. Look again at his statement that life is "extremely meaningful to most." This means that life can only have extrinsic value—as a tool for someone who wants it but not for someone who doesn't. If a person's opinion of life is what determines its value or lack thereof, then for the minority who do not find life "extremely meaningful," isn't it true that life itself is not? It seems that in Smullyan's view, he has no basis to say otherwise. And if that were the case, what obligation would he have to persuade such a person not to end his subjectively meaningless life if he so chooses?

The irony demands to be noted here. Krauss wants to convince us that all things came from nothing and that purpose comes from purposelessness. But atheist philosopher Julian Baggini abandons the double talk in his piece titled "Yes, life without God can be bleak. Atheism is about facing up to that." With remarkable candor, he notes, "Atheists should point out that life without God can be meaningful, moral and happy. But that's 'can' not 'is' or even 'should usually be.'" And that means it can just as easily be meaningless, nihilistic and miserable.[16]

Note carefully Baggini's words. He says that life can be meaningful and moral, but it's quite clear that he is referring to subjective meaning and morality. He even acknowledges that—without God—there is no reason to believe that life *should* be meaningful or moral. His honesty about this continues when he criticizes the atheist associations in London that placed prominent signs on buses reading, "There's probably no God. Now stop worrying and enjoy your life":

> Atheists have to live with the knowledge that there is no salvation, no redemption, no second chances. Lives can go terribly wrong in ways that can never be put right. Can you really tell the parents who lost their child to a suicide after years of depression that they should stop worrying and enjoy life?[17]

Baggini has no rose-colored view of what an atheistic worldview might mean. It could mean human progress (although by whose standards is yet to be determined), or it could mean that all will end in horrible tragedy. In other words, humanity has no undergirding purpose or intrinsic value, nor does any individual human life. While self-perceived fulfillment can be the result of our striving, the result can just as easily be despair.

Those who disbelieve in God's existence yet still persist in creating purpose or meaning in their own lives are leaning on an emotional crutch to help them stand up to the void. Ironically, atheists often chide Christians for creating delusions like God and redemption as emotional crutches because they fear death. But it is secular humanists who laudably want to ground a sense of purpose and meaning who create the crutch, because their very worldview does not allow for any real purpose or meaning.

It is, in fact, worse than a delusion. One who has a delusion actually believes the falsity he has created. But secular humanists are almost schizophrenic here, because they choose to believe the delusion of purpose and intrinsic value, yet at the same time openly deny they exist. If one is to remain a secular humanist, one must be prepared to live with the fact that in a secular humanist worldview, the Grand Central Question about human purpose and value has no answer. Actually, the answer is clear: there is none.

MORALITY IN SEARCH OF MOORINGS

Just as most secular humanists assert that humans have intrinsic value, it is (thankfully) far more common for secular humanists to affirm the existence of objective moral value and duties than to deny they exist. As a point of clarification, I mean that a moral value is "objective" in that it is always true, regardless of human opinion or belief. A moral value is objective because it is true even if every single human believes it is false. It is always wrong to drug and rape someone. You will scarcely find anyone who doesn't believe this to be true, but even if you did, it would still be wrong.

The same problem that confronts secular humanists when it comes to intrinsic value and objective purpose persists in the struggle to ground objective morality without God. Theists have long argued that atheists lack any grounding on which to base the existence of objective moral values and duties. Now, theists do not argue that atheists cannot act morally or recognize right and wrong; they only argue that atheists have no rational basis to affirm that right and wrong exist.

But secular humanists try to ground the existence of objective morality on "shared values" and applied reason. The problems loom large, however, because the notion of shared values is fleeting and, by itself, has no objective grounding. In other words, just because a value is shared by the majority of humanity does not mean it is actually objectively moral. For example, for much of human history, we shared the value that certain people could actually own other people. This was true in ancient Rome, ancient Near Eastern societies and even (gasp) Enlightenment-era Europe. Does the shared approval of (or even indifference to) slavery mean that it was objectively moral to own people as property at that time? To ask the question is to answer it. And that answer obviously implies that *accepted* morality is often quite different from *objective* morality.

Like Baggini, many prominent atheists are beginning to admit that there is no grounding for objective morality without a transcendent authority like God, who is beyond humanity. Consider the words of Joel Marks, professor emeritus of philosophy at University of New Haven, who readily acknowledges—and even argues—that morality simply does not exist in a universe without God:

> The long and the short of it is that I became convinced that atheism implies amorality; and since I am an atheist, I must therefore embrace amorality. I call the premise of this argument "hard atheism." . . . A "soft atheist" would hold that one could be an atheist and still believe in morality. And indeed, the whole crop of "New Atheists" are softies of this kind. So was I, until I experienced my shocking epiphany that the religious fundamentalists are correct: without God, there is no morality. But they are incorrect, I still believe, about there being a God. Hence, I believe, there is no morality.[18]

Interestingly, Marks was once quite the moralist, arguing for the atheistic justification for morality and ethics. But he suddenly realized, in what he has called his "anti-epiphany," that in a universe without God, there is no such thing as morality. He utterly rejects, as a matter of the logical outworking of his atheism, that there are any such things as "right" and "wrong." He explains that certain activities, like animal abuse, are not actually wrong; they are just not preferable. Perhaps they are not preferable because they are not conducive to human happiness or just because a person wants to save cute animals from suffering (and may have no interest in saving ugly ones).

Marks is not alone in telling us that secular humanists who desire to ground morality apart from God are chasing after the wind. Just as Baggini admits that meaning and purpose are illusions in an atheistic worldview, so philosopher Michael Ruse tells us that, if we are here because of Darwinian evolution, morality is just the illusion that serves as a survival characteristic:

> The position of the modern evolutionist . . . is that humans have an awareness of morality . . . because such an awareness is of biological worth. Morality is a biological adaptation no less than are hands and feet and teeth. . . . Considered as a rationally justifiable set of claims about an objective something, ethics is illusory. I appreciate that when somebody says "Love thy neighbor as thyself," they think they are referring above and beyond themselves. . . . Nevertheless, . . . such reference is truly without foundation. Morality is just an aid to survival and reproduction, . . . and any deeper meaning is illusory.[19]

Marks, Ruse and others are part of the growing number of academic voices still dwarfed by a more popular-level crowd of secular humanists who have not yet realized that their search for objective morality's foundation without God is in vain. The chorus coming from the ranks of secular humanists, be they scholars or popular bloggers, is that there is an objective morality even if there is no God. According to Marks and Ruse, this likely comes from the evolutionary development that humans need to live by a set of ethical rules. And so secular humanists need to invent the illusion of morality while at the same time denying any source for it.

But even the boisterous moralizers among the New Atheists are forced to concede that there is no right or wrong without God, even if they have to sneak that concession in. Recall Dawkins's words that the world we observe is full of meaningless fortune and meaningless misery. And he goes on to say that in this godless world "there is, at bottom, no design, no purpose, no evil and no good, nothing but blind pitiless indifference."[20] As the naked emperor of atheistic morality parades by, the secular humanist crowd sees what it wants to see, what it needs to see. But the voices of Marks, Ruse and perhaps even Dawkins have shouted from that crowd that the secular humanist emperor has no moral clothes.

JUSTIFICATIONS IN JEOPARDY

Reason. Quite literally, secular humanists have rallied behind the banner of reason to find the mooring for morality, thus Dawkins's Reason Rally. Indeed, without a transcendent, personal being to ground objective morality, it is hard to see any option other than reason. It is certainly not a new argument. Today the argument goes something like this: Through the use of our reason and sense of empathy, we can see that it is generally preferable to be happy rather than sad, comfortable rather than in pain, and alive rather than dead; morality is just the set of guiding principles that allows us to maximize the greatest amount of happiness, comfort and life for the greatest number of people. Through pure reason, unaided by divine revelation, we can know that rape is wrong, murder is wrong, and helping others is good.

Ironically, it is utterly unreasonable to believe this. Clearly we can use reason to recognize that happiness, comfort and life are usually preferable to sadness, pain and death. And we can use reason to recognize that certain things are wrong and others are right. But that only means that reason is the tool by which we see that these things are true. Reason doesn't establish their truth. We can use reason to recognize what is right and wrong, but we can't use reason as the foundation or source for objective morality.

Perhaps an illustration will help. The human eye allows us to recognize the visible light spectrum. But the human eye is not the source of that spectrum. The waves of light and the photons that create red, green and even ultraviolet light would still exist if no one had eyes. Reason is like the human eye. It allows us to recognize the existence of objective moral values, but it is not the source of those values. If everyone in the world were morally handicapped so that they were incapable of recognizing that raping babies was wrong, it would still be wrong. Guenter Lewy put it well: "Moral reasoning can inform a conscience; it cannot create one."[21]

And reason alone is notoriously fickle when it comes to arriving at even an accepted morality, let alone an objective morality. If reason is the source of morality, on what reasonable basis would I sacrifice my life for anyone? If this seventy-plus years is all I have, all I will ever have, and only oblivion awaits me upon death, why give up everything I will ever have for someone else's sake? I would not get any satisfaction or even knowledge that my sacrifice helped, and any help would be fleeting at best anyway. So why end the world from my perspective? It seems that such self-sacrifice would be categorically unreasonably. And if reason is the foundation of morality, then acting unreasonably by sacrificing myself would be the same as acting immorally. Can that be the case? In atheism, it must be. But it is unthinkable.

These inherent problems with reason as the foundation of morality have not been lost on atheist philosophers. Kai Nielsen, the noted atheist philosopher, admits as much when he says,

> We have not been able to show that reason requires the moral point of view, or that all really rational persons should not be individual egoists or classical amoralists. Reason doesn't decide here. The picture I have painted for you is not a pleasant one. Reflection on it depresses me. . . . Pure practical reason, even with a good knowledge of the facts, will not take you to morality.[22]

Putting it even more bluntly, Allan Bloom tells us that "reason cannot establish values, and the belief that it can is the stupidest and most pernicious illusion."[23]

Science. With unaided reason out of the running as the source for morality, secular humanists have turned to today's seeming savior—science—to rescue us from the pesky God who persists in our quest to ground moral values. In the past few years, as their public platforms grew, today's empiricism-influenced secular humanists have tried to offer scientific justifications for the objectivity of morality and human value to finally answer secular humanism's Grand Central Question.

Sam Harris, in *The Moral Landscape,* tries to give us such a scientific basis for morality. He argues that what is "good" is what is conducive to the greatest happiness for the greatest number of people. Since we can (at least roughly) measure human flourishing, we have a scientific basis for goodness or morality. Studies can be (and have been) done to determine the level of fulfillment, happiness and survival under certain conditions, and those conditions that produce the highest levels of fulfillment, happiness and survival are what we should strive for. Because studies show that acting with compassion, empathy and altruism produce biological benefits both to the actors and to the receivers of the acts, we can see that it is "good" to act in accordance with those virtues. This view looks at the consequences of an act or set of acts, determines if those consequences are optimized for human flourishing, and then labels them as morally good if they are.

But Harris's argument does not advance the ball toward secular humanism's goal of grounding human value and morality without God. For one thing, those who hold religious beliefs, particularly beliefs in an afterlife, have improved their qualities of life. Dinesh D'Souza cites Duke University Professor of Psychiatry and Behavioral Sciences Harold Koenig's compilation of impressive data showing that people who hold beliefs in the afterlife are "less likely to suffer from stress and depression, less likely to attempt suicide, less vulnerable to a host of other ailments, and are more likely to live longer."[24]

Koenig's findings are not isolated. Recent findings by Gallup, as part of its study on religiosity and well-being in America, show that religious people have higher well-being than the nonreligious.[25] Thus, if humanity's purpose is to "be well" or flourish, and that purpose somehow qualifies as objective, then it seems that religious beliefs ought to be fostered, not stifled. And in Harris's view, religious beliefs therefore would have objective moral value because there is good evidence that they contribute to human flourishing.

There is quite a gap in Harris's science-based argument, isn't there? While it might be empirically true that acting morally and trying to preserve human dignity makes us feel better and flourish, we are still faced with the more fundamental question of why human flourishing is objectively good in the first place. It is question-begging to assume that human flourishing is inherently or objectively "good," because the very thing we are looking for is an objective value to humanity, irrespective of human opinion. But if human flourishing is only important to human beings (and that would have to be so in a naturalistic framework) then the "goodness" of human flourishing is still subjective, not objective. Indeed, it is the very definition of subjective value. This means that we cannot be intrinsically valuable independent of human opinion, because our opinion is the only one there is. If a comet were suddenly to strike the Earth and wipe us all out, there would be no loss of value and no moral tragedy in the greater context of the reality of the mindless cosmos.

Can that really be the way it is with humanity? Is our value limited to our physical existence? And if it is, what then of justice, compassion and mercy? Mother Teresa's life of service to the orphans of India ultimately merits her oblivion, while Hitler's unspeakable cruelty to millions merits him the exact same reward. Is there justice in that? And there would be no lasting moral legacy to come from righting wrongs or feeding the hungry, because one day the entire universe will just cease to be. Those orphans Teresa helped will eventually cease to exist, as will their children and their children's children, ad infinitum. There is no ultimate meaning to any of these things because all of them are temporary, with temporary effects that will wink out of existence in either the near or distant future. And make no mistake: in the naturalistic view that underlies all of secular humanism, everything will die a heat death in the end. As Ernest Nagel unflinchingly states, according to atheism, humanity is "an episode between two oblivions."[26]

So why believe, in an objective sense apart from human opinion, that human flourishing is meaningful or good as opposed to the flourishing of the H1N1 virus or mosquitos? In fact, humans might greatly disagree over what it means to flourish. Why think that humans have the right to meaningful and enjoyable lives over, say, cows?

Harris acknowledges this problem deep within the endnotes of *The Moral Landscape*. He addresses philosopher Robert Nozick's term "utility monsters," which Nozick defines as creatures, like humans, who flourish at the expense of other creatures, like cows.[27] In that example, humans are the "utility monsters of cows." Assuming that the more advanced humans derive well-being from eating cows, it is ethical to sacrifice bovine well-being for our own.[28] While this might not trouble us humans as omnivores who enjoy the occasional steak, Harris acknowledges that it doesn't work out so well for cows. He even points out that if we can imagine cows suddenly realizing their plights, it may be *unethical* for such subservient creatures to revolt against their utility monsters, because the cows' well-being is outweighed by ours.[29]

Harris recognizes where this is headed philosophically when it comes to objective human purpose and morality and agrees with Nozick that if there were "superbeings" far more advanced than humans who derived well-being from consuming us, they would be our utility monsters, and it would be ethically permissible for them to use us for their happiness.[30] In such a situation, could we say, in any objective sense, that highly advanced extraterrestrials ought to respect our dignity as human beings or our right to life? In fact, would we even have such a right? If we have no obligation to respect the dignity of lower creatures like cows, chickens or even amoeba, why would beings far more advanced than us have an obligation to respect our dignity?

It seems that for secular humanism, without a transcendent authority like God, there would be no such obligation. As Harris puts it, "There seems no reason to suppose that we must occupy the highest peak on the moral landscape. If there are beings who stand in relation to us as we do to bacteria, it should be easy to admit that their interests must trump our own, and to a degree that we cannot possibly conceive."[31]

This discussion of utility monsters leads us once again to the conclusion that secular humanists who argue in favor of intrinsic human value and objective morality live in a state of cognitive dissonance. Science cannot help us escape the fact that, without a universally transcendent purpose-giver, purpose, value and ethics are all relative to the cognitive abilities of different species. Isn't Harris admitting that, on a conceptual level, ethics and morality are entirely situational and based on the subject? In other words, we have an ethical sense that things "lower" than us should serve us, while the lower things might think otherwise. So the morality is different based on the subject.

Further still, and perhaps even more fundamental, is the fact that in a secular humanist view, one species can define the very purpose of another species. Humanity, for instance, can define the purpose of cows to be merely livestock—nothing higher. Why couldn't it be the case that intellectually advanced extraterrestrials could define humanity's purpose as merely slaves or livestock? Without God, there really is nothing wrong with one set of creatures subjugating another set of creatures if the overlords derive a benefit from such actions. Western slave traders and owners could have argued that they were the utility monsters of the Africans (and to some degree they did). Again, it seems on the atheistic, naturalistic view that forms secular humanism's basis, the answer is yes, our purpose could be defined as something grossly inferior to what it is now (if there even is one). In other words, we could easily have only an extrinsic value. We would have no intrinsic value—no value as ends in ourselves.

Thankfully, save for a few, I know of no secular humanist who wouldn't have a visceral reaction to such implications. And, thankfully, the overwhelming majority of them, including Dawkins, Harris and their ranks, bristle at the ideas of racial subjugation. Indeed, human purpose, value and dignity are fundamental assumptions of secular humanism. The problematic implications arise when secular humanism tries to answers its Grand Central Question from the perspective that God does not exist.

As I said before, the question is not—and has never been— whether secular humanists have morals, can act morally or view humanity as intrinsically valuable. The question that we must struggle with—and that secular humanists have struggled with—is how do we justify the assumption that humans have intrinsic value, purpose and dignity? I am convinced that secular humanists' deeply felt need to find the source of human value and purpose is satisfied in the Christian worldview.

CONCLUSIONS AND CONSEQUENCES

An obvious response to all of this may be that, as long as secular humanists believe that humans have intrinsic value, what does it matter if they have no logical grounding for those beliefs? In other words, on a pragmatic level, why care about needing God for the foundation of meaning and morality as long as we live as if it has a foundation?

It matters quite a bit. The advances of every human endeavor— be it philosophy, engineering, medicine, theology or what have you—are determined by their foundations. In aeronautics, for example, it is not enough for us to know *that* planes fly because of the dynamics of air flowing past wings; we need to understand *how* and *why* that aids in flight. Pragmatically, we could have easily abandoned the search for the how and why. But, at best, that would have left us with useless kite-like contraptions.

The same is true of our worldviews. We need to understand the how and why of our worldviews, because we intuitively know that the foundations of our views have pragmatic implications on how we live our lives individually and corporately. Mere pragmatism does not help us progress. As G. K. Chesterton put it, "Pragmatism is a matter of human needs, and one of the first human needs is to be something more than a pragmatist."[32] Pragmatism, in other words, isn't as pragmatic as it needs to be for us to foster human value.

Ironically, the need to break free of useful fictions is itself pragmatic. What does it take for the fictional house of morality and value in the absence of God to come crashing down? Very little, as history has shown us. Bentley Hart rightly notes that human frameworks ungirded by a transcendent, value-giving authority are but "fragile fictions," easily toppled by a stumbling of human will:

> For every ethical theory developed apart from some account of transcendent truth—of, that is, the spiritual or metaphysical foundation of reality—is a fragile fiction, credible only to those sufficiently obstinate in their willing suspension of disbelief. If one does not wish to be convinced, however, a simple "I disagree" or "I refuse" is enough to exhaust the persuasive resources of any purely worldly ethics.[33]

These are not just alarmist predictions of someone who believes in God trying to convince secular humanists that the sky will fall unless they believe in God too. It is, rather, quite a real possibility that a world without ontic referents for human purpose, dignity and morals will go haywire because someone with impressive letters behind his name or with exceptional political prowess says, "I disagree," incredibly convincingly. In fact, this has already happened in the most educated countries in the world. And it can easily happen again. Baggini unblushingly recognized this fact, saying, "In an atheist universe, morality can be rejected without external sanction at any point, and without a clear, compelling reason to believe in its reality, that's exactly what will sometimes happen."[34]

Indeed, Stalin's murderous regime in Soviet Russia, with no higher power to account to other than the state, is an obvious example of a regime that stamped out millions of lives with impunity. Mao's China and Kim Jong Il's North Korea are further examples of basic human freedoms violated by an autocracy that held humans to be underneath it and nothing to be above it.[35]

But we need not look to oppressive regimes for examples of extremism to see that pure naturalism can logically lead to the abandonment of intrinsic human value and objective purpose. Prominent thinkers and scholars from some of our leading universities have claimed outright that certain humans have only extrinsic value— value determined by their usefulness to others. The autonomy of atheism has, as Krauss says, caused us to "think the unthinkable."

I think of Peter Singer, professor of bioethics at no less prestigious an institution than Princeton University. He has written and spoken much on the ethics of killing not just the unborn through abortions but also actually born people—infants. Infants are not self-aware, and so they cannot place value on themselves, Singer argues. Accordingly, they have value only if their parents give it to them. And so parents can kill infants within a month of being born if they burden the parents or society. Being human, by itself, is not enough to confer intrinsic value as a person.

In an op-ed piece written in *The Scotsman*, titled "Why it's Irrational to Risk Women's Lives for the Sake of the Unborn," Singer tells us that "membership of the species *Homo sapiens* is not enough to confer a right to life."[36] According to Singer, "we have no obligation to allow every being with the potential to become a rational being to realize that potential."[37]

Most bioethicists, including atheist bioethicists, disagree with Singer's view. But without a transcendent Value Giver, how can they disagree logically? Can we see what has happened here? Singer has shown us that without God to give us intrinsic worth, we can simply choose to confer worth on whomever we choose, provided they can think or are otherwise useful. Humans are like tools. They serve our purposes. They have no intrinsic value.

Amazingly, some medical ethicists are taking Singer's ideas seriously. Two such ethicists have argued that a woman can kill a newborn baby for the same reason that she can abort a preborn baby. In *The Journal of Medical Ethics*, Alberto Giubilini and Francesca Minerva argue that newborn children with Down syndrome may be killed after birth because "such children might be an unbearable burden on the family and on society as a whole, when the state economically provides for their care."[38] According to Giubilini and Minerva, such babies have value not intrinsically because they are human, but only insofar as they are not a burden. Newborns and others with severe mental impairments who can't yet cognitively ascribe value to their own lives have no right to that life.[39] They are somehow "less" than the rest of us. Indeed, newborns and the severely mentally handicapped are not actual persons.[40]

Giubilini and Minerva tell us that "a particular moral status can be attached to a nonperson [like a newborn] by virtue of the value an actual person (e.g., the mother) attributes to it."[41] Perhaps unwittingly, they actually argue that babies only have extrinsic value. They do not have value in themselves. And, in the secular humanist paradigm, those ethicists cannot be disputed. Ideas, it has famously been said, have consequences.

These are shocking—indeed, revolting—ideas. But they can result when one human being—who is no more an authority than any other—simply says, "I disagree." The fiction that humans have intrinsic value without God collapses at that moment. It collapses so easily because it is built on the shifting sand of human opinion. Singer's ideas are not human progress of any sort. In ancient times, tribes would sacrifice their children to gods to appease their wrath, get good crops or prevent wars. In other words, those children had only extrinsic value because they were a means to an end. Thousands of years later, our scholars and professors are calling for something eerily similar. They have just replaced the child-hungry gods of old with our contemporary personal desires for comfort and financial freedom. It is hardly the human progress to which most secular humanists aspire.

WHERE TO TURN?

All of this has not been to demean secular humanists' moral intuition and belief in human dignity and morality. Quite the opposite. Secular humanists have that recognition, that intuition that human beings are not valuable because they are merely means to an end, but ends in themselves. But the struggle remains as to how to understand that value in a world where there is no God. Secular humanists' struggle and desire to advance human dignity by understanding its source cannot find support on the foundation of atheism. Gould recognized that fact, and so he manufactured pleasant fictions of subjective value.

But is there a source for intrinsic human value? Is there somewhere we humans can find true humanness? I am convinced that it is not to be found in secular humanism. When we understand what value really is, we can begin to see that there is a place to turn for answers to this Grand Central Question. Value is quite simple, really. In our everyday lives, we measure value by what we are willing to pay for. But can we see in this simple fact a reflection of something greater, something ultimate in terms of value? Perhaps there is something in the gospel of Jesus Christ that uniquely speaks of the intrinsic value that we all look for.

WILL THE REAL HUMANISM PLEASE STAND UP?

THREE WORDS THAT MAKE IT MATTER

As I sat at a table at a nice restaurant, catching up with a classmate who was in town on business, the subject of intrinsic human value and purpose was suddenly thrust into real life. The hour grew late on that weekday evening as we enjoyed talking about our families and careers. All the other patrons had long since gone, leaving only us and the staff, when our discussion turned to spiritual matters. He knew of my conversion to Christianity from Islam and had learned that I started a ministry, so he naturally asked me why I followed Jesus. I knew from our time in school that he was agnostic, leaning more toward atheism, and he always had a way of making philosophical conversations more personal.

As we talked about the possibility of God's existence, the look in his eyes and the tone of his voice took on a subtle hint of somberness. That tone peaked when we began discussing human suffering. Looking down at his coffee, he asked me how I could believe that an all-powerful, loving God exists given the amount of suffering and evil in the world. His tone was almost apologetic, as if he was sorry that he had to ask me that question, knowing how difficult it can be to answer.

But he wanted an answer. Perhaps he even needed one.

He was interested in the theological and philosophical answers, but I sensed that there was more to it than that. His concern over the so-called "problem of evil" was intensely personal. So I fidgeted just a bit more as I provided some of the philosophical and theological responses. I hoped that he would reveal why the issue was so important to him while fearing that he wouldn't.

But he did.

"It's hard for me to believe that a loving God exists after my mom died when I was just ten years old," he told me. "You can call that a life-shaping moment."

He spoke those three words softly, but with an intensity that made me mentally capitalize them. Life-shaping moment. Those words connected the intellectual and emotional aspects of our humanity. At a tender age, my friend lost someone he valued as a person in her own right, but more specifically as his mother. She had value to him, but did she have ultimate value and purpose? How could she if God let her die so young? And how could my friend have ultimate value and purpose if God let him suffer through that loss when he was so young? The problem of evil is really a restatement of the Grand Central Question, do we have intrinsic value and objective purpose?

How does one answer at that moment? To trot out more syllogisms to defend God's existence in response to such an anguish-laden statement would have been insensitive, perhaps even cold. But a mere "God works in mysterious ways" would have been vapid and equally insensitive. How can we address life-shaping moments in ways that touch the mind and the heart?

The quandary is not for the theist alone. Secular humanists want to offer a satisfying answer too. When someone asks whether his mother's death had meaning or was just random, what can secular humanists say? Dawkins tells us emphatically that tragedy is ultimately meaningless. Gould could tell my bereaved friend only to conjure up his own meaning for his mother's death. But the tone of my friend's statement suggested that he had tried but was unable to do so these many years. He couldn't see any meaning in it unless God exists. But if God does exist, what could the meaning and purpose of his mother's life and death possibly be?

There is something about death that makes us think hard about life and ask the difficult questions. If a person dies young, before having the chance to contribute something to society or find a sense of self-fulfillment, did her life have meaning and purpose? Does her death? After all, if life is to have objective purpose and meaning, shouldn't a person's death also have meaning? Indeed, a meaningless death seems to be one of the worst tragedies we can think of. Is there anything sadder than the words "she died for nothing" or "he died in vain"?

A popular song aptly calls this the "sharp knife of a short life." It is part of our humanness to look for meaning in life and death—especially death. That stems from something deeper than just a fear of the unknown. There is something innate in us that recognizes that this universe, this planet and our bodies have the fingerprints of intention all over them. As John Templeton put it, "Would it not be strange if a universe without purpose accidentally created humans so obsessed with purpose?"[1]

THE HALLMARK OF PURPOSE

Abstract paintings have never really captured my eye, but as I look more carefully and begin to understand what the artist is trying to express, I can understand why some pieces fetch a high price in the art world. Even the most abstract or impressionistic paintings have purpose behind them. Art worth looking at shows purpose and choices. One color may be used to show contrast, while a streak of subdued paint might show depth. Each choice is a purposeful expression. We give our attention to a piece of art not because it is random, but because it was purposefully made.

In the Christian worldview, every bit of creation was intentionally made, as evidenced by the appearance of design in every object from the largest to the infinitesimal. And so, in the Christian view, the universe in general and humanity specifically have purpose. God's purpose in designing all of this demonstrates our intrinsic value and our objective purpose.

THE OUTER LIMITS OF PURPOSE

The Bible's 3,500-year-old opening lines tell us that the universe had a beginning and that its formation, and the formation of the world, was sequential. In the very first line of Genesis, we read, "In the beginning, God created the heavens and the earth. The earth was without form and void, and darkness was over the face of the deep" (Genesis 1:1-2). Setting aside for a moment that the Bible records God as the creative agent, let's just focus on the opening words: "In the beginning." There is something remarkable in those words, especially given that they were written so long ago.

It's remarkable because, millennia ago, the Bible recorded that time, space and matter sprang into existence at a point in the finite past. And they didn't spring into existence by mindless accident. No, they came to be by a timeless, spaceless, powerful being's design. In the not-so-distant past, cosmologists once thought the physical universe to be infinitely old—that it had no beginning. Since the days of Einstein's theories of general and special relativity, we now understand that the universe indeed had a beginning in the finite past. As Stephen Hawking has put it, "Almost everyone now believes that the universe, *and time itself*, had a beginning at the Big Bang."[2] What science once thought to be a gross error in the Bible has turned out to be verified by top scientists, including those who don't believe in God.

The point is that a beginning of everything in the physical universe implies a beginner to get it all started. If the Bible is correct that the cause of the universe's beginning is God—an immaterial, omnipotent and timeless being—then we would expect to see supporting evidence. We already have evidence that the universe—including all matter, energy and time—began at a point in the finite past. From what is popularly known as the *kalam* cosmological argument, we can infer that the first cause of all causes looks very much like the God of the Bible. The argument provides that everything that begins to exist has a cause. We now know that the universe began to exist, and thus we can know that the universe had a cause.[3] And as a matter of logic, the cause of the universe would have to be transcendent; it would be spaceless (because there was no space when there was no universe), timeless (because time did not exist when there was no universe) and immaterial (because there was no matter yet). And this cause would have to be immeasurably powerful to be able to create everything from literally nothing. More can be said about this, but suffice it to say that mindless physical forces, laws and conditions cannot be the candidates for the cause of everything, since they could not have existed without a universe. The best and most plausible option left, then, is a transcendent, powerful and personal being—God.

We actually have good evidence of intelligent handiwork in the creation of the universe. All scientists, theists and atheists alike, believe that the universe was finely tuned for the advent of life on this Earth, especially in the initial conditions and forces at its very beginning. Now, the term *fine-tuning* is, in and of itself, a theologically neutral phrase. It simply means that, as a matter of fact, the conditions and forces at the universe's beginning fall within an exquisitely narrow, or fine, range to allow for life to develop. If those conditions and forces were slightly different, life in the universe would be impossible.[4]

Consider just a few examples of how finely tuned the universe is to allow for life.

Stephen Hawking has estimated that if the rate of the universe's expansion one second after the Big Bang had been smaller by even one part in a hundred thousand million million, the universe would have re-collapsed into a hot fireball. British physicist P. C. W. Davies has calculated that in order to be suitable for later star formation (without which planets could not exist) the relevant initial conditions must be fine-tuned to a precision of one followed by a thousand billion billion zeroes, at least. He also estimates that a change in the strength of gravity or of the weak force by one part in 10^{100} would have prevented a life-permitting universe. Roger Penrose of Oxford University has calculated that the odds of the Big Bang's low entropy condition existing by chance are on the order of one out of $10^{10(123)}$. There are around 50 such quantities and constants present in the Big Bang that must be fine-tuned this way if the universe is to permit life.[5]

The sheer force of this kind of data compels even atheist scientists like Hawking to make some candid admissions: "The remarkable fact is that the values of these numbers seem to have been very finely adjusted to make possible the development of life."[6] The fine-tuning is not in dispute. What is in dispute is the conclusion we can draw from it. A secular humanist would make the inference that the conditions and values at the start of the universe, though fantastically improbable, resulted from mere chance or necessity. But the theist would draw a different inference, not based on what we don't know, but on what we do know. We know, from observations, that information specifically ordered to fit a given set of circumstances arises from an intelligence, not from mindless chance. Thus the best explanation of the fantastic improbabilities is that a divine intelligence chose the values and conditions purposefully.

We regularly infer the actions of an intelligent being as a better explanation than mere chance. If we found a body in a shallow grave with three bullet holes in the chest, would it be better to infer that the person accidentally fell into a shallow hole onto some bullets forcefully enough to drive the bullets into his body and then the hole got covered with dirt due to the wind? Or would the more rational inference be that the person was shot and thrown into a shallow grave that the murderer covered to hide the body? Had we seen the investigators on our favorite television police drama chalk it up to a natural accident, we'd likely change the channel in disgust.

We are certainly within reason to infer that the universe was finely tuned for life on purpose. So compelling is the inference that a designer specifically chose the values and conditions of the universe such that life would be possible, that prominent scientists admit the case for design. The British physicist Paul Davies comments that the initial conditions of the universe are so finely tuned that "It is hard to resist the impression that the present structure of the universe, apparently so sensitive to minor alterations in numbers, has been rather carefully thought out."[7]

After centuries of effort, we are only starting to unlock the mysteries of our universe and formulate equations to try to explain the phenomena we see. The findings fill both scientists and laypeople with awe and wonder. As someone who used his considerable intellect over his entire career seeking explanations about our universe, Davies offers a penetrating insight:

> A common reaction among physicists to remarkable discoveries . . . is a mixture of delight at the subtlety and elegance of nature, and of stupefaction: "I would never have thought of doing it that way." If nature is so "clever" it can exploit mechanisms that amaze us with their ingenuity, is that not persuasive evidence for the existence of intelligent design behind the physical universe? *If the world's finest minds can unravel only with difficulty the deeper workings of nature, how could it be supposed that those workings are merely a mindless accident, a product of blind chance?*[8]

It is critical that we understand what Davies is asking. How can our collective intelligence as a species be stymied by nonintelligence? The best answer is that an intelligence far greater than our combined intelligence was behind it all. We have such great difficulty, despite the genius of men and women like Newton, Einstein, Curie and Hawking, because we are playing catch-up with the very Creator of our minds.

Since the Enlightenment, secular thinkers have charged religious believers, specifically Christians, with backward-thinking superstition that holds back scientific discovery. Yet in his most recent book, Hawking has to admit that such ancient ideas are not so backward after all, given that "the discovery relatively recently of the extreme fine-tuning of so many of the laws of nature could lead at least some of us back to the old idea that this grand design is the work of some grand designer."[9] It is strangely poetic that secularists tell us how backward Christians are when science is only now catching up to what the Bible said so many centuries ago: "The heavens declare the glory of God, and the sky above proclaims his handiwork" (Psalm 19:1).

The strength of the design inference is highlighted by the competing inferences atheist scientists are willing to make—just so long as a purposeful designer is not allowed in the door. Unable to retreat to the once safe haven that the universe is eternal, such scientists posit the existence of a multiverse, also known as the many worlds hypothesis. These theories try to explain away the fantastic improbabilities of our life-permitting universe by saying that there are an infinite number of universes coming into and going out of existence all the time. Because there is an infinite number of them, it is inevitable that one of them would be a life-permitting universe, and ours is that universe.

Is the problem with such a theory not incredibly obvious? Does the irony not leap out at us? It is utterly unscientific to explain away the highly improbable existence of our life-permitting universe by relying on the existence of utterly unknown multiverses. Such scientists chide theists for inserting God into the gaps of our understanding of unexplained phenomena. Yet those same scientists are willing to plug unwarranted multiverses into those gaps with abandon. The fact that atheist scientists have to resort to such theories shows how strong the design inference actually is.

Lawrence Krauss's effort to tell us that everything came from nothing also highlights the strength of the design inference. In *A Universe from Nothing*, Krauss argues that quantum mechanics has shown us that subatomic particles pop into and out of existence all the time within certain arrangements of quantum fields of subatomic energy. By extrapolation, Krauss proposes that in the beginning of the universe, there was nothing but a "vacuum" of quantum energy with no actual physical particles in it at all, and eventually the quantum energy vacuum arranged itself in such a way that—poof!—matter formed out of nothing.[10]

But Krauss is playing games with the word *nothing*. He does not mean "not anything" for the simple reason that the quantum vacuum is actually something. As David Albert has pointed out, the quantum vacuum field is actually an arrangement of physical matter.[11] So desperate is Krauss to exclude God as the fine tuner of the universe that he asks us not only to believe that everything sprang mindlessly from nothing, but also that nothing actually is something.

The willingness of scientists to retreat to such logically and empirically bankrupt explanations tells us much about the strength of the design inference. But there is more to it than that. The inference that can be made from the scientific data goes beyond a powerful designer of some sort that is equally likely to be purposeless as purposeful. The universe is finely tuned not for just any state of affairs. It is not finely tuned for the existence of comets and stars and quasars. It is finely tuned—exquisitely tuned—to support life.

The life-permitting properties of the universe are so narrow in their ranges and so sensitive to deviations that even the slightest change would be catastrophic to life. From that we can quite reasonably infer that the designer made choices—specific and narrow choices—in making a universe that allowed humanity to be possible. Choices imply a mind. They imply a will. They imply purpose.

THE INNER BEAUTY OF PURPOSE

How strange it would seem that God would pay any attention to us given the immensity and splendor of the cosmos. In the Psalms, David asks, "O LORD, our Lord, how majestic is your name in all the earth! You have set your glory above the heavens. . . . When I look at your heavens, the work of your fingers, the moon and the stars, which you have set in place, what is man that you are mindful of him, and the son of man that you care for him?" (Psalm 8:1, 3-4). We seem so insignificant compared to the red giant stars, the super-sized galaxies and the nebulae from which stars are born. Krauss says that in comparison to the cosmos, we are a "bit of pollution." But the Bible answers its own question—what is man that God cares for him?—differently.

Long before television turned DNA into the magical elixir that solves crimes in just under an hour, King David glorified God as the designer of humanity's most intricate building blocks:

> For You formed my inward parts;
> You wove me in my mother's womb.
> I will give thanks to You, for I am fearfully and wonderfully
>   made . . .
> My frame was not hidden from You,
> When I was made in secret,
> And skillfully wrought in the depths of the earth. (Psalm
>   139:13-15 NASB).

If the Bible is right about the intentional design of human beings, what would we expect to see? We would expect to see choices made about how the biological and chemical mechanisms for life would work and interact. We would expect to see the highly improbable actually happen to form life. If a divine intelligence were responsible for life, we would expect to see life characterized by highly specific, ordered information. And science once again has shown us exactly that.

Not long ago, geneticists finally completed mapping the human genome. The sheer amount of information found in human DNA, which is floating in the trillions of cells in each of our bodies, was so staggering that Francis Collins, one of the directors of the Human Genome Project, was compelled to tell us about the findings:

> This newly revealed text was 3 billion letters long, and written in a strange and cryptographic four-letter code. Such is the amazing complexity of the information carried within each cell of the human body, that a live reading of that code at a rate of three letters per second would take thirty-one years, even if reading continued day and night. Printing these letters out in regular font size on normal bond paper and binding them all together would result in a tower the height of the Washington Monument. For the first time on that summer morning this amazing script, carrying within it all of the instruction for building a human being, was available to the world.[12]

Does that not inspire awe? It is not just that the human genetic code's complexity makes it interesting or shows that it is intentionally designed. The fact that it is highly complex and specified *information* shows the *purpose* behind it. DNA is a self-replicating chemical compound that provides the information to allow proteins to be built. They in turn encode the material that makes up our genes, which in turn determines how tall we are, how far our eyes are set apart, our genders and our ethnicities.

From this highly complex ordering of three billion letters we can certainly infer intentional design. We have never observed an environment where there is this kind of ordered information, so highly specified, where there wasn't also an intelligence behind that ordering. If science is about drawing inferences from observable facts, and we have never observed an ordered set of information arising without an intelligence behind it, then the scientific inference to draw from the amazingly voluminous and ordered library of information that makes up every human is that we are designed. Choices were made to ensure that it would all work together to create us. And where choices are made, there is purpose.

Still, there are those who dismiss this as an unwarranted inference. So they come up with competing theories about how DNA could have formed from the "prebiotic soup" that allegedly existed on the Earth so many eons ago. But each of these has its own problems. The theory that DNA formed by random chance has been all but abandoned in academic circles because the probability of amino acids forming even a single protein by blind chance is less than 1 in 10^{125} (that's a 10 followed by 125 zeros). Still others want to apply ideas of natural selection to the chemicals that make up DNA. But, as Stephen Meyer has pointed out, this is utterly circular, because to get natural selection to develop chemicals that self-replicate, the self-replicating system that is found in DNA needs to be in place already. Because this kind of chemical natural selection is impossible, Theodosius Dobzhansky concluded that "prebiotic natural selection is a contradiction in terms."[13]

Still another naturalistic theory has been offered to avoid the design inference. Some have suggested that the chemicals or molecules that make up DNA are structured so that they had to combine because they have natural attractions to each other. In water molecules, for example, hydrogen and oxygen naturally form bonds with each other. And when we see the molecules binding to each other, we can get structured patterns in, say, ice crystals.

But there is a looming problem. While a matrix of water molecules is certainly an ordered arrangement, it isn't anything remotely like the irregular and complex arrangement of chemicals in DNA. In water, we just get repeated patterns, over and over again: H-O-H, H-O-H and so on. Michael Polanyi points this out when he asks, "What would happen if we could explain the sequencing in DNA and proteins as a result of self-organization properties? Wouldn't we end up with something like a crystal of salt, where there's merely a repetitive sequence?"[14] But DNA is ordered far differently. Its four amino acids combine in utterly irregular, nonpatterned combinations. And those irregularities don't result in nonsense and nonfunction. They result in specified information used to make proteins, which in turn build functioning organisms.[15]

Ever resistant to the idea that DNA could have been purposefully designed by a transcendent intelligence, some scientists have argued that most of our DNA does not encode proteins and is thus "junk DNA." They argue that if our DNA were designed, it wouldn't have so much useless information in it. But, they argue, if our DNA evolved through natural selection and random mutations, we would expect to see leftover useless information. The idea of junk DNA recently has been debunked, as scientists in the Encyclopedia of DNA Elements (ENCODE) project provided evidence that up to 80 percent of our DNA actually has functionality.[16]

This is all terribly ironic, of course. Those scientists who accuse those who believe in God of halting scientific progress by inserting God into the gaps of our scientific knowledge have done something far more egregious. They did not know what the function of most DNA was, so they concluded that there must not be any function (after all, there is no God). And in so doing, they held back scientific inquiry into whether such functions exist. But lo and behold, they do exist.

In the end, we can reasonably infer that the building blocks of humanity arose not by mindless forces, but by an intelligent agent.

I want to be careful here, because I am not arguing in favor of God's having designed us because we currently don't know otherwise. Like those scientists who advocate intelligent design, I'm not arguing based on what we don't know, but rather on what we do know. We know that DNA is information, an incredible set of highly specified and uniquely ordered information. And all the evidence we have is that such information comes from the work of intelligence.

Indeed, biochemist Michael Denton tells us that the complexity of the smallest element of life "excels in every sense anything produced by the intelligence of man."[17] Denton says of DNA what Davies says of the universe: it strains common sense to think that something that our finest minds can't fully understand came about through mindless processes. It is this fact that caused Francis Crick, himself a committed atheist, to admit that "the origin of life appears at the moment to be almost a miracle, so many are the conditions which would have had to have been satisfied to get it going."[18]

IMPLICATIONS OF DESIGN

I find two related facts absolutely fascinating. The human eye can see neither the far reaches of the universe nor the inner workings of the human cell without the aid of ingenuously designed instruments. And God tells us in the Bible that as we use our intellect to discover what's "out there" and what's "in here," we will discover purpose. We look outwardly to answer the mysteries of the universe. We look inwardly to understand the mysteries of biological life. What we have found by looking in both directions is that we look Godward to find an answer to the Grand Central Question.

In the movie *Contact*, the protagonist is Dr. Ellie Arroway, an ambitious and idealistic astronomer who is given the extraordinary opportunity to make first contact with an alien intelligence. At the end of the movie, Ellie is instructing a group of children, and one asks if there is life on other planets. She says something that Carl

Sagan—the author of the book on which *Contact* is based—often said in his *Cosmos* series: "The universe is a pretty big place. It's bigger than anything anyone has ever dreamed of before. So if it's just us . . . seems like an awful waste of space, right?"[19]

Many others have echoed this same sentiment, and it is fascinating to me that they would come to that conclusion instead of another. Why can't it be that God made the universe, with all its celestial bodies and amazing properties, specifically so that humanity could exist on this precious, rare, amazing planet? Indeed, as we understand the fine-tuning of the universe more and more, we begin to see that so many things in the universe, millions and even billions of miles away, have made conditions just right for the universe to sustain life on our very planet. In other words, instead of the universe being a colossal waste of space if we are the only intelligent life, would it not be amazing to see that God created all of this, with its marvelous complexity and fine-tuning, just for us?

At the end of *Contact*, Ellie (as Carl Sagan's fictional surrogate) tells a crowd of reporters that her experience with the alien intelligence showed her how "insignificant" yet how "rare and precious" humanity is. In a sense, she's right, but not because there is so much life out there. She's right because God shows us how valuable and precious we are through all that he has created, just so that humanity can live and seek him. He purposefully ordered the universe—with all of its gravitational pulls and energy fields and magnetism and photons—for us. And the vast array of its splendor and power shows us how valuable we are to him.

The design of humanity's building blocks has similar implications. The genetic code within each one of us, as diverse as we all are, tells us about the purpose and dignity in each of us. If our genetic code was specifically chosen, that means that the results of those choices have sacred value to them. Race and ethnicity are not accidents, mere quirks of blind evolutionary processes. They are purposeful and sacred. That's why racial prejudice and ethnic cleansing are inherently immoral. A person's gender is not accidental—it is purposeful and sacred. That's why it is wrong to discriminate against women or kill firstborn infant girls. And sexuality is designed and therefore sacred. It's biological purpose of procreation—to create more valuable humans—and its emotional component—to create a bond between a man and a woman—tell us that it is sacred and should not be violated.

Jesus takes all these sacred purposes and treats them with dignity. In chapter four of John's Gospel, Jesus encounters a Samaritan woman at Jacob's well. Ethnic, gender and sexual tensions all come up in the conversation. At that time, Jews would have nothing to do with Samaritans, and men and women who did not know each other would not talk alone. Yet Jesus talks to this Samaritan woman, and she marvels at it (John 4:9). Jesus unmasks the sexual violations of her past, pointing out her many husbands and her living with a man who is not her husband (vv. 16-18). Yet the Jew from Nazareth tells the woman of a despised ethnicity and with a checkered past that God values her and wants eternal, holy relationship with her in spirit and truth (vv. 23-24). And all her feelings of worthlessness fall away as she realizes the value she has in the sight of God. Jesus tells her—and us—that we are sacred because we bear the image of God.

I have often marveled that for some atheists this seems to come as bad news, a conclusion that must be fought and countered. But how is that bad news, exactly? Should it not be exhilarating and liberating to know that we are not accidents, cosmic orphans with no place but the existence we eke out? Humanism—by its very name—is an endeavor to find objective purpose and intrinsic value for every human. For the humanist who truly wants to find the source that grounds her affirmation that we are invested with intrinsic value and purpose, the fact that God serves as that grounding brings her home. It brings her to true humanism.

THE REALITY OF MORALITY

Our desire to protect race, ethnicity, gender and sexuality as objectively valuable traits derives from the existence of objective morality. In other words, if there is no objective morality, then why not just redefine the purposes for which we were created? Why not violate those objective purposes to suit our subjective ones? The existence of an objective morality—derived from God—is the answer. There is no objective moral value without God, as we've seen. And the rejection of God requires that we reject objective moral values that secure our purpose and dignity. Jerry Walls and David Baggett put it well:

> The attempt to define morality in terms of the satisfaction of our desires tries to replace theism's objective account of value and meaning with subjective satisfaction, but the exchange leaves us worse off. It remains a leap of blind faith to affirm that anything like objective obligation would emerge from such empirical properties. For that matter, persons themselves, especially persons with intrinsic value and dignity, seem much less likely to emerge from valueless impersonal stuff than from the intentional hand of a personal Creator.[20]

Still, secular humanists might argue that we don't need God for objective morality by arguing that moral values "just exist." They derive this argument from something Plato wrote so many centuries ago: the so-called Euthyphro dilemma. In one of Plato's writings, a character he calls Euthyphro asks this question: Is something good because the gods will it, or do the gods will something because it is good? Applied to God, this is meant to point out that neither choice bodes well for the theist. If something is good just because God wills it, then its goodness is arbitrary, because God could have commanded something terrible, like rape, making it good. And if God commands something because it is good, then that means that the good exists outside of God, which means we don't need him to have objective moral values.

But, as many have pointed out, this presents a false dilemma, because there are other options. An answer to the supposed dilemma is that God's commands are moral because he is good. In other words, his nature is goodness—he is the Good—and so it is not that he commands things because they are good, it's that his commands are moral because he is good.[21]

Indeed, the dilemma is even more of a problem for the atheist. If the mere fact that God commanding something makes it arbitrarily moral, what saves morality from arbitrariness? Certainly not naturalism. In naturalism, something is moral only because it has survival value. But if we could wind the evolutionary clock back and set it in motion again, we would likely arrive at a species with different survival characteristics. It could be that rape promotes the survival of certain species, making rape moral. What is "moral" in that case would be driven primarily by chance. And that would be even more arbitrary than morality commanded by a sentient being like God.

We simply cannot ground morality in something mindless. And here is where the Euthyphro dilemma actually helps further belief in God's existence. Secular humanists who believe in objective moral values want us to pick the second horn of the dilemma—that God commands something because it is moral—to show us that morality exists as an abstract concept outside of God, making him unnecessary. Morality—or as Plato originally called it, "the Good"— exists only as an abstract object.

But how is this intelligible? First, picking a mindless abstraction and calling it the Good doesn't provide any better of a stopping point than God. The dilemma would persist. Is something good because the Good commands it, or does the Good command it because it is already good? If it's the second one, then there is something good outside the Good, and we can continue to ask the question endlessly.

Objective moral values and duties are saved, however, if they are rooted in a personality. As Paul Copan says, "Personhood and morality are necessarily connected."[22] Justice isn't just. A person is just. Mercy isn't merciful, but a person is. And the Good, for that matter, isn't good. But a person can be. To be objective, moral values must be transcendent. To be truly moral, the values must be rooted in a person. And a truly transcendent person is exactly what God is. So the Euthyphro dilemma doesn't point us away from God; it highlights why we need him in order to make any sense of morality.

THE REALITY OF EQUALITY

Without a robust understanding of morality's foundation in God, we lose humanity's value, especially humanity's equality. Let's consider America's founding principle expressed in the Declaration of Independence: every human has inalienable rights. By definition, a right is inalienable only if it cannot be taken away. Put another way, a right is inalienable because a person or group of persons (like a government) cannot take them away.

But if a group of humans, like a society or government, is the source of our rights, then humans can take those rights away. After all, that which has the authority to give something has the authority to take it away. And if humans have the authority to give inalienable rights, then humans can take away those rights. Thus they would not be inalienable. And if inalienable rights don't exist, then America, as a country founded upon inalienable rights, is an illusion. If we don't have inalienable rights, then what value and dignity do we have that cannot be plucked from us by a persuasive despot? For rights to be inalienable, their source must be beyond humanity. They must come from God.

That every human is "created equal" is also the building block—the DNA if you will—of the American experiment. But in a naturalistic view, where survival of the fittest is the guiding force for life, in what sense are we equal? According to naturalism, some are stronger, some are smarter, some are better looking and some are faster. And some have profound developmental disabilities. When we look at only the material world, we see there is no such thing as equality.

Dawkins may try to label genetic mistakes as "blessed" and "precious" Darwinian misfirings, but he cannot do so without smuggling in a preference and a moral assessment that he has already admitted doesn't exist. Even Dawkins cannot live with the implications of his own worldview, because deep down he, like most of us, wants to cherish equality for everyone. But without God, there is no true equality. As Peter Singer concludes, without God, just being human isn't enough.

But with God, there is fundamental equality in virtue of what and who we are. The Bible says that God made us, both men and women, in his image—we have the *imago Dei* (Genesis 1:26-27). We have intrinsic value and purpose because the transcendent being put his seal of purpose and value on each one of us, regardless of our differences. Jesus teaches human equality regardless of gender, race, social status or ethnicity. "Many who are first will be last, and the last first," Jesus tells us (Matthew 19:30). And in him, "there is neither Jew nor Greek, there is neither slave nor free, there is no male and female, for you are all one in Christ Jesus" (Galatians 3:28). With God, we are all equal. There is nothing more humanistic than that.

If true value and purpose come from God, a question arises: which God? Do we find intrinsic value and objective purpose in the God of Islam, the pantheistic impersonal absolute or "Mother Earth"? Religious systems are not very uniform in their moral systems, as anyone who has studied comparative religion knows. So isn't religion just as shaky at arriving at human purpose and value as irreligion? It is true that religion can be an inconsistent determiner of value and purpose. But that does not mean that value and purpose are relative. Rather, it means that the existence of God is a necessary condition to ground the existence of value and purpose. I am convinced that in the gospel, specifically the incarnation of Christ and his suffering on the cross, we find the true value and purpose of our lives.

Not long ago, I was flipping through television stations while traveling, just to have some background noise while I worked (it's funny that having children has caused me to find total silence disconcerting). As I did so, I came across an episode of the sitcom *Everybody Loves Raymond*. Raymond, the main character, was put into a sticky parental situation when his young daughter asked him where babies come from. After screwing up his courage, Raymond plodded upstairs to his little girl's room to have the "sex talk."

He was taken quite aback, however, when he found out that her question wasn't about sex after all, but about the meaning of life. "Why does God put us here?" she asked. Raymond stumbled over his words for some time, only to tell her, "Because heaven is crowded." It was funny because we often think that "the meaning of life" is the deepest and hardest question to answer. We think of gurus sitting at the top of mountains meditating in the lotus position who may know the answer, but may not.

It's actually not that difficult, if I may be so bold. Humanity's purpose was summed up well in the Westminster Shorter Catechism: "Man's chief end is to glorify God and enjoy Him forever." In other words, our purpose is relationship with the Divine. Our purpose is not to be happy in this life or to acquire stuff. No, our purpose is much greater than physical happiness or sensual fulfillment. We are made for relationships; our desire for fulfilling relationships is universal.

That desire in us is explained by looking to our Designer, who is a relational Being. In Christianity, there is only one God. But while God has only one nature, he exists with three distinct personages—the Father, Son and Holy Spirit. This is a community of relationships within a single Being. This makes relationships fundamental to reality and thus makes relationships the ultimate purpose of existence. Walls and Baggett had it right when they said,

> Ethics [is] about relationship with the God whose triune nature enabled him to be a God of perfect love before any human beings were created. As much as human nature might provide clues to the content of morality, this is why, at the end of the day, we are inclined to say that it's God's nature and image, in whose ours was created, that ultimately reveal the most veridical picture of moral reality. The Trinity is the ultimate reality, if Christianity is true, a God whose nature is reciprocal self-giving love. The bedrock of reality is this personal God with whom we are invited to be in relationship.[23]

The Bible tells us that one of the persons in the triune Godhead incarnated himself in Jesus of Nazareth. He took on a human nature while maintaining his divine nature so that we can relate to God. And through that relationship, we find objective fulfillment. Even if every other human rejects us, we can find acceptance in Christ because our value does not depend on human opinion. Our value transcends it.

THE HALLMARK OF VALUE

How much does God value that relationship? What shows us that we have intrinsic value as opposed to just extrinsic value? What tells us that we are not just tools that God uses for some other end? What tells us that, to God, we are ends in ourselves, that we are valuable to him for our own sake?

Intuitively we judge how valuable something is by how much we are willing to pay or sacrifice for it. According to Jesus' self-understanding, he was the incarnation of the God of the universe (see, for example, John 8:58). And the Bible tells us that the incarnation, in and of itself, is something that the second person of the Trinity, God the Son, did as an act of sacrifice to have relationship with us. The apostle Paul writes, "Though he was in the form of God, [he] did not count equality with God a thing to be grasped, but emptied himself, by taking the form of a servant, being born in the likeness of men" (Philippians 2:6-7).

Think of what it means for God—the Being to whom all devotion is due—to incarnate himself in Jesus, a servant. Incarnated in this way, Jesus is the "image of the invisible God" (Colossians 1:15) and so shows us what God is really like, in a relational way that we can grasp. There is a majestic humility inherent in the very act of incarnation. There is an expression of his value for us in that act alone.

But there is far more to the payment than just the incarnation. Our value is proven by the conclusion of that payment. The incarnation, where it ultimately led and indeed its very purpose, tell us something deeply impactful. Hundreds of years before Jesus' earthly ministry, the psalmist beautifully described the infinite preciousness each human has and what it takes to redeem us: "Truly no man can ransom another, or give to God the price of his life, for the ransom of their life is costly and can never suffice, that he should live on forever and never see the pit" (Psalm 49:7-9).

The original Hebrew powerfully captures what this passage expresses. The word *ransom* means "the price for a life" or the price to free someone from captivity. The King James Version captures the essence of the words well in translating the passage as telling us that "the redemption of their soul is precious" (v. 8). Each one of us, though captive in this world to our own desires and sin, is *precious.* We are so precious that the payment for our freedom "can never suffice." From our perspective, the payment can never be enough, because we are infinitely valuable.

But an infinite payment is found at the cross. Nowhere else.

Human sin is not just a moral failing or a mere lapse in judgment. It is a rebellion against the One who gives us purpose. It is, in this sense, the very violation of purpose. God has created us for relationship with himself, but in choosing our own way, we have taken it upon ourselves to tell God that we do not need him. He is not good enough for us, as it were. That is obviously offensive. And an offense against an infinite God would naturally require an infinite payment.

So in an act that demonstrates our value in God's eyes, God the Son incarnates himself in Jesus and pays the terrible price by suffering and dying on that cross. That pain was not just physical; it was beyond that. Now, please don't misunderstand. Jesus did not die spiritually. But there was forsakenness at the cross. God the Father forsakes his Son Jesus because Jesus has taken our place as the guilty party. That's why Jesus cries out, "Why have you forsaken me?" God the Son, who from infinity past knew only harmony in relationship with God the Father, experiences the forsakenness all humanity deserved at the cross. Because that relationship between Father and Son is infinite, the pain is infinite.

The incarnation and the cross are profound demonstrations of the value we have in God's eyes and of our inherent dignity. They tell us that our actions are significant because they have consequences. And they tell us that God must address those consequences, but in a way that saves us from ourselves—because he values us. At the cross, we see the confluence of what gives us purpose and dignity. We see a price paid to demonstrate the value God has for us. And all of this is wrapped up in the perfect fulfillment of the moral values of justice, love and mercy.

How can we know that we are intrinsically valuable, and not just means to one of God's ends? Because at the cross God paid an infinite price to show our infinite value. As a triune being, he does not need relationship with us to have relationship. He has it within himself in the eternal community of the Trinity. And so relationship with him does not benefit him or satisfy some need he has. He offers us relationship through the cross, not for his sake, but for our sake. And in that, we are an end in and of ourselves.

The gospel shows us that true humanism has a Christian foundation. To even speak of the value of persons is to borrow from Jesus' impact on the world through his cross. Bentley Hart says that we use the word *person* with "a splendidly indiscriminate generosity, applying it without hesitation to everyone, regardless of social station, race, or sex" in modern times because Christianity changed the fact that, in Jesus' time, only a Roman citizen was considered a true person.[24] The point is that what seems self-evident to us is only that way because the West—in fact, the world—has been utterly changed to such a profound degree by the gospel that human value is a given. We have the gospel to thank for that.

God came to Earth in Jesus, forsaking the majesty of heaven, exchanging the form of God for the form of a slave, to achieve salvation for us. As Bentley Hart says, God overthrew oppression in the form of a slave, not by the power of the lofty.[25] It is a poetic picture of what humanity's preciousness is and of how much God values it. Secular humanism tries to provide us with intrinsic value and objective purpose, but without God. Because that is impossible, *secular humanism* is a contradiction in terms. The only true humanism—a worldview that truly affirms human existence and dignity—is Christian humanism. Those who seek a foundation for our value and purpose can find it in the gospel—specifically at the cross.

THREE WORDS REVISITED

Life-shaping moment. We come back to the three words that my friend uttered when telling me about the impact his mother's death had on him. In the moments before he arrested my comments with those words, we were discussing the problem of evil, the ages-old question of how an all-loving, all-powerful God could exist while suffering also exists. He asked me how I had reconciled the seeming difficulty or contradiction in my mind to allow me to continue believing in God.

I pointed out that the question itself assumes the existence of objective moral values (like suffering should be stopped), which can exist only if God exists. Thus the problem of evil doesn't actually disprove God's existence, but instead goes toward proving it. I focused my attention on the fact that the problem of evil has an underlying flawed assumption. It presumes that God, an all-knowing being, couldn't allow certain instances of suffering, even great suffering, to accomplish an immeasurably greater good in the future. We, as beings of limited intelligence, can't see how all future contingent events might play out, but God can. So we're not in a good position to say that God couldn't have a morally sufficient reason to allow certain suffering. If we say we can know such a thing, we are putting ourselves in the place of an omniscient being—the very being the problem of evil is meant to disprove.

I hadn't fully finished my philosophical soliloquy when my friend hit me with his life-shaping moment. He didn't do it to trump me or stun me into silence. He was pointing out something that we often miss: the problem of evil is actually a question about human purpose and intrinsic value. If we have objective dignity, value and purpose, then how can God let such things happen to us?

Secular humanists want to have an answer for my friend and others who have lost someone dear to them. Secular humanists rightly want an answer that satisfies the mind and the heart. But is there such an answer? Dawkins would have to tell my friend that his mother's death was a "meaningless tragedy" to go along with "equally meaningless good fortune." Gould could only retreat to utter subjectivism. And Baggini's answer would be even grimmer. Christians would answer quite differently, but is there more to it than straightforward theology and logic?

Sitting at that table as my coffee got cold, I swallowed hard and prayed quickly for wisdom. Philosophical sparring would have been profane at that moment, but something needed to be said. "I can't imagine what that's like," I began. "But can I offer you something that might bring some hope and not just logic?"

"Sure," he replied.

"As a Christian, I don't have to rely on the logical possibility that God could allow suffering to exist for a greater possible good that I can't see. I don't have to rely on the mere possibility, because history tells me that it is a reality."

"Go on," he said.

"Jesus suffered on the cross. Evil men condemned him to die as a criminal, even though he was guiltless. God could have stopped it, but he let it happen. I can trust that God can allow suffering for a greater good, because at the cross he allowed a terrible evil to happen to his Son. And he let it happen not just for some good that might happen in the future, but for the greatest possible good: the salvation of anyone who believes in Jesus. I don't rely just on theory to tell me that we are all valuable to God, that your mom has value in God's eyes. I have the reality of the cross to demonstrate it to me. And you can have that too."

If something's value is determined by its price, what more could we ask for in the cross to see how precious humanity is? My friend's mother has intrinsic value not just because he loved her, but because she is transcendently loved. It has become trite nowadays to quote John 3:16, but I think it's particularly appropriate. In giving his Son to us, in that sacrifice that showed us that "God so loved the world," God identifies with our pain, which tells us so much about his love and our value. The words of Frank Graeff's hymn "Does Jesus Care?" come to mind:

> Does Jesus care when my heart is pained
> Too deeply for mirth or song,
> As the burdens press, and the cares distress,
> And the way grows weary and long?

> *Chorus*
> O yes, He cares, I know He cares,
> His heart is touched with my grief;
> When the days are weary, the long night dreary,

I know my Savior cares.

Does Jesus care when my way is dark
With names dread and fear?
As the daylight fades into deep night shades,
Does He care enough to be near?

Does Jesus care when I've tried and failed
To resist some temptation strong;
When for my deep grief there is no relief,
Though my tears flow all night long?

Does Jesus care when I've said good-bye
To the dearest on earth to me,
And my sad heart aches till it nearly breaks,
Is it aught to Him? Does He see?

As we left the restaurant, my friend turned to me and said something else I won't soon forget. "I'm not totally convinced yet," he said. "But you've given me a lot to think about." God's love for us has a way of doing that. It stirs the heart and the mind. There is emotional satisfaction in the intellectual realization that we are infinitely valued. The answer to secular humanists' Grand Central Question about human value and purpose is found in the One who dwelt among us, full of grace and truth.

Part Two

EASTERN AND
WESTERN SPIRITUALITY
OR THE GOSPEL

Which Gives Real Answers to Suffering?

PANTHEISM AND PAIN

At a gathering of the world's foremost religious experts, a rather unassuming figure strode onto the stage to speak—uninvited. He stood there in his traditional Eastern garb and boldly addressed the crowd gathered there with eloquence and confidence as if he were a scheduled speaker. "Sisters and brothers of America," he began. "It fills my heart with joy unspeakable to rise in response to the warm and cordial welcome which you have given us. I thank you in the name of the most ancient order of monks in the world; I thank you in the name of the mother of religions; and I thank you in the name of millions and millions of Hindu people of all classes and sects." With those words, Swami Vivekananda pricked the ears and captivated the hearts of those attending the World's Parliament of Religions on September 11, 1893, in Chicago.[1]

Over the next several days, Vivekananda spoke at the Parliament numerous times to enraptured audiences about the virtues of Hinduism. He preached the universality of Hinduism, its connection with Buddhism, and how all the renowned religious teachers and founders, including Jesus, were really proponents of Hindu pantheism. He chastised Christians and Muslims in the audience for extolling the virtues of each other's faith while ignoring the "Mother Religion"—Hinduism. And in the very same speeches he legitimized the Hindu philosophy in the eyes of his audience by likening Jesus' and Paul's teachings to Eastern pantheism. Audiences all over North America responded, inviting Vivekananda to speak at universities and conventions. A new era had begun, and the Western fascination with all things Eastern has lived on to this day.

Vivekananda's success owes largely to pantheism's apparent inclusivism and its ability to chameleon itself to look so similar to other worldviews that we might ask ourselves why we ever thought pantheism was wrong.

> He proclaimed, how, then, can the Hindu, whose whole fabric of thought centres in God, believe in Buddhism which is agnostic, or in Jainism which is atheistic? The Buddhists or the Jains do not depend upon God; but the whole force of their religion is directed to the great central truth in every religion, to evolve a God out of man. *They have not seen the Father, but they have seen the Son. And he that hath seen the Son hath seen the Father also.*[2]

Vivekananda snuck in the (erroneous) claim that all religions seek to evolve a God out of man, and he cannibalized Jesus' words in John 14:8-10 to make that idea appealing to Westerners. After all, if Hindu pantheism is just like Christianity in so many ways, why not embrace some of its ideas? In fact, unsatisfied with merely appealing to the religiously minded, Vivekananda argued that pantheism was the spiritual sister of scientific evolutionary theory.

In the decades since his arrival, mystics, gurus, swamis and even talk show hosts who extol pantheism's virtues have captured the minds and hearts of Westerners looking for something exotic to follow. Pantheism's star began to rise in 1893 with Vivekananda, and it has not yet waned.

The bloom has not fallen off pantheism's rose for another reason.

It claims to address a basic human instinct: the avoidance of pain and suffering. Indeed, that is pantheism's Grand Central Question: *how do we escape suffering?*

PANTHEISM UNPACKED

Of course, to understand pantheism's answer, we must understand what pantheism is. I use the term broadly to include ancient Eastern religious views like Hinduism, Buddhism and Taoism. But I am also including the younger daughters of those ancient systems, like the New Age movement, the New Spirituality (a more mature version of the New Age) and new religions like L. Ron Hubbard's Scientology. These huddle under the same umbrella because they share some of the same fundamental beliefs, even though they are diverse in their details and rich complexities.

In general terms, the most common fundamental belief among them is that the reality we experience is to some degree an illusion. The world around us is but a shadow of reality. We think that we are individuals, only incidentally connected to each other. We are under the illusion that we are limited in power and knowledge. But, according to pantheism, the reality is that we are infinitely powerful beings connected to each other in profound ways. We are actually divine beings, or, in the case of Hinduism and some forms of Buddhism, we are identical with the divine singularity.

Pantheists avow that the divine is all there really is. Everything is part of the divine; everything is a manifestation of the single divine reality. There is no reality other than the divine. We are simply mistaken to think that there is a difference between anything. And when we realize that—when we realize our true divine, powerful nature—we are freed from this life of suffering.

Strictly speaking, the moniker *pantheism* applies most directly to Hinduism, some forms of Buddhism and some of the beliefs of New Spirituality practitioners. In Hinduism's oldest writings, the Vedas, we are told that the essence of every human being is the Atman. The

Vedas culminate in the Upanishads, doctrinal writings teaching that
the essence of all reality—in fact, the only thing that is actually
real—is the Brahman, the impersonal absolute.[3]

Further, each person is under the illusion that his or her self is
an individual and personal soul. The reality, for the Hindu, is that
the self—the Atman—is really one with the Brahman, and therefore
every human's essence is not really personal, it is impersonal.[4] Buddhism in its original form, as well as Scientology, is a nontheistic
religion in that it does not specifically deny that there is a divine
being. Like the Hindu, the Buddhist believes that the world we see
around us is illusory. But the Buddhist would go further than the
Hindu and claim not only that we mistakenly perceive an individual
self, but we are mistaken that we have a self at all; our perception
that we actually have a self is an illusion. In both Hinduism and
Buddhism, these illusions we have about ultimate reality and about
ourselves are called *maya*.

The more popular advocates of the New Spirituality, people like
Deepak Chopra and Eckhart Tolle, whose books have sold millions
of copies, would adopt wholesale the Hindu and Buddhist ideas of
maya while calling their view by a different name. Other modern
pantheists, like New Age pundits and Scientologists, also tell us
that we are under the illusion that we are limited beings and that
we are subject to the external forces of the world, when in fact it is
the other way around.

Some New Spirituality advocates (those who have meshed
Eastern religion and Western ideas) cling to the Western emphasis
on human individuality, so they do not teach that we lose our
identity when we "become." Yet they still believe that we can attain
a higher state that is "one with the universe" while retaining our
individuality. We can see the New Spirituality's connection with
Hindu pantheism in the way it co-opts Hindu language. Hinduism
tells us that the illusory world is like a *lela*, a stage play, while reality
takes place behind the curtain. Ken Wilber, a widely followed

pundit of the New Spirituality, adopts that idea: "At that frothy, foaming, chaotic emerging edge of spirits unfolding is where lela, the creative play, is."[5]

As Sire puts it, "One could define new consciousness as a Western version of Eastern mysticism in which the metaphysical emphasis of the East (its assertion that Atman is Brahman) is replaced by an emphasis on epistemology (seeing, experiencing or perceiving the unity of reality is what life is all about)."[6] So in all these views there remains a sense of the oneness or monism of all creation; thus they are all pantheistic to some degree.

All these views share the belief that maya—these illusions about reality, ourselves or both—play a role in human misery. We are trapped in a seemingly endless cycle of death and rebirth, having to live life after life until we break free from the illusion. For the Hindu and Buddhist, this cycle is called *samsara*, and it is characterized by suffering and misery. For the more contemporary pantheists, the cycle does not necessarily have a name, but it does entail reincarnation on the road to total enlightenment. Even Scientology—the youngest of Hinduism's daughters—ascribes to the idea that we are in a cycle of reincarnation.

Our level of enlightenment, and thus our level of suffering in any life, is determined by our *karma*—the sum total of the good and the bad deeds of our previous lives. For most pantheists, we are the cause of our own suffering; there is no external cause. And so pantheism looks inward for the answer to its Grand Central Question of how we escape suffering.

Freedom from the cycle is every living thing's goal. The Hindu and the Buddhist call that liberation *moksha*. For the Hindu, this means oneness with the Brahman, the impersonal absolute unity of reality. As the Upanishads say, "Beyond the great self is the unmanifest; beyond the unmanifest is the spirit. Beyond the spirit there is nothing. That is the end (of the journey); that is the final goal."[7]

But moksha for the Buddhist is akin to annihilation. It entails casting off the illusion that we are actually selves when in reality we are just embodied karma. Our goal is not union with God per se, but to be extinguished like a candle's flame. New Spirituality advocates like Chopra would agree with the Hindus that we are to become like God—the absolute. Tolle's views are a bit more muddled in that he claims we are to become like God, but God in fact is nothing. Others would say that release comes from becoming one with the universe.

For the Scientologist, we are "clear" when we are freed from that which holds us back from our full potential. Once the Scientologist's "Thetan" self (the pure, powerful human self) is freed from the illusions of this life, he or she progresses up the levels to become an Operating Thetan VIII, a godlike being in control of the MEST—Matter, Energy, Space and Time.[8]

To break free from the cycle of samsara, we must see through the fog of maya. And to do that, we have to pull ourselves up by our own bootstraps. Hinduism teaches that the path to moksha involves working off the negative karma from a previous life. Several roads are open to us, including *jnana* (the maya way of knowledge), karma (the way of works) and *bhakti* (the way of devotion and love). Buddha described the means of escape as the Eightfold Path, in which one must have right views, right aspirations, right speech, right conduct, right livelihood, right effort, right mindfulness and right contemplation. Those of the New Spirituality focus on meditation, positive thinking, physical health and charitable work as paths to enlightenment. The point, though, is that for pantheists, escape from this illusory state to realize their true nature is the goal of life. But they have to merit that becoming.

INTO THE WEST

The number of pantheists around us is quite surprising, and thus the depth of pantheism's influence is profound when we stop to think about it. Consider for a moment that there are roughly one billion Hindus in the world. Consider further that there are probably over four hundred million Buddhists. And consider further still that in the West, millions of people ascribe to Westernized versions of these religions in the forms of the New Age, New Spirituality and Scientology. When we add these together, we quickly see that pantheism is the second largest—if not the largest—worldview.

Even for those who would not necessarily affirm that they are actually pantheists in the formal sense, there can be no denying that they are heavily influenced by it. We often hear one another talk about our good karma or bad karma or even flippantly talk about our past lives. Both concepts are specifically rooted in Eastern pantheism, yet even self-identified Christians use them with surprising ease and regularity. So when we add to the mix those who at least believe in some aspects of pantheism, we can see just how pervasive it is. Our neighbors, our coworkers and even our relatives may be at least a touch pantheistic.

Though Vivekananda is largely responsible for pantheism's initial allure, sixty years later it exploded in popular culture in the wake of the mass American protest movement. Sire writes,

> On a sociological level, we can trace the interest in the East to the rejection of middle-class values by the young generation of the 1960s. . . . The Vietnam War (young Americans had not personally experienced earlier conflicts) is a result of reason. So let us abandon reason. Second, Western economics has led to gross inequity and economic oppression of masses of people. So let us reject the presuppositions from which such a system developed. Third, Western religion has seemed largely to support those in control of technology and the economic system. So let us not fall into that trap. The swing to Eastern thought since the 1960s is, therefore, primarily a retreat from Western thought. The West ends in a maze of con-

tradictions, acts of intellectual suicide and a specter of nihilism that haunts the dark edges of all our thought. Is there not another way?[9]

At that point, the ground for pantheistic ideas was fertile. We were enchanted by anything new and exotic. And there was nothing quite as exotic to Westerners as the Far East.

In the midst of this enchantment, Easterners did a very Western thing: they slightly changed the system to make it even more appealing to Westerners. Authentic foreign cuisines are often changed in America to make them more acceptable to Western palates, so why not do the same with foreign belief systems?

Scientology provides a very nice illustration of the Western adoption of this Eastern idea. Its founder, L. Ron Hubbard, repeatedly claimed that the tenets of Scientology were extensions of ancient pantheistic teachings.[10] Instead of telling us that bad karma holds us back, he tells us how negative forces called "engrams" have infected our minds because of the pollutants around us. Instead of meditating or chanting to get rid of engrams, we should hook ourselves up to machines called e-meters and undergo mental "audits." When we have been thoroughly audited and have successfully navigated Scientology's program, we are "clear." Scientology's techno-speak replaces Eastern pantheism's foreign words in the consummate American way.

But, again, this all started with Vivekananda. He was a master at taking monotheistic biblical teachings and twisting them so that they affirmed Hindu pantheistic doctrine. For example, he explained Hinduism's central goal of realizing inner divinity in these words: "The whole object of their system is by constant struggle to become perfect, to become divine, to reach God and see God, and this reaching God, seeing God, becoming perfect even as the Father in Heaven is prefect, constitutes the religion of the Hindus."[11] Vivekananda used Matthew 5:48, in which Jesus makes the point that we can only be saved if we are perfect—which is impossible without God's grace—to imply that Jesus taught that we will one day become God. Jesus' point is that we are definitely not God, but Vivekananda morphed the meaning to make pantheism appealing.

This kind of appeal has been quite effective in Western culture. Popular authors, like Tolle and Chopra, have sold millions upon millions of copies of their self-help books by removing some of the spice of Eastern pantheism to make it taste more Western. In his wildly popular book *The Power of Now*, Tolle tells us that we are under the illusion that there is a separation between us and God: "The word God is limiting not only because of thousands of years of misperception and misuse, but also because it implies an entity other than you. God is Being itself, not a being. There can be no subject-object relationship here, no duality, no you and God."[12]

Chopra continues the thought when he tells us,

> Success in life could be defined as the continued expansion of happiness and the progressive realization of worthy goals. . . . Even with the experience of all these things, we will remain unfulfilled unless we nurture the seeds of divinity inside us. *In reality, we are divinity in disguise, and the gods and goddesses in embryo that are contained within us seek to be fully materialized.*[13]

Interestingly, Chopra claims that he is offering ancient wisdom in a new way so that all of us can see that we are truly divine. He has taken great pains to avoid having this worldview pinned down to any "ism" so that he can make it as universally appealing as possible. But there is no escaping the fact that he is pushing Hinduism's version of monistic pantheism. Ravi Zacharias has pointed out that other Hindu scholars and writers have taken Chopra to task on this, calling for "credit where credit is due."[14] It turns out that neither Chopra nor Tolle offer us anything original. They are simply repackaging Eastern pantheism for Western consumption.

In fact, Chopra's *The Third Jesus: The Christ We Cannot Ignore* is entirely devoted to turning Jesus—the fiercely monotheistic Jew—into a pantheistic monist. Like Vivekananda before him, Chopra takes Jesus' words and other biblical passages, gives them a pantheistic twist and makes it appear that Jesus agrees with the Hindu Vedas, the Buddha and other Eastern sages. For example, Chopra, like all Hindus, believes that our pain and our struggles in this life are largely an illusion caused by the fact that we have not yet realized our inner god. To make this idea appeal to Western minds, he makes Jesus its champion.

Chopra twists the most widely known Bible verses, John 3:16-17, to make them mean precisely the opposite of what they say. Those verses read, "For God so loved the world that he gave his only Son, that whoever believes in him should not perish but have eternal life. For God did not send his Son into the world to condemn the world, but in order that the world might be saved through him." These verses are clearly making a subject-object distinction between God and the world to show that the world is incapable of saving itself without believing in the Son. But according to Chopra, these words somehow mean that "Jesus bolsters his divine identity in the strongest, most eloquent terms. Higher consciousness saves a person from the illusion of death, and this gift comes from a loving God."[15]

Come again? How did Chopra arrive at such a meaning from those words? Does this not seem like the height of arrogance? He is telling billions of Christians that they have misunderstood these words for two thousand years and that it is only the enlightened Chopra who finally understands them. Perhaps the real illusion is Chopra's belief that Jesus would agree with him.

In taking the Bible's words out of all context and infusing them with a meaning completely foreign to their original intent, Chopra is not doing anything new. He is simply imitating the methods of Vivekananda, whose brilliant prose gave a voice to pantheism in the West.

Though he says that he is espousing an unlabeled, universal religion, Chopra is really offering Hinduism to spiritually minded Westerners, just as Vivekananda did over one hundred years ago. And just like Vivekananda, Chopra misuses the Bible to do so. I cannot resist commenting that even Chopra's unoriginality lacks originality.

Pantheism's influence and appeal are not limited to best-selling self-help books. The wildly popular *Star Wars* saga of films incorporates various forms of pantheism, from Hinduism's belief that ultimate reality is an impersonal, absolute state of being that we must aspire to (the Force) to Buddhism's belief that ultimate enlightenment comes from a life free from attachments to material things or even people (the Jedi Code). *Star Wars* brought Eastern ideas and New Age philosophies into the imaginations of many, including and especially young people.

I can recall my friends and I fantasizing about "using the Force." I wanted to feel the connection between me and all other things in existence so that I could make them fly across the room like Luke Skywalker. And like so many, I was enamored of the sagacious guru, Yoda, with his tiny body and strange manner of speaking that exhibited the enlightened calm of a warrior philosopher.

In *Star Wars*, everything is connected, and the ultimate truth is not to be found in a person, but in the impersonal creative Force. That is just the science fiction version of the Brahman. Hinduism and Buddhism tell us that enlightenment comes from detachment, and suffering comes from attachment. Yoda tells the troubled young Jedi, Anakin Skywalker, not to become attached to people, because that leads to the dark side of the Force. Jedi, like enlightened Buddhists and Hindus, must divorce themselves from attachments so that they are unfettered in their communion with the Force. And when they die, they are absorbed into the Force. "Mourn them, do not. Miss them, do not," Yoda tells Anakin.[16] They have achieved enlightenment through absorption into the impersonal absolute.

The Matrix films of the late 1990s and mid-2000s were a gritty answer to *Star Wars*. Although the films contain a mishmash of different philosophies and religious views, the main character, Neo (an anagram for *One*), has an inner divinity that he must eventually realize to break humanity free from the Matrix, a computer-generated dream world that we all think is real (read, maya). The *Matrix* films make explicit references to reincarnation, the cycle of death and rebirth, and karma (though that last concept is horribly mangled in the films).

And in one of the most popular movies of all time, *Avatar*, the protagonists are aliens that have a spiritual and physical connection to their planet, called Eywa, which has its own divine qualities (much like the Gaia worshipers of the New Age). The main characters are on a journey toward connection with the impersonal deity of that planet and finally realize who they are when they fully attain that connection.

There is an allure to all of this, isn't there? The human heart craves connectedness with the transcendent, but it also craves freedom from suffering. In a pantheistic view, we can be compassionate to others without being attached.[17] Yet we can be connected in the sense that we are connected to each other because we are all one—we are all *the One*. And we can feel this connectedness while being countercultural by rejecting the "traditional" belief system of Christianity.

It bears repeating that the deep allure of all of this, from the Eastern religious systems to their popularized Western versions, is that we can be free of suffering and strife if we just strive to become something greater. That question, of how to be free from suffering and pain, is central to all forms of pantheism.

PERVASIVE PAIN

The pantheistic religions are as varied within themselves as they are among each other. In his massive survey of Hinduism and Buddhism, Sir Charles Eliot observed that general statements about

Hinduism are impossible because Hinduism always offers an exception.[18] The same can be said of Buddhism. In its original form, today called Theravada, Buddhism was very much like Hinduism, except that Gautama Buddha rejected several important ideas. He rejected the idea that an actual self exists. We are only under the illusion that we have a self; there is no Atman. Instead, there is only emptiness that we need to realize.

Buddhism, it can be said, is not strictly pantheistic, because in its original form it did not acknowledge the existence of anything godlike. While Buddhism maintained many elements common to Hindu pantheism, it largely ignored the theistic element. The majority of Buddhist sects have veered from the original Theravadic teachings. Tibetan Buddhism affirms that the Dalai Lama is the incarnation of the Buddha sent to guide humanity, while the largest sect, Mahayana Buddhism, deifies the Buddha and asks for his blessing. So it seems there are exceptions to almost every rule in pantheism.

But not every rule has an exception. The common threads between all pantheistic views reveal to us pantheism's Grand Central Question. Every pantheistic view claims that this world is full of pain, suffering and limitations because we have not yet seen our sufferings and limitations for what they really are. When we see through that illusion, and when we see that we are immensely powerful, divine beings, we can break free from the suffering.

The Hindu forms of pantheism agree that karma and samsara are real conditions of the self and that they cause the illusion of pain from which we must be liberated. Mariasusai Dhavamony points out that "the main purpose of every Indian philosophical system is precisely to free man from the bonds of karma and samsara and to enable him to attain liberation. Most of the Hindus accept his doctrine as [a] self-evident first principle and adhere to it at all costs."[19]

To make the point that pain is the central illusion from which we must be cured, Hinduism teaches the following:

Man is caught in the wheel of *samsara* which is full of desire, anger, delusion, covetousness, fear, depression, envy, union with undesirable and separation from desirable, hunger, thirst, old age, death, disease and sorrow. Desire binds man to the endlass [sic] prolongation of life which is swamped with the unpleasant things. Hence liberation consists in getting rid of the root-cause of such an evil.[20]

I have heard it said that Buddhism is the tender heart of Hinduism. And so it is no surprise that Buddhism places even more focus on alleviating our pain. Buddhism places reincarnation, karma and moksha squarely in the center of how to deal with pain. Release for the Buddhist comes from believing the Four Noble Truths: (1) life is suffering, (2) suffering is caused by craving or desire, (3) suffering will cease when we cease desiring, and (4) we can be free from desire only by following the Eightfold Path.

Every step along the Path requires perfection of the mind and body. In other words, freedom comes from our efforts. But the freedom we are seeking is, ultimately, a freedom from pain. The Tibetan Buddhist monk Geshe Kelsang Gyatso repeats throughout his writings that everyone's goal is to be free from suffering and pain:

Each and every living being has the sincere wish to avoid all suffering and problems permanently. Normally we try to do this by using external methods, but no matter how successful we are from a worldly point of view—no matter how materially wealthy, powerful or highly respected we become—we shall never find permanent liberation from suffering and problems. In reality, all the problems we experience day to day come from our self-cherishing and self-grasping—misconceptions that exaggerate our own importance. However, because we do not understand this, we usually blame others for our problems, and this just makes them worse. From these two basic misconceptions arise all our other delusions, such as anger and attachment, causing us to experience endless problems.[21]

The New Agers of the 1960s, 1970s and 1980s sought release from a life of depression and pain by realizing their transcendent consciousness and oneness with the universe (often spelled with a capital U). Scientology's aim is to evolve the human mind past the illusions of its limitations, caused by the engrams that fester there and keep us from our true potential to become masters of all reality. And the New Spiritualists, people like Tolle and Chopra, are continuously publishing books on mental and physical wellness that tell us how to achieve happiness in a world of pain.

Ever eloquent with his words (and always a champion of both Hinduism and Buddhism), Vivekananda pulled all of this together to present pantheism's Grand Central Question at the World's Parliament of Religions:

Is man a tiny boat in a tempest, raised one moment on the foamy crest of a billow and dashed down into a yawning chasm the next, rolling to and fro at the mercy of good and bad actions—a powerless, helpless wreck in an ever-raging, ever-rushing, uncompromising current of cause and effect; a little moth placed under the wheel of causation which rolls on crushing everything in its way and waits not for the widow's tears or the orphan's cry? The heart sinks at the idea, yet this is the law of Nature. Is there no hope? Is there no escape?—was the cry that went up from the bottom of the heart of despair. It reached the throne of mercy, and words of hope and consolation came down and inspired a Vedic sage, and he stood up before the world and in trumpet voice proclaimed the glad tidings: "Hear, ye children of immortal bliss! even ye that reside in higher spheres! I have found the Ancient One who is beyond all darkness, all delusion: knowing Him alone you shall be saved from death over again."[22]

Note carefully what Vivekananda said. He accurately summed up the questions we all have about suffering and pain, but then positioned those questions in pantheistic terms. He asked, "Is there no hope?" and then coupled it with a more Hindu-sounding question, *"Is there no escape?"* That is pantheism's Grand Central Question.

THE ROAD TO CLARITY

We cannot—I would even say we dare not—begrudge pantheists their aim to address human suffering. It is, in and of itself, something that every worldview strives to address. We all seek to understand the cause of our pain and what can be done about it. And ultimately we want to know if there is a place or a state of being of peace that is devoid of the pains that plague us. Though every view seeks answers, pantheism makes this quest its main focus. Christians can affirm the quest while offering a fundamentally different path through the gospel.

If we truly care about the solution, all of us must ask these questions: Does pantheism provide a coherent and satisfactory answer? Does it address the pain and suffering we all deal with in a way that satisfies the whole person—heart and mind? Does the gospel? We have to ask ourselves these questions not just in the realm of theory, but also in the midst of our struggles. Can we really buy into the fact that life is an illusion? Or, more pointedly, can we really believe that our suffering is only a temporary illusion that we can get over, that we can whisk away with enough meditation, yoga or good deeds? Is there a deeper understanding of pain and suffering and its reality?

More to the point, are pain and suffering more profound because they are real and not mere illusions? Does the reality of pain tell us something deeper about ourselves, God and the nature of true peace beyond the idea that we need to escape it? Is pantheism's Grand Central Question answered in our efforts to rise above it by becoming God or in God's initiative to deal with it on our behalf?

Pain and suffering are central to all worldviews, but no worldview puts its God in the midst of pain like the gospel. And so we will see if the gospel can satisfy the heart's cry and the mind's questions in a world of pain.

ESCAPING THE ESCAPISM

TRANSFORMATION AND RENEWAL

The paradoxical allure to Westerners about ancient Eastern religion is that it is exotic, so it is like trying something new. The gospel is too traditional, too old-school, so we must look elsewhere for answers to be "deep" people. C. S. Lewis warned us that our love of the exotic and our "horror of the Same Old Thing" can entice us away to explore seemingly novel ideas that end up providing nothing new compared to our everyday experiences.[1]

The gospel seems like the "same old thing," the been-there-done-that of past generations that we've grown tired of. And so we look elsewhere, like Eastern religious ideas, to find seemingly novel spirituality. The ideas of becoming one with the universe, of being absorbed into the Brahman and of achieving a state of nothingness in the Buddhist Nirvana seem so mystical, so mind blowing and so hard to understand that they must be true. That is the insidious trap, because as we'll shortly see, there is nothing "same old" about the gospel when it comes to answers about pain and suffering. And as we'll also soon see, when we compare the core of pantheism's solution to pain and suffering with the solutions of other world-views, there is nothing terribly unique about pantheism.

In contrast to Paul's statement to each of us to "be transformed by the renewal of your mind" (Romans 12:2), much of pantheistic thinking tells us to be transformed by the *removal* of our mind. I'm not saying that in the pejorative sense. I'm saying that in the descriptive sense. To become one with the impersonal is to lose all sense of mind and self. To become nothing is to do the same, by definition. And in this we don't renew our minds, we lose them. That might sound exotic and new, but is that really something that we all strive for in understanding the origins, meaning and destiny of ourselves, our friends and our children? Is that really the kind of answer we are looking for in trying to make sense of suffering and pain?

THE KARMA CHAMELEON

Pantheism's teaching about how we are to achieve a sense of unity with the divine is not new or exotic. Karma is, at its core, a works-based belief system that says what almost every other religion and worldview says: if you are a good enough person, you can achieve heaven, enlightenment, bliss, Nirvana, whatever. Islamic salvation is based on a person's merit in following God's will. Modern Judaism says that our eternal reward is based on our works, and the largest religion in the world—Good Personism—tells us that we'll get to heaven if we're good people. Karma is a chameleon doctrine because it can be adopted and adapted to fit every worldview. And so pantheism isn't all that exotic after all.

Some have tried to put the Christian faith into a karmic paradigm by arguing that the Bible, too, teaches that "what goes around comes around." A verse they rely on is Galatians 6:7, which reads, "For whatever one sows, that will he also reap." But the context of this passage reveals that it is not referring to the consequences of our actions in some next life. Paul is talking about ultimate justice in an eternal hereafter. The very next verse says that "the one who sows to his own flesh will from the flesh reap corruption, but the one who sows to the Spirit will from the Spirit reap eternal life" (v. 8).

Karma is not about that at all. It is about the actions in one life affecting the circumstances in the next. Eventually everyone will work out his or her bad karma, resulting in impersonal absorption or nothingness, which means that there is no eternality to justice. Bliss or nothingness may be eternal in a pantheistic view, but justice is not. The karmic view of justice is totally at odds with the biblical view.

Jesus makes the point quite clear when dealing with the man born blind in John 9.

> As he passed by, he saw a man blind from birth. And his disciples asked him, "Rabbi, who sinned, this man or his parents, that he was born blind?" Jesus answered, "It was not that this man sinned, or his parents, but that the works of God might be displayed in him. We must work the works of him who sent me while it is day; night is coming, when no one can work. As long as I am in the world, I am the light of the world." Having said these things, he spat on the ground and made mud with the saliva. Then he anointed the man's eyes with the mud and said to him, "Go, wash in the pool of Siloam" (which means Sent). So he went and washed and came back seeing. (John 9:1-7)

The man wasn't born blind to pay off the bad karma from his previous lives, and his parents were not paying off their karmic debt in having to take care of a blind child. Nor was the blindness just an illusion. Jesus did not use the suffering to make a speech about the illusions of life or about our inner divinity. No, he acted toward real suffering in a real way. He pointed out that the suffering and pain were quite real and that those circumstances would eventually lead to the glory of God. Then he put his hands on the man to heal him.

THERE CAN BE ONLY ONE

In Matthew 11, Jesus makes a very exclusive and yet paradoxically inclusive claim. He tells the crowd that has gathered to hear him preach that no one can know the Father except those to whom the Son chooses to revel him (Matthew 11:27). In other words, the only way to know God is to know God the Son, who is Jesus. There are no spiritual paths or works or methods to enlightenment that gain us some kind of secret knowledge or mystical realization about our own divinity. Here, as he has done in many places, Jesus claims to be the exclusive means to salvation and the answer to our struggles. But he follows his statement up with an inclusive invitation. He says, "Come to me, *all* who labor and are heavy laden, and I will give you rest. Take my yoke upon you, and learn from me, for I am gentle and lowly in heart, and you will find rest for your souls. For my yoke is easy, and my burden is light" (Matthew 11:28-30, emphasis mine).

Jesus weaves an interlacing pattern of seeming paradoxes here that give us insight into what it means to find release from the burdens of this life. He says that he is the exclusive means by which people come to know salvation. But he invites *all* to come and know him, to follow him and to bear his light burden. He provides an inclusive invitation for us all to come to the exclusive means of salvation.

Men like Vivekananda, Chopra and Tolle want to take Jesus' invitation to those of us who are heavy laden and twist it into something esoteric and nebulous. Vivekananda equates Jesus' statement with an invitation to become one with the Impersonal Absolute—the Brahman—to find escape from maya by finding rest in realizing your own divinity. That could not be further from what Jesus meant. When he said, "Come unto me," we should take him at face value and see that he is referring to himself when he says "me." To claim that Jesus does not mean "me" when he says "me" defies both logic and grammar.

There is something fascinating in what Jesus says about the rest he invites us to partake in and the easy yoke he invites us to take up. He relinquished his glorious state with the Father to live among us and die a sinner's death. If we are to follow his sacrificial example, how exactly is such a burden light and such a yoke easy?

The answer is far deeper and more profound than platitudes about obtaining inner peace or quieting the mind. The true peace that Jesus offers has nothing to do with being so enlightened as to be free of strife and pain. It has everything to do with embracing them with his strength, not ours. Let me explain. Better yet, I'll let Jesus do that.

On the night before his crucifixion, which Jesus knew was coming, he talked with his disciples about the necessity of the cross. On the eve of his death—by the most excruciating torture the world's mightiest empire could devise—Jesus made a remarkable statement to his disciples: "Peace I leave with you; my peace I give to you. Not as the world gives do I give to you. Let not your hearts be troubled, neither let them be afraid" (John 14:27).

This should peak our interest, because of all the people in that discussion, Jesus—the one who should have been the most troubled and afraid, the one who should have had the least amount of peace—was the only one who had true peace. He had peace enough to offer it to the disciples. That word for peace in the Greek is *eirene*, which does not just mean a lack of conflict, but also a state of being "set at one" in a relationship.[2] Jesus, as the incarnation of God the Son, has that perfect relationship with God the Father, and he is offering the peace, the tranquility of mind and spirit, that comes with that kind of relationship.

But notice something critical. Jesus is not offering peace by saying that he is in a state of undifferentiated unity with God and we can be too. It is true that as the incarnation of God the Son, Jesus' divine nature is identical to the Father's divine nature. (We will explore that in greater detail in later chapters.) But there is an eternal distinction between the Father and the Son. They are not the same personhood. This allows for relationship between the Father and the Son.

In that sense, Jesus' peace in terms of being "set at one" with the Father requires a subject-object distinction. Reconciliation is not the lack of distinctions between two things. Reconciliation requires relationship, and relationship requires distinctions between the two persons in that relationship. So, what Jesus offered his disciples was the kind of peace that comes from being in a perfect relationship with God, by being submitted to the Father's will.

Eastern religions tell us to attain "inner peace" by denying the existence of suffering or conflict as mere illusions. But Jesus offers a peace that is profound because it does not run from suffering. No, the peace Christ offers blossoms in the presence of suffering. This is why I believe Jesus offered not just peace but *his* peace—peace that comes with a true relationship with God—to the disciples on the eve of the most violent encounter of his earthly ministry. Before his death, Jesus promised to give his disciples peace "not as the world gives" so that they could be sustained in the midst of their suffering. That peace came from Jesus' reconciling work on the cross. He offered it to his disciples, and he offers it to us.

KEEPING IT REAL

This is a fundamental distinction between pantheistic and gospel-centered views of suffering and pain. Pantheism tells us that suffering and pain are mere illusions because life is basically an illusion. Or it tells us that we can overcome pain and suffering by realizing our inner divinity and power. But as appealing as the pantheistic view might sound with all its exotic esoterica, the idea that the suffering we experience is all an illusion to wake up from simply cannot be lived out.

The idea that human (or even animal) suffering is but an illusion implies that morality itself is illusory. As Dhavamony explains, according to Hinduism, moral categories of good and evil apply only in our lower state; they do not apply when it comes to the absolute—the Brahman—we are all trying to attain unity with: "Until [a man] reaches the state of oneness with God he is subject to the pairs of opposite like good and evil."[3]

But wouldn't this mean that morality is ultimately unreal if it does not apply to the ultimate reality we are trying to attain? And if that is the case, then there is nothing "wrong" with human suffering and pain, even the suffering we inflict on each other. They may be unpleasant illusions, but they are not moral wrongs that need to be righted. In the pantheistic view, pain and suffering are only experiences on the way to realizing that experiences do not matter.

Can such a view provide us with real, existential answers in the passages of our lives? After all, when suffering confronts us, it forces us to be real. In his semiautobiographical novel about pantheistic ideas like Zen Buddhism, Robert Pirsig's fictional surrogate, Phaedrus, asked a Hindu professor whether the bombs dropped on Hiroshima and Nagasaki were just illusions. When the professor affirmed that they were, Phaedrus got up, left and "gave up."[4] That is quite a natural reaction, I would submit, especially when we start to look inward at our own pain. Of course we'd like an escape. Of course we'd like to run to the idea that these things are just illusory and that we can overcome them with a mind trick. But if I can be so bold, I would say that the idea that our most intense pains and sufferings are just in our heads isn't mystical or deep— it's offensive.

Allow me to be even more transparent in saying that I cannot imagine this to be any kind of real hope. Brahmans—those of the highest Hindu caste and those supposed to be closest to enlightenment—weep at their children's funerals. Even Vivekananda thundered away at the West for building churches instead of food banks in India. Why the moral outrage if this is all just an illusion and if morality is ultimately illusory? If doing good is merely a way for the doer to exercise karma (Vivekananda is quick to point out that we don't actually benefit anyone, we only work out our karma) so as to attain a higher station the next go-round, then why is he upset at the suffering around him? If suffering is an unpleasant (but karmically deserved) illusion, then why are the moral sensibilities of a man as enlightened as Vivekananda so enflamed?

One can only speculate, but the circumstantial evidence points to the conclusion that even for pantheists, suffering is nothing like an illusion. It is quite real. It cannot be merely wished away through meditation, good works and devotions. It has to be dealt with in a meaningful way. Two questions arise from this: How is suffering meaningfully dealt with? And what do we mean by "meaningful" anyway?

THE POWER OF HOW

Let us address the differences between pantheism's solutions to how we are to deal with pain and how the gospel deals with the issue. As we begin, we must consider some basic and intuitive truths. Suffering and pain can be dealt with only by a being who is capable of handling it. So it simply stands to reason that we humans, who are the problem, cannot possibly be the solution. Yet, with its systems of karma and self-actualization, the pantheistic worldview claims that we can be the solution. From the Hindu belief that we will attain godlike status, to the Buddhist claim that we can be emptied of self to attain nothingness, to the New Age and New Spirituality view that we can become a personal god or one with the universe, pantheists propose that humans can and must be the solution. But we ourselves have created and re-created (*ad nauseum*) the problems. If we are the problem, then how is it possible that we can be trusted to be the solution too?

Consider also the fundamental problems with the logic behind the pantheistic system. The various systems teach that we are one with absolute reality, we are nothing, or we are as powerful as the universe itself. And they teach that we do not know our true state because we are beset with the illusion that we are finite. In regard to Hinduism and New Age/New Spirituality, we have to ask, How, exactly, does the perfect being get so deluded? If the divine mind is perfect, then it seems unthinkable that it would believe false information or be tricked into thinking it is something that it definitely is not. Who could have pulled the wool over our divine eyes? As for Buddhism, it is hard to even comprehend who is beset with the delusion of selfhood if there is no selfhood. How does a nonpersonal nonself ever acquire a belief at all, let alone a false one? What accounts for the very inception of the delusion?

How did we ever arrive at this painful existence? It's interesting that Vivekananda admits that pantheism provides no answer to its own Grand Central Question:

> How can the perfect become the quasi-perfect; how can the pure, the absolute, change even a microscopic particle of its nature? But the Hindu is sincere. He does not want to take shelter under sophistry. He is brave enough to face the question in a manly fashion; and his answer is: "I do not know. I do not know how the perfect being, the soul, came to think of itself as imperfect, as joined to and conditioned by matter." But the fact is a fact for all that. It is a fact in everybody's consciousness that one thinks of oneself as the body. The Hindu does not attempt to explain why one thinks one is the body.[5]

Not only does Hindu pantheism not provide an answer, it doesn't even try.

In addition to the logical problems, we can see that even pantheistic systems recognize the need for "divine" intervention in the midst of pain. The divine intervener just happens to be us. Let us revisit Eckhart Tolle's words, only partly quoted in the previous chapter:

> There are many accounts of people who say they have found God through their deep suffering, and there is the Christian expression "the way of the cross," which I suppose points to the same thing. . . . Strictly speaking, they did not find God through their suffering. . . . I don't call it finding God, because how can you find that which was never lost, the very life that you are? The word God is limiting not only because

of thousands of years of misperception and misuse, but also because it implies an entity other than you. God is Being itself, not a being. There can be no subject-object relationship here, no duality, no you and God. . . . The worst thing in your life, your cross, turns into the best thing that ever happened to you, by forcing you into surrender, into "death," forcing you to become as nothing, to become as God—because God, too, is nothing.[6]

Tolle can suppose all he wants, but the "way of the cross" has nothing whatsoever to do with finding our inner God through deep suffering. Tolle seems to adopt Chopra's marketing formula: use Christian-esque language and you might win some people over to your view. Tolle says that we are the cause of our own pain; all our pain is self-inflicted because we allow it to have power over us. He tells us that we "surrender" to reality through pain when we cannot stand it any longer. We suddenly give up, unable to give pain any more energy, which leads to our becoming God, which is nothing. How exactly? Well, that's not entirely clear. But what is clear is that he thinks suffering is an illusion that you just have to get over.

That is the fundamental distinction between the gospel and pantheism. For pantheists, pain and suffering arise because they have forgotten that they are God. According to the gospel, pain and suffering arose because we wanted to be God. God created Adam and Eve to exist in a state of bliss and happiness amid a garden of tranquility. There was nothing forbidden to them except the fruit of the tree of the knowledge of good and evil (Genesis 2:17). If they ate this fruit death would come, not from acquiring knowledge, but from rebelling against God.

God had but one commandment for our first parents to follow to continue to enjoy their sublime relationship with God. Satan later came and tempted Adam and Eve away, twisting God's words and telling them that they would not die if they ate the fruit, but they would become like God (Genesis 3:1-5). It is at that enticement—to become like God—that the fruit suddenly took on an appeal. They ate the fruit not because they were hungry for physical nourishment, but because they were hungry for their spiritual autonomy. Adam and Eve did not want relationship with God—they wanted to be like him and be his rival.

God respected their desire for their own way and their rejection of a pure relationship with him. He cast them out of the garden they thought so little of. And this world of pain and suffering resulted. We have each inherited that pain and suffering, being born not into the garden but into this world, which is quite far from Edenic.

Thus, in one sense, pantheists and Christians have a similarity: we acknowledge that we are the cause of our own suffering. But Christians recognize that suffering has resulted from our corporate actions, inherited from the choice of our first parents to rebel and reject relationship with God, and we have perpetuated that choice. True, sin in our lives has its consequences here as well as in eternity. But we are not paying for sins from a past life.

For pantheists, all our pain and misfortune is our own doing, but not in a corporate sense. The pain of this life, regardless of whether it comes directly from us or from an external source, always comes back to our individual actions. Our actions in past lives have resulted in the horrors—as illusory as pantheists claim them to be—of this life. From the common ground that humanity is its own worst enemy, we can see that it simply does not add up that humanity can save itself. Pain is not an illusion. It is very real. And we need a very real savior to lift us up out of the mire.

MEANINGFUL SUFFERING

There is something more to explore in confronting the reality of pain and suffering. Pain and suffering are not cognitive defects we can cure by detaching ourselves from the world. They are the indicators of what really matters. We feel pain as a natural and important way to understand the value of those things that we are at risk of losing or have already lost.

As I sit and write this, there is a fresh wound in the American psyche and soul. A young man burst into an elementary school and murdered twenty children—yes, *children*—and six adults. Before that, he murdered his mother, the woman who had taken care of him in his troubled days and was at that very time thinking of ways to help her son. Can we look at the pain of those parents who lost little ones that day and say that what they are going through is an illusion? Can we tell them that this is just the bad karma of a previous life rearing its head in this life in some form of impersonal cosmic justice? Or perhaps the children were visited by some bad karma of their own. The children who survived that terrible ordeal, who saw the blood, heard the screams and witnessed the death, are indelibly scarred by what they saw and cannot be consoled with the idea that this is all an illusion that they can overcome with good deeds and right thinking.

In fact, the pain of that day, and the pain of every day after that, might be one of the most real things those left behind can experience. It is difficult for any worldview to address the questions that come from such tragedy. But if you will indulge me, allow me to underscore something important for pantheists to consider in all of this.

In his book *The Problem of Pain*, C. S. Lewis remarked that "God whispers to us in our pleasure, speaks in our conscience, but shouts in our pain; it is his megaphone to rouse a deaf world."[7] Having experienced intense loss in his own life, Lewis was not being glib or clever. He was saying something profound. Pain arouses the senses and tells us what is important. It visits us even if we do everything right, take every precaution and say our prayers. That is the effect of sin from the beginning. Pain is the unpleasant measure of reality.

The loss of things we don't really care about barely registers, if at all, with any pain. But take away something we care deeply about, and the pain is immeasurable. Pain tells us how real, how valuable and how important another person is to us. That's why the loss of a parent is so intensely painful, and that's why the loss of a child is unfathomable.

If pain and suffering are only illusions, then the pain we feel over the severed connections with lost loved ones is also illusory. Can that really be the way things are? Can anyone really be so detached as to say that those connections are illusory in favor of the idea that we are all connected as part of the One? Tolle seems to think so. He says,

> Enlightenment consciously chosen means to relinquish your attachment to past and future and to make the Now the main focus of your life. It means choosing to dwell in the state of presence rather than in time. It means saying yes to what *is*. You then don't need pain anymore. How much more time do you think you will need before you are able to say, "I will create no more pain, no more suffering"? How much more pain do you need before you can make that choice?[8]

Did we catch that? Tolle is saying that we create pain because we have attachments to those things we have lost in the past and concern for what such a loss could mean for our future. If we apply this situation to those parents who lost their five-, six- and ten-year old children in Newtown, Connecticut, then we can only conclude that they are going to feel pain because they are attached to the past they had with their child and are sorrowful about a future without them. They will get over that pain only when they choose not to dwell on such attachments. I don't want to paint Tolle as unfeeling, but can he really be serious? Frankly, it borders on the outrageous to think that the losses those parents feel are simply because of selfish attachments.

Their pain is more than that. It is the natural feeling that follows the severing of the inherently valuable connection made between two beings who are inherently valuable. Our human experience and our own intuition stand defiantly shaking their fists at the notion that a mother's connection to her son or a father's connection to his daughter is illusory. The intensity of the pain is directly proportional to the reality of our connections. In that way, pain is meaningful.

Buddhists and Hindus are noted for their intense compassion and empathy. But true compassion and empathy imply the reality of pain and suffering. I find it hard to believe that any pantheist— Tolle, Chopra or any other—who lost a child would sit back, even years later, and say that the pain of that loss is just a dream to wake up from. Pain shouts louder than any such sophistry, no matter how well meaning. And rightly so.

Jesus listens to the shout because he treats pain and suffering as meaningful realities of the human condition. He came down to Earth to deal with them for us. Pantheism says that desire results in bad behavior, which results in karma, which results in the illusion of our nondivinity and our pain. The gospel says that human rebellion—the desire to be like God—corrupted us, leading to sin and separation from God, which causes us pain.

But rather than have us reach up to divinity to escape pain, the gospel tells us that God came down to us to rescue us from it. The Bible tells us of the death of Jesus' friend Lazarus (John 11:1-44). Jesus arrives at Lazarus's tomb, knowing full well that he intends to raise Lazarus back to life. Yet, amid Lazarus's mourning family and friends, Jesus is brought to tears (v. 35). Perhaps Jesus wept because, although he knew that Lazarus would walk out of the tomb, he also knew that death and sorrow were not what was intended for humanity. But our individual and corporate corruption made them happen. Jesus wept not just for his friend, but for all of us who pass under the shadow of pain and death. He cried real tears because our pain is real.

Krishna is the most cherished and revered deity in Hinduism. His interaction with humanity is told in the *Bhagavad-Gita*, the "Song of God," in which he says that we need to sacrifice as part of the process of working out karma, but he also says that he himself is a sacrifice for us. But look as we might to find out what that means, no explanation surfaces. It's just baldly stated. This is a clue to pantheism's view of the illusory nature of suffering. Karma is real, our suffering seems real, and we need a sacrifice for it. But even the sacrifice itself is illusory—nebulous and unexplained—because the suffering it is called on to alleviate is just as nebulous.

The gospel shows us that both the suffering is real and the sacrifice needed to alleviate it is real. Dhavamony describes the differences well:

> However divine and merciful be Krishna presented in the Hindu Scriptures and in the theologies which commented on them, he is never a "redeemer" in the sense of personally taking on himself the responsibility of human race [sic] and saving it from the consequences of sin. For Krishna is the God that has never borne on his shoulders the guilt of the world and consequences of sin. Radhakrishnan ventures to remark: "A suffering God, the deity with a crown of thorns, cannot satisfy the religious soul." Here lies an essential difference between the Hindu and Christian religious sentiment. This religious sentiment, of course, is based on the religious conception of man, for when man is naturally divine, sin does not affect him in his inner structure and salvation cannot consist except in making man aware of his natural divineness and to help him realize it.[9]

There you have it. In every pantheistic system, humanity is essentially divine and so needs no redeemer. Tolle and Chopra would agree, and Scientologists tell us we are immeasurably powerful Thetans in the rough. But the sharp reality of pain and suffering and our utter inability to deal with them tells us that we need someone real and more powerful to deal with them. The cross is where we find the Powerful One who took suffering seriously by taking it upon himself so that we would not have to and so that one day we will be totally free.

REVISITING TRUE RENEWAL

And so we come back to the difference between renewing our minds by seeing that we need a divine savior (Romans 12:2) and emptying our minds so we can believe that we are the impersonal divine.

As a worldview, pantheism in all its forms tells us that we have to work to achieve our salvation—that we have to pull ourselves up by our own bootstraps. That is not exotic. We've heard it all before. Pantheism, especially its Western daughters, has just told us the same old things we've told ourselves for millennia, but in more mystical language.

But consider the gospel. It is the only worldview that tells us the sheer, stark truth that we are inherently sinful and that we need to be saved from ourselves. True spiritual transformation happens when our minds are renewed—perhaps even rescued—from the illusion that our works will save us and that we can be free from suffering if we just try hard enough. God's renewal of our minds into understanding that we need the unmerited grace of the cross is unique and fresh.

The Hindu philosopher Radhakrishnan says that a suffering God doesn't satisfy the religious soul. But in a pantheistic view, there really is no satisfaction for the soul that looks for answers in the morally charged, love-ridden question of human suffering. If we are all part of the impersonal, absolute of the universe, the Brahman, then where is true morality? Doing good things, working off our karma by helping others, isn't done for their sake but for ours, so that we can attain godhood. It is a self-help system meant to help us achieve a state of unity with the divine, not to help the poor or unfortunate for their sake. James Sire puts it well:

> But two things should be noted about this system. First, the basis for doing good is not so that the good will be done or so

that you benefit another person. Karma demands that every soul suffer for its past "sins," so there is no value in alleviating suffering. The soul so helped will have to suffer later. So there is no agape love, giving love, nor would any such love benefit the recipient. One does good deeds in order to attain unity with the One. Doing good is first and foremost a self-helping way of life.[10]

Our deeds portray only the illusion of altruism, but they are really the shadows of self-interest. And so the illusory prison of samsara leads to the very real prison of selfishness, because one is not truly free to act in someone else's best interests for that person's sake. That is ironic, because in Buddhism the only way to escape is to be free of desire. But the entire system is set up so that every action is done out of the desire to be free. The lack of distinctions between God and self in Hinduism and the total denial of self in Buddhism are what imprison the self to an existence of self-centered conundrums. Strange, isn't it, that pantheists try to escape the painful cycle of death and rebirth only to be sucked into the vicious cycle of a desire to be free from desire?

In the gospel, however, neither suffering nor good deeds are an illusion, because our minds are renewed to finally see the reality. We see that we are not God. We see that we need God to transform us. And we see that he dealt with suffering on Calvary's hill. Because he has done so, we can be free to act toward others in gratitude and for their sakes. We do not do good to one another to escape endless suffering. God has already rescued believers in Christ from that eternal pain by embracing the pain of our penalty himself. The gospel—which tells us that we give, not to get, but because we are grateful—is what can satisfy the religious soul.

TRUTH THAT TRANSFORMS

It is true that suffering and death remain in this world. But our liberation from it is both "already" and "not yet." Jesus has already freed us from the ultimate consequence of eternal pain and suffering through his self-sacrifice. We are not yet at the time when there are no more tears and no more death (Revelation 21:4). But that is the ultimate state for those who trust Jesus. The pain in our lives is real and may seem relentless, but the joys of knowing that it has an end and an answer make them bearable.

John Newton, who wrote the famous hymn "Amazing Grace," penned another hymn that poignantly describes our once and future hope:

How tedious and tasteless the hours,
when Jesus no longer I see!
Sweet prospects, sweet birds, and sweet flowers,
have all lost their sweetness to me.

The mid-summer sun shines but dim;
the fields strive in vain to look gay;
but when I am happy with Him,
December's as pleasant as May.

Content with beholding his face,
my all to his pleasure resigned,
no changes of season or place
would make any change in my mind:

While blest with a sense of his love
a palace a toy would appear;
and prisons would palaces prove,
if Jesus would dwell with me there.

Dear Lord, if indeed I am Thine,
if Thou art my sun and my song,
say, why do I languish and pine,
and why are my winters so long?

Oh, drive these dark clouds from my sky;
Thy soul-cheering presence restore;
or take me unto Thee on high,
where winter and clouds are no more.[11]

Perhaps there is a reason that Vivekananda, Chopra and Tolle rely on Jesus so much to try to tell us how to deal with suffering. Perhaps it is because Jesus actually provides the answers and the means to truly and profoundly deal with them. Jesus doesn't offer platitudes or kitsch. He doesn't offer pretty crystals or mystical experiences. He doesn't offer a *way* of dealing with suffering. He offers himself as *the way*. Pantheism's Grand Central Question of how to deal with pain and suffering finds its answer not in a *how* but in a *who*.

Part Three

ISLAM OR THE GOSPEL

Which Tells Us About God's Greatness?

FROM WHENCE COMES GOD'S GREATNESS?

WORDS OF MY FOREBEARS

How is God great? That is Islam's Grand Central Question. In the years of my life when I followed Islam, two special Arabic words were so important that they almost appeared to take on a physical form when spoken. When the resonant voice of the *muezzin* said the words in the not-quite-musical, not-quite-atonal call to prayer, the words seemed to hang in the air like smoky vapors in the serpentine Arabic script. "Allahu Akbar," the muezzin's voice would call out—"God is great." As the words left his throat, he would draw them out in a long atonal chant that steadily rose in pitch and ended suddenly, almost as if it were a defiant declaration.

"Allaaaaaah Akbar . . . Allaaaaaaahu Akbar!"

So begins the Islamic call to prayer as the muezzin sits atop the minaret and calls to the faithful. Upon hearing the words, Muslims who take their devotions seriously stop what they are doing, look toward the sound, rise and begin washing themselves for the ritual prayer. To me, the sound of those words was haunting and inspiring. The tone of the muezzin's voice, coupled with the words' meaning, beckoned reverence.

Those words—Allahu Akbar—literally mean "God is greater."[1]

So important to Islam is this phrase that it actually has a name—Takbir. Many Westerners have heard these words uttered, especially since September 11, 2001. What was once unheard to Western ears has now become familiar. Perhaps there is no religious verbal expression that creates such opposite reactions. For many non-Muslims, the words have become associated with violence and acts of terrorism, shouted by robed men with long, straggly beards who shoot bullets in the air to proclaim their intentions to dominate the West. They shout "Allahu Akbar" as a means of proclaiming to non-Muslims that Allah is greater than Western imperialist powers and that Islam will subdue them one day. And save for a few exceptions, the media has not worked hard to disabuse us of the association.

It is true that some Muslims use those words as a battle cry. But for many other Muslims, the words have a far different association. They do not inspire dread, fear, rage or violence. For most (but not all) Muslims, the words inspire reverence, awe and humility. Allahu Akbar, "as the briefest expression of the absolute superiority of the One God, is used in Muslim life in different circumstances, in which the idea of God, his greatness and goodness is suggested."[2] The Takbir "is a part of the call to prayer repeated five times a day, and faithful believers may use it as an exclamation in response to anything out of the ordinary, whether good or ill."[3]

I can recall those close to me saying "Allahu Akbar" as they walked into someone's home as a way to ask for a blessing on those who lived there. Many Muslims I know and love use the words to express delight when surprised by a pleasant turn of events. And when told of bad news, perhaps that they or a loved one are facing a grave illness, they say Allahu Akbar as a declaration that God is greater than their daunting circumstances. So to most Muslims, the Takbir, the proclamation that God is greater, is both an expression of praise and a short prayer. Those words express the most elemental beliefs of every Muslim, not just that God is great but that he is greater—he is greater than anything we can conceive. He is the Greatest Possible Being.

DIVINE GREATNESS AS THE ROOT OF ISLAM

Like Christianity and biblical Judaism, Islam is a monotheistic faith. But to the Muslim mind, the Islamic version of monotheism is what distinguishes it from all other such faiths. In Islam, God is an absolute oneness in his nature and in his personhood. His mind, will and actions have no separation or differentiation. "The Unity of Allah is the distinguishing characteristic of Islam. This is the purest form of monotheism, i.e., worship of Allah Who is neither begotten nor beget nor had any associates with Him in His Godhead. Islam teaches this in the most unequivocal terms."[4]

Like the Takbir, the doctrine of God's oneness has a name: Tawhid. God is one and only one, and that oneness is an element of his majesty. As one Muslim scholar puts it: "God is the essence of existence. His Arabic name is Allah. He is the First and the Last. He is unique and nothing resembles Him in any respect. He is One and The One. He is self-sustained, does not need anything but everything needs Him."[5]

This is a concise summary of the ideas that come directly from the most important chapter of the Qur'an, Sura 112, which says in its entirety: "Say: He is Allah, the One, the Only. The Eternal, the Absolute. He begets not, nor is He begotten. And there is none like unto Him."

The well-known Muslim commentator Zamakshari tells us that when Muhammad was asked to describe Allah, this *sura* was revealed to him as the perfect description.[6] The Islamic traditions tell us that Muhammad viewed Sura 112 as worth one-third of the entire Qur'an and that its recitation remits sins.[7]

Sura 112 is so important because it weaves two fundamental Islamic doctrines together. It declares that God is an absolute, undifferentiated unity. And it declares that God, in his unity, is utterly independent of anything; he is self-subsisting and self-sufficient. But Takbir is the foundation for all of this:

> The unequaled greatness of Allah becomes the linchpin of all further considerations of his nature. Anything that could conceivably be construed as detracting from his greatness must be considered to be false, or even offensive. The worst sin in Islam is *shirk*, which is commonly translated as "idolatry," but literally means "association" and thus implies far more than the common understanding of idolatry, such as worshiping statues of deities. Shirk means to conjoin Allah with any of his creatures, to ascribe a partner to him, or to understand him to possess limitations that are characteristic of his creatures but not of him.[8]

Thus even the fundamental doctrines of Tawhid and God's self-subsistence have still a deeper root—God's greatness—which permeates them. In other words, God is one and self-subsistent because God is the Greatest Possible Being.

The conception of God's greatness is so central to the Islamic way of life that it is a virtuous act for a Muslim to know and recite God's Ninety-Nine Beautiful Names. These names are meant to approximate in the mind of the believer who God is and what he does. The fact that God has such attributes and is described in those "names" comes from the Qur'an itself:

> Allah is He, than Whom There is no other god; Who knows (all things) both secret and open; He, Most Gracious, Most Merciful. Allah is He, Whom there is no other god; the Sovereign, the Holy One, the Source of Peace (and Perfection), the Guardian of Faith, the Preserver of Safety, the Exalted in Might, the Irresistible, the Supreme: Glory to Allah! (High is He) above the partners they attribute to Him. He is Allah, the Creator, the Evolver, the Bestower of Form (Or Colours). To Him belong the Most Beautiful Names: whatever is in the

heavens and on earth, doth declare his Praises and Glory: And He is the Exalted in Might, the Wise. (Sura 59:22-24)

The Hadith, the Muslim traditions about Muhammad's life and sayings apart from the Qur'an itself, tell us that Muhammad said, "Verily, there are ninety-nine names of God and whoever recites them shall enter Paradise."[9] This is how fundamental God's greatness is to Islam. To recite a list of his great attributes is tantamount to achieving everlasting life in paradise.[10] Indeed, one of those "beautiful names" is that God is great—Al-Kabir (Sura 22:62).

For the devout Muslim, even to say the word for *God* in Arabic—Allah—requires reverence and ritual. Muslims will follow the word Allah with the *subhana wa ta'alah*, meaning "God: glory to Him the exalted or High," which is taken from Sura 17:43 of the Qur'an. The notion of God's infinite greatness comes through at the very mention of God. For Muslims, God is above everything we can think about him, and Muslims are reminded of that every time they say the Arabic word for God.

God's greatness forms the way Muslims can (or, more accurately, cannot) relate to him. Islamic classical theology holds that God is so great that it is impossible for the human heart and mind to grasp anything about him beyond the superficial. This makes it impossible to have a relationship with him. Although God is personal in that he is conscious and expresses a will, no one can know his personality to any meaningful degree. We can only catch imperfect glimpses of God's character through the commands he gives in the Qur'an. In that way, we can know *about* God. But in no real sense can we know *God*.

This fact may trouble some Muslims who feel that they have a relationship with God to some degree. But one of Islam's premier theologians and philosophers, al-Ghazali, tells us that those with the most knowledge of God know that they have no way to really know him at all: "The end result of the knowledge of the *arifin* [those who have knowledge] is their inability to know Him, and their knowledge is, in truth, that they do not know Him and that it is absolutely impossible for them to know Him."[11]

There is something in this with which the gospel agrees, of course. In Christianity, God is transcendent and above humanity in infinite ways that make it impossible to ever know him in an exhaustive sense. God's ways are higher than our ways, the Bible tells us, and his thoughts are higher than our thoughts (Isaiah 55:9). So great, so incomprehensible is God that should anyone see God in his full glory, he would die, because the infinite glory is simply too much for the finite mind to grasp (Exodus 33:18-20). Even in the instance in which Moses saw a mitigated glimpse of God's glory, his face glowed with the aftereffects of having seen something so grand (Exodus 34:29-35).

For Christians, this gives a picture of our existence in heaven, where we will have eternity to learn new things about the infinitely searchable God. That never-ending exploration of the divine fulfills the very purpose of our existence. Yet despite God's transcendent and unfathomable grandeur, the Bible tells us that God condescends to allow us to know something profound: not just his qualities, but also his personality. Indeed, the very incarnation of God in Jesus of Nazareth is an expression of that condescension as the "image of the invisible God" (Colossians 1:15). But there will be more on that later.

In orthodox Islam, however, God does not condescend so that we can encounter him personally. Islamic scholars tell us "it is even difficult to find an appropriate Arabic or Persian expression for 'experience of God' without running the risk of encroaching upon the absolute transcendence of the God of Islam, of anthropomorphizing him."[12] So great, so wholly other is Allah that language fails us because there is no analogy in human experience to use to understand him. Duncan Black McDonald sums it up well:

This is one of the most fundamental and characteristic points in Muslim theology. No terms applicable to a created being may be applied to him [God], or if they are—as so often in the Qur'an—it must be clearly understood that their meaning as applied to created things is no clue to their meaning when applied to Allah.[13]

This is the idea, again sprouting from the root doctrine of God's greatness, that God is so different from creation that we cannot make any analogies with which to mentally apprehend God, except for what God says in the Qur'an.

Though in Islam God is a personal being, he is not worshiped and obeyed with any personal interaction. He is more of a will to be followed, a master to serve. In Islam,

law is more central, broadly speaking, than theology, and knowledge of the divine will and our obedience more crucial than knowledge of the divine nature and our experience. Worship, in Islam, even though phrased in the divine Names, is concerned with God's sovereignty over our wills, rather than his fellowship with our spirits.[14]

This shows itself in the everyday life of Muslims. They pray at specified times of the day (five, to be exact). And they perform those prayers ritualistically, prostrating, kneeling and bowing a certain number of times, placing their hands in certain places when they say certain phrases. Even the content of their words is prescribed with limited room for deviation. Most Muslims recite Sura 112 during their prayers to get the benefits of praising God's oneness and self-dependence through a sura worth one-third of the whole Qur'an.

There is an interesting fact about Islamic prayer that hearkens back to the Mosaic laws of physical purification and uncleanness. Muslims must cleanse themelves in a specifically prescribed manner before praying and submitting to God. Looking back on it now, having come out of Islam and into the Christian idea of praying "just as I am," I am struck by the fact that Muslims must clean themselves before they can even prostrate before God. In a way, the humility is admirable. But there is a strange paradox that diminishes the worship experience, is there not? A person is penitent before God and humble in supplication because he recognizes his uncleanness—a state that only God can fix. Yet in Islam, Muslims bear the responsibility of cleaning themselves up to approach the great God, even in a state of abject humility.

In the Old Testament, the faithful had to purify themselves before they could come to God to sacrifice animals to atone for sin. But those purification laws served to foreshadow a time when God himself would provide a lasting sacrifice that would wash sin away. Now the follower of Christ enjoying the grace of the new covenant comes to prayer realizing her sullied state and realizing that God makes her clean spiritually rather than physically. When accused of irreverence for not washing his hands before a meal, Jesus responded that the physical does not defile the spiritual. Rather, it is the other way around (Matthew 15:1-20).

THE CONTEXT OF GREATNESS

The importance of Takbir did not arise in a vacuum. It has a specific historical context for Muslims. Islam sprang up in the midst of a seventh-century pagan culture, in a state of competition as it were. And the competitors were well established. In addition to the polytheists of Arabia, there were Jews and Christians. Islam made no bones about the fact that it was offering these groups a conception of a better, more worship-worthy God. Thus today's politically correct sensitivities that make it unfashionable to compare different religious systems do not apply to Islam, and comparisons should not offend Muslims. Winfried Corduan has it right:

Now to approach the study of Allah and Islam on a comparative basis is not to do it an injustice. A great amount of the content of the Qur'an consists of demonstrating that Islam is better than any other religion, and that God, as portrayed in Islam, is greater than any other deity that human beings may have imagined. Islam arose in the context of rivalry. Muhammad was proclaiming monotheism as he understood it against the polytheism that dominated Mecca in his day, the monotheism of Judaism, which he considered to be hypocritical, and the Trinitarian monotheism of Christianity, which he censured as both idolatrous and absurd.[15]

In this light, we see that the Takbir phrase is not best understood woodenly as "God is greater." Rather, "[Allahu Akbar] actually implies 'God is greater than all others,' or 'God is the one and only supreme being.' We see, then, that at the very foundation of Islam is the conviction that Allah's greatness is understood by way of contrast to all other inferior beings."[16] And, according to Islam, those supposedly inferior beings include the trinitarian God of the Bible.

COMMON AND UNCOMMON GROUND

An understanding of the commonalities and differences between Islam and Christianity is critical if we are to see whether the gospel can answer Islam's Grand Central Question of God's greatness with any compelling substance. Let's begin with the common ground.

In both Christianity and Islam, there is one God, and he is the only uncreated being. He is omnipotent, omniscient and omnipresent. For both Christians and Muslims, God is transcendent. He is just and merciful. God has revealed himself and his will through certain inspired texts. While Christians believe that God inspired his self-disclosure in the Old and New Testaments, it often comes as a surprise to Christians to learn that according to Islam, God inspired the Torah (called the *Taurat* in the Qur'an), the Psalms of David (the *Zabur*) and a text the Qur'an refers to as the Gospel (the

Injeel) as well as the Qur'an. (See Sura 3:3; 5:43-44, 47, 58.)

Like Christians, Muslims believe that Jesus was born of a virgin named Mary (Sura 3:33-60). Jesus is a prophet and a powerful messenger; he is sinless and worked miracles according to the Qur'an. Christianity and Islam share a sense of God's greatness, his transcendence. Indeed, the view that God is the greatest possible being is the most important commonality we share.

As important as they are, the similarities are superficial. The Islamic and biblical views of God have fundamental and important differences that bear on Muslims' and Christians' answers to the Grand Central Question of God's greatness. In other words, while the common ground for Christians and Muslims is their shared conviction that God is the greatest possible being, Islam and the gospel clash in their understanding of *how* God is great and what makes him great. The paradox is that the most important point of agreement is also the greatest point of departure between the two faiths.

In Islam, God is not triune. He is an absolute unity, utterly without any differentiation within himself. To have any differentiation within God would be to diminish his greatness, and so Islam denies that God has any differentiation, whether in knowledge, emotion, will or interaction with humanity. He is one through and through. But Islam's fervor for God's oneness—his Tawhid—goes further than just a fear of lessening his greatness. For Islam, differentiation is the greatest possible blasphemy, called *shirk*, which is to ascribe associates or partners to God. The Qur'an, although seeming to refer to the Trinity as God, Jesus and Mary (Sura 5:116), denies it in the most unequivocal terms: "They do blaspheme who say: Allah is one of three in a Trinity:[17] for there is no god except One Allah. If they desist not from their word (of blasphemy), verily a grievous penalty will befall the blasphemers among them" (Sura 5:73).

As with the Trinity, the Qur'an condemns the very idea of God's incarnation. In several places, it says that those who believe such a thing are blasphemers (Sura 5:72). Islam's rejection of the incarnation again stems from Takbir. For Muslims, God would never condescend to his creation by appearing as a human, as one of us. He would never allow himself to be subjected to the frailties of the human experience, like walking, sweating and feeling pain. And of course it is inconceivable to Muslims that God would subject himself to the humiliation of death on a cross at the hands of wicked men. These distinctions show that in many ways Islam is defined by what it rejects. As Corduan summarizes, "Islam did not so much define itself internally as externally against the other existing options."[18]

The very language the Qur'an uses to express its repugnance to the incarnation reveals something fascinating when we compare it to the biblical account of Jesus' triumphal entry into Jerusalem. As Jesus proceeded into Jerusalem, he was met with the crowd's praise and adoration as the king. Appalled, the Jewish leaders demanded that Jesus silence the crowd's apparent blasphemies. But Jesus refused, saying that creation would wail in protest if the praises that were given to him—praises that are due to God—halted. "I tell you," Jesus said, "if these were silent, the very stones would cry out" (Luke 19:37-40).

In a complete contrast, the Qur'an says that at the very idea that God would have a son (either as offspring or incarnation) the "skies are ready to burst, the earth to split asunder, and the mountains to fall down in utter ruin" (Sura 19:89-92). In the Bible, nature would cry out praises to Jesus if the people stopped, because God is great and due all praise. In the Qur'an, nature cries out in protest if Jesus is praised, because it denigrates God. Islam tells us that the incarnation diminishes God's greatness, while the gospel tells us that the incarnation is an expression of that greatness. The two views could not be more opposite. The question is, which is right?

THE STRUGGLE TO UNDERSTAND

In Islam, while God is utter transcendence and aloofness, there remains at least a modicum of personal interaction between God and humanity, even though it is mediated by angels. One Muslim commentator tells us that God is utterly transcendent in Islam yet near to us in a personal way:

> God is High and Supreme, but He is very near to the pious thoughtful people; He answers their prayers and helps them. He loves the people who love Him and forgives their sins. . . . Because He is so Good and Loving, He recommends and accepts only the good and right things. The door of his mercy is always open to any who sincerely seek his support and protection.[19]

These kinds of statements that tell us that God is utterly transcendent yet somehow near to pious people seem to help us understand the mystery of God's greatness a little better. But careful consideration reveals that they do not. Islam tells us *that* God is transcendent yet near, but it does not tell us *how* that can be. This creates a tension for Muslims who sincerely seek to worship God as great, yet wrestle with how worshiping an utterly unknowable God can possibly be intelligible.

As with Christianity, God in Islam is great in the sense that he is maximally perfect and uncompromising in the qualities that make him great. In other words, if Allahu Akbar—God is greatest—then none can surpass him in his great-making qualities, and he cannot compromise or diminish any of those qualities. In Islam, God is Al-Wadud, full of loving kindness—in a maximal way. God is Ar-Rahman, the Merciful One, in a way that cannot be compromised. Yet He is Al-Adl, the Maximally Just One.

The paradoxes and possible contradictions leap out, do they not? How is it that God is uncompromisingly merciful yet uncompromisingly just at the same time? Does not one seem to cancel out the other? Indeed, this plunges Muslims into a struggle to understand this very relationship to God.

On one hand, orthodox Muslims tell us that God is utterly unknowable and that he does not condescend to interact with us. "Men are servants of a just master," one scholar tells us. "They cannot, in orthodox Islam, typically attain any greater degree of intimacy with their creator."[20] And al-Ghazali says that "it is absolutely impossible for [Muslims] to know Him." Yet somehow God "loves the people who love Him and forgives their sins." How are we to come to terms with these ideas if we are truly to affirm God's greatness?

It makes sense, of course, that we cannot expect to have a comprehensive understanding of the infinite. But the struggle for a coherent view of God's greatness that satisfies Muslims' rational mind and devotional heart can be intense. I vividly recall struggling to make sense of all of this as a Muslim. I wanted to express adoration to the personal Supreme Being, yet I could not help but believe that such a thing was beyond me. I so desired to tell of God's infinite mercy, yet also wanted to proclaim his uncompromising justice. The dilemmas that emerged from that struggle seemed inescapable from the Islamic perspective. So I was forced to retreat to escapist answers that really were no answers at all. To avoid the dilemma, I had to believe that attributes like justice, love and compassion are not remotely the same for God as they are for humanity. I hoped that this retreat would solve the issue for me. But it did not.

Chalking the dilemma up to a mystery was not enough for me, and from the writings I have read and the looks in the eyes of Muslims I have talked with, I know that it is not enough for them either. Like all who sincerely want to believe in one God, Muslims yearn to acknowledge God's greatness. They do not pretend to fully understand it, nor should they expect to. But there is something about us, in our experience of personal relationships, that senses the tug for divine relationship. Something within us knows that although we cannot fully comprehend God's ways and how his mercy interacts with his justice, there must be a way to reconcile them if God is truly great. We must be able to do so without sacrificing reason on the altar of mysterious reverence. Though God's greatness might transcend our reason, it must not defy it. On this Muslims and Christians can agree.

So the Grand Central Question is, how are we to come to grips with God's greatness in a way that satisfies our mind's God-given rational capacity and our soul's realization that what is worthy of worship is that which is beyond us? Does Islam's affirmation of God's greatness—in its denial of Christian doctrine—get us there? Or is it possible that the gospel—preserved by a God who is capable and who cares, with its doctrine of God's triunity and its proclamation that God gives of himself—gives us a fuller picture of divine greatness? Can the gospel satisfy the Muslim mind's desire to apprehend God's greatness while satisfying the Muslim heart's longing to submit to it in awe?

In Acts 17, we read of Paul's famous encounter with the Athenian philosophers on Mars Hill. When he got to Athens, Paul perused the city and saw the various idols representing the various Greek pagan deities. In that city of philosophers, Paul addressed those who wanted to hear more about Jesus and his resurrection. Paul opened his dialogue with the Athenians by remarking that they seemed very religious, with all their idols and altars of worship (Acts 17:22-23). He specifically called out one altar with a particular inscription: "To the unknown god" (v. 23). Likely they erected that altar to avoid offending a possibly powerful yet unknown deity. They made sure that all their religious bases were covered, as it were.

And with this fact, Paul did something remarkable. He told the Athenians that the God unknown to the Athenians is Yahweh, the only God who really exists (vv. 23-26). None of their other gods were worthy of worship, because they had no power or character. But Paul showed them that the God who was unknown to them has both. In fact, in Acts 17, Paul did not just point to the theological differences between pagan idol worship and biblical monotheism. He pointed to something more profound. He pointed to events in history, telling of how God has interacted with humanity in creating, guiding and relating to us.

Paul told them that God has determined certain dwelling places for each of us so that we "should seek God, in the hope that [we] feel [our] way toward him and find him. Yet he is actually not far from each one of us" (vv. 26-27). We are made to look for God, but God comes alongside us and draws near to us in intimate ways. For Paul, God was not an aloof character sitting on high, observing us as we stumble about. God was close. He was intimate. He engaged in human history. In fact, in that first century, God had directly engaged in very recent history, having incarnated himself in Jesus of Nazareth and rising from the dead just a few years earlier. Ironically, the "unknown god" the Greeks referred to was far more knowable than they could have imagined.

I do not for a moment think that Muslims worship Allah in the same way the pagan Greeks worshiped their idols. But as we consider whether the gospel can provide an answer to Islam's Grand Central Question, I would like to indulge in a comparison. Islam tells us that God is great, yet unknowable. While Muslims do not conceive of God as one among many pagan deities, in some sense Allah is an "unknown God" to Muslims. Unlike the ancient Greeks, who called their god "unknown" because they had no knowledge of who he might be (or if he even existed), Muslims claim to know that God exists and that he has dealt with humanity in the past and will deal with us again in the future.

But while Muslims can know *about* God—his existence and his commands—they cannot *know* him relationally. Christians can commend Muslims' religiosity and devotion even to a God they cannot know. But the gospel offers Muslims a great One who has expressed that greatness by making himself known in a relational way. Perhaps Muslims' quest to glorify God as great is found in the very gospel Islam denies. We will look to see if that is so.

GOD'S GREATNESS AND THE PRESERVATION OF THE GOSPEL

"Why do you think the Bible is God's Word? Don't you know it's been changed over the centuries?" I would ask. Even Western biblical scholars agree that it has been changed, I would say, referring to the likes of Bart Ehrman and, before him, Walter Bauer. These were typical challenges I would barrage Christians with in the years that I embraced Islam. And deafeningly silent responses from Christians were, sadly, also typical. Once I had done my job in dismantling (or at least severely damaging) Christians' faith in the Bible, I would offer them a counter—the Qur'an. I would claim that Christians could trust the Qur'an because it had not been changed since its revelation to Muhammad 1,400 years ago.[1]

Over the course of some years of study, I discovered that precisely the opposite is true. The historical evidence for the reliable transmission of the Bible is remarkable. I will not delve deeply into the historical evidence for this transmission, its historical accuracy or the historical evidence for the Qur'an. I commend the works of other fine scholars to interested readers.[2] My aim here is to address the issue of the Bible's preservation within the framework of Islam's Grand Central Question of God's greatness.

The question is, can a Muslim who fully believes that God is great also believe that the Bible has been so badly corrupted that it contains damnable blasphemies about God? Without over-stating the case, I think that, in terms of Islamic belief, the question of the Bible's reliability and authority really does come down to that one question.

How does Islam's Grand Central Question of God's greatness fit into how we look at the Bible's history? It becomes clear when we look at the most common Muslim arguments against Christianity. Muslims have explained the divergences between Christianity and Islam by claiming that Islam is the original monotheistic religion of the Middle East and that Christians have corrupted the historical records and inspired texts to suit their own theological needs. This accounts, for example, for the difference between Christian rev-erence for Jesus as God and the Muslim belief that Jesus was a prophet but only a man.

For centuries, Muslims have claimed that Jesus' original message was changed and that error crept in during the years between Jesus' ministry and the first writings of his life. This supposedly led to the development of legends and embellishments including Jesus' claims to divinity, teachings about the Trinity, and even the historicity of Jesus' death by crucifixion and his later resurrection. Nearly every Muslim I know and have met has been taught to argue against the gospel in this way at least to some degree. I was no exception.

The Qur'an itself—Islam's foundational document—refers to certain biblical documents as revealed by God, including the Torah (*Taurat* in the Qur'an), the Psalms of David (*Zabur*) and the Gospel (*Injeel*). The fact that the Qur'an actually references the Judeo-Christian Scriptures often surprises most Christians (and even a few Muslims). The Qur'an not only references them, but explicitly states that they were "sent by God." For example, the Qur'an says about the Torah: "It was We [a plural of majesty referring to God] who revealed the law (to Moses): therein is guidance and light" (Sura 5:44). The Qur'an affirms the divine origin of the Torah and the Gospel together: "And We caused Jesus, son of Mary, to follow in their footsteps, confirming that which was (revealed) before him in the Torah, and We bestowed on him the gospel wherein is guidance and light" (Sura 5:46).[3] And again, the Qur'an says, "[God] sent down the law (of Moses) and the Gospel (of Jesus) as a guide to mankind" (Sura 3:3).

A serious tension arises when we see that the Bible and the Qur'an contradict each other on the important points we discussed in the previous chapter, such as the deity of Christ, the Trinity and Jesus' death and resurrection. To resolve the tension, Muslims teach that the Bible has been changed over time, either intentionally or unintentionally, to include these ideas. For Muslims, who must affirm the Qur'an, God's revelations in the Bible had to have been corrupted. Otherwise God's revelations—the Bible and the Qur'an—would be self-contradictory. In the Muslim mind, it simply cannot be that the Qur'an is wrong. And since the Qur'an and the Bible are in conflict over these ideas, it must be the Bible that contains the errors. Those errors crept in through human corruption, and the Qur'an was sent to correct those corruptions and bring us all back to true monotheism.

This is a critical issue if we are to understand where the truth lies when it comes to Islam's Grand Central Question. If God truly is great, how can it be that his self-revelation has been so fundamentally changed as Muslims claim? Thus the reliability of the Bible is crucial for both Christians and Muslims: "Without a reliable New Testament we have no objective, historical way to know what Jesus said or did. We cannot establish whether he was God, what he taught, or what his followers did and taught."[4]

For Christians, if the Bible has been faithfully transmitted through the ages, the doctrines that form the heart of the gospel are vouchsafed. But for Muslims, the Bible's preservation presents a stickier problem. If the Bible has been preserved, and it contradicts the very Qur'an that affirms it, the necessary implication for Muslims can be faith shattering. But there is solace to be found, even if finding it is uncomfortable. If God is great, then his revelation has been preserved. And we can find solace in the fact that God is, indeed, great.

AN UNLIKELY CHALLENGER

I read the Qur'an several times through as a young boy and into my twenties. In my late teens and early twenties, I began to study Arabic so that I could understand the original language of the book that was at the center of my devotional life. I believed that the Qur'an taught what Muslims have believed for years—that the Bible has been corrupted, necessitating the revelation of the Qur'an as God's pure message. *Sure, the Bible we have may contain some true statements*, I thought. *It is highly unlikely that all of it was lost. But it cannot be trusted on the most important aspects of faith in God. We have the Qur'an for that.*

While deeply entrenched in those beliefs in my college days, I met two Baptist men. They went door to door to the student apartments at the University of Michigan, asking people to talk about Jesus. Ann Arbor being the town that it is, most students said no, and some not all that politely. But I didn't say no. I eagerly welcomed the two men in, happy to have an opportunity to extol the virtues of Islam and the Qur'an.

Our discussions were long and arduous. I made those two men quite uncomfortable, challenging them at every corner, yet inviting them to come back week after week. And they did. They came back numerous times to continue our conversations. Their willingness to endure the tortuous discussions was quite a testimony to their commitment.

For some time before that I had been reading the Bible, not to gain spiritual insight about deep truths, but to find the flaws in it. With the various courses I was taking in New Testament studies (with a decidedly liberal bent to the perspective), I was arming myself for our continued discussions. That's when I was challenged in a very profound way by the very book I was seeking to debunk. I came across Luke's account of John the Baptist addressing the religious leaders of his day, chastising them and others for their lack of penitence:

> He said therefore to the crowds that came out to be baptized by him, "You brood of vipers! Who warned you to flee from the wrath to come? Bear fruits in keeping with repentance. And do not begin to say to yourselves, 'We have Abraham as our father.' For I tell you, God is able from these stones to raise up children for Abraham." (Luke 3:7-8)

Those words leapt out at me as I sat in the long-past-its-prime armchair in my apartment. John the Baptist was telling the Jews who relied on their traditions that their DNA would not save them from God's judgment for what they deserved. Their allegiance to truth—not mere tradition—is what would save them. John the Baptist's words reached out to me across the centuries. He challenged my personal basis for believing in Islam. For years I had challenged others that being a Christian based merely on parental upbringing was intellectually insufficient. Yet there I was, sitting in that chair, suddenly facing the same challenge.

I was right, you see, to challenge others to reconsider their traditions in the light of truth. Believing something just because it is your tradition is not a sufficient reason. It may be that your tradition happens to be true, but it may not be. The consequences are too dire to rely on earthly convenience and comfort. The tables were suddenly turned on me, and I was forced to address those same questions and issues. Though I had tried over the years to justify my belief in Islam with evidence, I suddenly knew that the chief reason I was a Muslim was the same reason that the Pharisees were Jews. Because I was born that way.

What happened to me that evening was a slight—but profound—change in mentality. I found myself applying the same kind of critical thinking to Islam and the Qur'an as I did to every other faith and worldview. I had nothing to fear, I told myself, because if the Qur'an is true, then it should stand up to the toughest scrutiny and I would come out in the end with more confidence in Islam than ever.

That's when I was blindsided by an unlikely challenger, a challenger that shook my beliefs to their foundations. I was blindsided because I entrusted my faith, character development and identity to the challenger. I would turn to the challenger for comfort, guidance, wisdom and the rule of my faith in Islam. This challenger was not a Muslim, a Christian, a Jew, a Buddhist or an atheist. In fact, the challenger wasn't even a person. It was my Qur'an—the holy book in which I had placed all my faith.

With the slightly shifted attitude brought about by John the Baptist's words, verses of the Qur'an that I once took for granted suddenly took on new, even startling meanings. And so I came across this verse of the Qur'an:

> And We caused Jesus, son of Mary to follow in their footsteps, confirming that which was (revealed) before him in the Torah, and We bestowed on him the gospel wherein is guidance and light, confirming that which was (revealed) before it in the Torah—a guidance and an admonition unto those who ward off (evil). *Let the People of the Gospel judge by what Allah hath revealed therein.* Whoso judgeth not by that which Allah hath revealed: such are the evil-livers. (Sura 5:46-47)[5]

The words challenged everything I believed about the Bible as a Muslim. As a Muslim, I believed that the Qur'an was not just the inspired word of God, but God's literal words recited by Muhammad as he received them from the archangel Gabriel. That is fundamental to the Muslim understanding of the Qur'an. God chose to reveal the Qur'an in Arabic and gave the message to Gabriel, who in turn gave it to Muhammad to recite word for word. In the Christian view of inspiration, God uses the literary styles and personalities of various people to convey his message, but Islam views scriptural revelation as a matter of mere dictation. The prophet is nothing more than a human mouthpiece for the divine. In fact, that's what the word *Qur'an* means: recitation.

For Muslims, then, the Qur'an is perfect because God speaks perfectly. Every sura is perfect in content and form. Every verse in every sura is perfect, and no other will do. And every word, including the verb tenses—past, present, future and imperative—is perfect, and no other will do. With that view in mind, we can see just how pivotal and world changing my reading of Sura 5:46-47 was for me. Muslims the world over believe that the Bible was once God's revelation to humankind. The Torah, Psalms and Gospel were his limited divine self-disclosures and the means by which certain people could know God's character and his will.

But, according to Muslims, that message was corrupted over time, which necessitated the revelation of the Qur'an as the final, forever-to-be-preserved word of God. But how could that even possibly be true if these verses in Sura 5 were true? The Qur'an does not say that the People of the Gospel—Christians—*should have* judged between truth and error by the gospel they once had. No, the Qur'an gives a present-tense imperative to Christians. It commands them to judge—right at that time—by what God had revealed in the Gospel.

According to the Qur'an, there must have been a divine message, called the Gospel, that Christians could have turned to and judged by in the seventh century, *at the time the Qur'an was spoken by Muhammad.* And if that was the case, the Gospel couldn't have been corrupted at the time of the Qur'an. Otherwise those verses would make no sense, because God would then be commanding Christians to judge by a hopelessly corrupted text. In fact, the passage concludes by saying that those who do not judge by what God has revealed are rebelliously evil. In those verses, the Qur'an could not be more clear that the Gospel was a trustworthy message from God that Christians could—and should—turn to for divine guidance and truth.

I read and reread that sura, hoping to find some kind of explanation of what I was reading that would confirm what Muslims had been taught for centuries—that the Bible was corrupted before the Qur'an's advent. But I was coming up empty. The immediately preceding verses state that the Torah and the Gospel were presently available Scriptures in the possession of the Jews and Christians in which there "is the (plain) command of Allah" (Sura 5:43). And the Torah is a book in which there "is [present tense] guidance and light" (Sura 5:44).[6]

Several verses later, the Qur'an addresses Christians and Jews (called the "People of the Book"): "People of the Book! Ye have no ground to stand upon unless ye stand fast by the Law [Torah], the Gospel, and the revelation that has come to you from your Lord" (Sura 5:68). The Qur'an admonishes Christians and Jews to "stand fast"—again present tense—by the Torah and the Gospel. So important is this that unless they do it, they have no other ground to stand on.

Thus began my search through the text of the Qur'an to find out why I had been taught for so long that the Bible had been corrupted and changed. But I could find no such thing in the Qur'an. Rather, the opposite proved true. In sura after sura and verse after verse, I found support for exactly the opposite—that the Bible had been preserved and should be followed. In fact, the Qur'anic text assumed that the Bible was consistent with it. In Sura 5:46 we read the following: "And in their footsteps We sent Jesus the son of Mary, confirming the Law *that had come before him*: We sent him the gospel: therein was guidance and light, and confirmation of *the Law that had come before him:* a guidance and an admonition to those who fear Allah" (emphasis mine).

This is from the most commonly used English translation of the Qur'an (the Abdullah Yusuf Ali translation). Most other Muslim translators give the same or a similar translation. But this translation is not faithful to literal Arabic. The phrases (mis)translated to read that Jesus and his Gospel were confirming the law that "had come before him" in Arabic are *ma beyna yadihi*, literally "that which is between his hands." So, literally, the verse should be translated to say that Jesus and his Gospel confirmed the law "that was between his hands." That is an Arabic idiom that describes when two different things are present together. If something is "between the hands" of something else, it means that they exist alongside each other.

The verse *does not say* that Jesus and his Gospel confirmed the law that was before him *chronologically*. It says that Jesus confirmed the law that was before him *spatially*—just as a lectern spatially stands before a person on a stage. Thus the Qur'an is saying that Jesus confirmed the uncorrupted law that he had in his own hands.

When we look at verse 48 (just two verses later) with this understanding, we see that the Qur'an claims to confirm the Gospel. It says, "To thee (Muhammad) We sent the Scripture (the Qur'an) confirming the scripture that came before it." Again, "the scripture that came before it" is literally the scripture "between its hands," meaning the scripture (the Gospel) that existed simultaneously with the Qur'an. The Qur'an assumed that the Bible existed in the possession of the People of the Book and that the Qur'an was consistent with it.

This forced me to reexamine my prior suppositions about the Bible, including my interpretations of Qur'anic verses that I once thought supported the idea of biblical corruption. For example, Muslims will refer to Sura 2:79 to support their argument that the Qur'an teaches the actual corruption of the text of the Bible. That passage reads, "Then woe to those who write the Book with their own hands, and then say: 'This is from Allah,' to traffic it for a miserable price. Woe to them for what their hands do write, and for the gain they make thereby."

But from the Qur'anic context and the historical context, we see that this verse does not support the Muslim argument. The verses that precede Sura 2:79 are important. They state,

> Behold! When they meet the men of Faith, they say: "We believe": But when they meet each other in private, they say: "Shall you tell them what Allah hath revealed to you, that they may engage you in argument about it before your Lord?"—Do ye not understand (their aim)? Know they not that Allah knoweth what they conceal and what they reveal? And there are among them illiterates, *who know not the Book, but (see therein their own) desires*, and they do nothing but conjecture." (Sura 2:76-78, emphasis mine)

The full context says that there are those who do not know the true text but write original material and say it is from God. These verses actually make reference to something quite common and quite well-known in the seventh-century Arab world: the Jewish Targums and Midrash. No one considered those documents to be actual holy writ or part of the Old Testament. They were only important theological stories and commentaries written by Jews and Jewish rabbis. Some rank-and-file Jews passed them along as fables and legends, and some of those who were not learned ("illiterate," as the Qur'an calls them) may even have believed that these stories were true and in the Old Testament texts. But they were never intended to be historical, and they most certainly are not in the original text.

Commentaries from some of Islam's earliest authorities provide little support for the idea that the Qur'an teaches that the biblical text (as opposed to the meaning) was corrupted.

Gordon Nickel conducted a detailed study both of the Qur'anic verses Muslims use to support the idea of corruption and of the works of Islam's earliest and most well-known commentators, Muqatil ibn Sulayman and Abu Ja'far ibn Jarir al-Tabari, to see whether they understood the Qur'an to say that the biblical text had been changed.

Nickel concludes that these seminal Muslim thinkers were very reluctant to read the Qur'an as accusing the Bible of having been textually changed.[7] Rather, they interpreted the Qur'anic verses as charges against Jews and Christians who allegedly changed the meaning of the text to hide supposed prophecies about the coming of Muhammad and certain God-given laws that they did not want to apply.[8] And even these alleged changes were done around Muhammad's time in the seventh century, well after the New Testament canonization. At least one Muslim scholar agrees that the Qur'an doesn't teach biblical corruption:

> Contrary to the general Islamic view, the Qur'an does not accuse Jews and Christians of altering the text of their scriptures, but rather of altering the truth which those scriptures contain. The people do this by concealing some of the sacred texts, by misapplying their precepts, or by "altering words from their right position." However, this refers more to interpretation than to actual addition or deletion of words from the sacred books.[9]

Not only does the Qur'an call the Torah, the Psalms and the Gospel God's word, but it also says in at least two places that "None can change God's words" (Sura 6:115; 18:27). Islam's most well-known commentator, Ibn Kathir, explains this verse:

> Al-Bukhari [perhaps the most trusted early Islamic scholar], reports [that] Ibn 'Abbas said that the [verse] means they alter and add although none among Allah's creation can remove the Words of Allah from his Books. They alter and distort the

apparent *meanings*. Wahb bin Munabih said, "*The Tawrah and
the Injil remain as Allah revealed them, and no letter in them was
removed*. However, the people misguide others by addition
and *false interpretation*, relying on books that they wrote
themselves. They say, "this is from Allah," but it is not from
Allah; as for Allah's Books, *they are still preserved and cannot
be changed*.[10]

Every argument I had once used to convince Christians that the
Bible had been corrupted was being dismantled one by one—by the
very sources I relied on as a Muslim.

As I discovered this kind of information, the common Muslim
belief that Paul hijacked Christianity in its early stages no longer
made any sense. The Qur'an specifically says in two places that
Jesus and his followers were not defeated by those who sought to
corrupt God's message.

Behold! Allah said: "O Jesus! I will take thee and raise thee to
Myself and clear thee (of the falsehoods) of those who blaspheme; *I will make those who follow thee superior to those who
reject faith, to the Day of Resurrection*: Then shall ye all return
unto Me, and I will judge between you of the matters wherein
ye dispute." (Sura 3:55, emphasis mine)

O ye who believe! Be ye helpers of Allah: as said Jesus the son
of Mary to the Disciples, "Who will be my helpers to (the
work of) Allah?" Said the Disciples, "We are Allah's helpers!"
Then a portion of the Children of Israel believed, and a portion
disbelieved: *But We gave power to those who believed against
their enemies, and they became the ones that prevailed*. (Sura
61:14, emphasis mine)

Well-known Muslim commentator Al-Qurtubi says that Sura
61:14's reference to the disciples included Paul:

It was said that this verse was revealed *about the apostles of*

Jesus, may peace and blessing be upon him. Ibn Ishaq stated that of the apostles and disciples that Jesus sent (to preach) there were Peter *and Paul* who went to Rome. . . . Allah supported them (the apostles) with evidence so that *they prevailed*, meaning they became the party with the upper hand.[11]

If a Muslim is to take these verses seriously, he simply cannot believe that someone like Paul came along in the earliest days following Jesus' ministry and completely took it over, corrupting Jesus' original message while the disciples were still alive to oppose him. If that had happened, in what sense could Jesus' disciples have been granted victory to the "Day of Resurrection"? If Paul had hijacked Jesus' message, would this not have made Jesus and his disciples abject failures? To suggest such a thing flies directly in the face of the Qur'anic text and Muslim beliefs that Jesus was a great prophet.

The New Testament text leaves no real room for this argument either. For Paul to have been the founder of Christianity by hijacking Jesus' message, we would have to see evidence in Paul's writings that he was uninterested in Jesus' life and teachings and that he espoused teachings inconsistent with Jesus' core teaching. But we see nothing of the kind. In fact, we find that Paul was interested in Jesus' life, referring to specific events recorded in the Gospels.

In Colossians 3:13, Paul makes a reference to Jesus' teaching in the Lord's Prayer that we are forgiven as we forgive (see Mark 11:25). In Galatians 5:13-14, Paul practically quotes Jesus' teaching that loving our neighbor as we love ourselves fulfills the entire law (see Matthew 22:38-40). Paul specifically mentions several facts in Jesus' life, including the Last Supper, in which Jesus broke bread and drank wine to show the symbols of the new covenant (compare 1 Corinthians 11:23-26; Matthew 26:26-29). And when we look at Jesus' core teachings, we find Paul to be perfectly consistent (see table 8.1).

Table 8.1. Parallels Between Jesus' and Paul's Teaching

Core Teaching	Jesus	Paul
Man is in need of a savior	Mark 10:45; Luke 5:31; 18:19	Romans 3:23-25
Jesus is that savior as God incarnate	Matthew 16; John 8:58	Colossians 1:13-17; 2:9; 1 Timothy 2:3-6
Jesus came to sacrifice himself in payment of our sins	Matthew 20:18-19; John 10:15-16; Mark 10:45	1 Corinthians 15:3-7
Jesus rose again from the dead that we would have eternal life and to vindicate his claims to divinity	Matthew 20:18-19; John 2:18-22	1 Corinthians 15:3-7

Neither the text of the Bible nor the text of the Qur'an nor the early Muslim commentaries support the view that Paul hijacked Christianity.[12] As N. T. Wright noted during his debate on that very subject with (now former) atheist A. N. Wilson, "Paul was one true voice in a rich harmony of true voices of the early church, but the writer of the song was Jesus."[13]

From where, then, does the Muslim view of biblical corruption come if not from the Qur'an and the early Muslim sources? Translations of the New Testament were not available in Arabic until the ninth century. Until that time, Muslims had basically assumed that the Gospel was consistent with the Qur'an and that Christians and Jews had distorted the meanings in oral exposition or by coming up with Targums and the like. But in the ninth century, things changed because the Bible was finally translated into Arabic.

As Muslims began reading the actual text, they could not help but notice the glaring differences between the Bible and the Qur'an. It was then that a Spanish Muslim named Ibn Khazem systematized and popularized the argument that the biblical text was corrupted.[14] In his view, it simply had to be the case that the Bible had been corrupted, because otherwise the Qur'an would have been wrong all those years about historical facts concerning the life, death and resurrection of Jesus. And for Muslims, it cannot be the case that the Qur'an is wrong. So Muslims came to believe that the Bible was changed, despite all the evidence to the contrary.

AN INCONVENIENT TRUTH

The Muslim belief that the Bible is corrupt (to resolve the Bible's contradiction of the Qur'an) creates a thorny theological problem. The Qur'an says that God revealed the *Taurat, Zabur* and *Injeel.* In other words, the Bible is God's revealed word, his very self-revelation to humankind. But if the Bible was corrupted, then one of two consequences necessarily follows: either (1) God was unable to preserve the Bible, or (2) God was unwilling to preserve the Bible. There is no third option.

If God was unable to preserve the Bible, then he is not all powerful. But no Muslim would believe that. Indeed, for Muslims, a god who is not almighty is no god at all. If God is not able to preserve his self-revelation in the Bible, why should we think that he has the power to preserve the Qur'an? If God does not have the power to protect his self-revelation, then we cannot have any confidence in him. This first option being totally unacceptable, we must look to the second option: that God was able to preserve the Bible but he was unwilling to do so.

Is this choice any better? Does it allow us to believe that God is great? If God is unwilling to protect his revelations, he is utterly untrustworthy, because he allowed the books that told millions of people about him to profess what Muslims consider to be outright blasphemies, like the incarnation, the Trinity and the crucifixion. But if God was willing to let his revelation in the Bible become corrupted, then he is responsible for such blasphemies. And if he is willing to allow the Bible to become hopelessly corrupted, what would give a Muslim any confidence that he would not allow (or has not already allowed) the Qur'an to become corrupted as well?

As a Muslim, I simply could not believe that God was so impotent that he could not preserve the Bible, nor was he so cruel and untrust-worthy that he would not preserve it. No Muslim can believe in an all-powerful and all-good God and believe that the Bible has been corrupted. Thus only one avenue remains for any Muslim who be-lieves that God is truly great: the Bible could not have been corrupted.

In trying to escape this dilemma myself, I would respond (as I've heard Muslims today respond) that this is really a false dilemma, much like the dilemma posed by the problem of evil, which says that if God is all good and all powerful, then his goodness would compel him to want to stop evil and his power would provide him with the ability to do so. Since he has not stopped evil, either he does not want to stop it or he cannot stop it (or he just doesn't exist). Theists have correctly countered that it could easily be the case that God has sufficient moral reasons for allowing certain evils if they bring about a greater possible good. Based on this logic, Muslims might argue that God could allow his revelation to be cor-rupted if a greater possible good could later come.

But this fails to provide an escape to the conundrum. The cor-ruption of God's revelation to the point of espousing abhorrent blasphemies that lead to damnation is quite different from allowing an evil to take place for some greater good. In allowing certain evils, God might be allowing some people to undergo temporary physical or emotional suffering to bring about a greater, permanent benefit in terms of salvation. But if God allows his self-revelation to be so corrupted that millions, if not billions, go to an everlasting hell due to believing the corruptions, then God is responsible for their false beliefs and their eternal damnation.

And if God's revelations could be easily corrupted because he does not care to protect them, then he would be impossible to obey or follow with any certainty, and we would therefore have no trust-worthy source for spiritual truth. To believe such things would be to do something no Muslim would do. It would be to deny that God is great.

The tension remains for Muslims at this point, does it not? The Bible teaches things about God that Muslims do not find to be great. The Bible teaches that God is a triune being—one being who exists with three distinct personages or centers of consciousness. For Muslims, this doctrine sounds at best like a confused monotheism or, at worst, actual polytheism. The Bible teaches that God is incarnational, that he actually condescended to take on a human nature and live among us in Jesus of Nazareth. Yet for Muslims, this doctrine diminishes God's greatness, because as the Master he would never condescend to humanity in that way. And the very idea of the cross—that God the Son subjected himself to an unspeakably humiliating death at the hands of his own creation, is the antithesis of God's greatness for Muslims. But the Bible teaches all these things. Yet the Qur'an—which affirms the Bible—denies them all. And so the tension persists. And it is profound.

There is a satisfying way out of the dilemmas and the tensions. The very same doctrines that Islam rejects—the Trinity, the incarnation and the cross—actually highlight God's greatness. In this way, the gospel message folds greatness upon greatness. God is greater—Allahu Akbar—in that he is able and willing to protect his self-revelation. And that very self-revelation teaches us unique things about God's nature, character and actions that prove him to be the greatest possible being. In these doctrines, the tension Muslims feel—between wanting to affirm God's greatness yet fearing that the Bible lessens it—is resolved and fulfilled. The beautiful nature and character of God are taught to us in the Bible that God the Great has preserved. And that nature and character we will now explore.

GOD'S TRIUNE GREATNESS

I have had many debates and discussions about the Trinity—perhaps the most challenging idea in Christianity. Looking back on all those debates and all the books and articles I've read on the subject, especially between Muslims and Christians, I have come to the conclusion that Islam's rejection of the Trinity is one of the most profound ironies in comparative religion. Islam rejects the Trinity out of a fear that it leads to the unforgiveable sin of *shirk*, which is saying that God has partners. *Shirk* is Islam's cardinal sin because it diminishes God's greatness by saying that he is equaled by another or that he needs associates to do what he wants or to be who he is. The irony is that, when properly understood, the Trinity is the very doctrine that glorifies God as the self-subsisting, coherent yet completely transcendent being that Muslims claim him to be.

In several passages, the Qur'an seems to address the Trinity to debunk it. Consider the following Qur'anic passages:

> O People of the Scripture! Do not exaggerate in your religion
> nor utter aught concerning Allah save the truth. The Messiah,
> Jesus son of Mary, was only a messenger of Allah, and his

word, which He conveyed unto Mary, and a spirit from Him. *So believe in Allah and his messengers, and say not "Three"—* Cease! (it is) better for you!—Allah is only one Allah. Far is it removed from his Transcendent Majesty that He should have a son. His is all that is in the heavens and all that is in the earth. And Allah is sufficient as a Defender. (Sura 4:171)[1]

They surely disbelieve who say: Lo! *Allah is the third of three*: when there is no Allah save the One Allah. If they desist not from so saying a painful doom will fall on those of them who disbelieve. (Sura 5:73)[2]

While it is true that Islam, as practiced and believed by Muslims today, denies the biblical Trinity, we can see from these passages that Islam's critique of the Trinity starts from a fundamental misconception. These verses warn Christians not to believe in "three" and castigate as blasphemers those who say that God is "the third of three." But does the Bible teach anything even remotely like the idea that God is "a third of three" separate beings or that the Trinity is God plus two other beings?

It is even more interesting that the Qur'an seems to view the Trinity as made up of God, Mary and Jesus. In Sura 5:116, we read, "And behold! Allah will say: 'O Jesus the son of Mary! Didst thou say unto men, worship me and my mother as gods in derogation of Allah?'"[3] The fact that God would supposedly ask Jesus this question strongly implies that the Qur'an considers this to have been what the Trinity actually is. Even a cursory reading of the Bible shows that it teaches nothing of the sort.

From such misconceptions, some of Islam's greatest apologists and theologians have attacked the Trinity. Ibn Taymiyya, a prolific and widely known Muslim scholar of the twelfth century, criticized the Trinity as the illogical belief that God is one in one sense and three in the same sense: "It is a fact that their view combines making God one and proving three gods, holding for one substance and proving three gods, holding for one substance and proving three substances."[4]

But as we will soon see, the Bible teaches nothing like what the Qur'an denies. The Bible does not teach that God is one of three separate divine beings joined together in a triad. It does not teach that Mary, Jesus and God are a triumvirate of divine beings. Nor does the Bible teach that God is one in one sense and three in that same sense. By criticizing the Trinity on these grounds, Islam rejects beliefs that no Christian holds. Or, put another way, Islam attacks a hill that no one defends.

For those Muslims who see what the Bible teaches, the Trinity puts them in a difficult position. To reject the Trinity, a Muslim may resort to claiming that it is a corruption of the Bible, but he cannot do so, because the Qur'an does not allow Muslims to believe in biblical corruption. So Muslims who truly understand this tension are left with only one avenue: they must reinterpret the Bible so that it does not teach the Trinity.

Ibn Taymiyya thought the Bible was corrupted but hedged his bets by misinterpreting the Bible's trinitarian language and arguing that Matthew 28:19—which specifically mentions the Father, the Son and the Holy Spirit—does not teach trinitarian doctrine. He argued,

> If it is true that this expression truly comes from Christ who is inerrant, what he meant by it must correspond to the rest of his teaching. . . . The meaning of "Baptize people in the name of the Father, the son, and the Holy Spirit" is that they command people to believe in God and his prophet which God sent and in the angel by which God sent down the revelation which he brought. That would be a command for them to believe in God and his angels, books, and messengers. . . .
>
> Is this anything but the act of corrupting the speech of the prophets and perpetrating a lie against them? The evident

meaning of this speech is that by the word "father" the prophets intended in their language "Lord"; by "son" in their language is meant "him who is governed, reared," that is, Christ; by "Holy Spirit" is meant the angel, the revelation, etc., by which God supported Christ.[5]

That is all terribly ironic, of course. In fact, there is a double irony here. The Qur'an and the Islamic traditions claim that Christians and Jews changed the meanings of God's revelation. But this is exactly what Ibn Taymiyya tried to do in the twelfth century. He took Jesus' words on the Trinity in Matthew 28 and reinterpreted them to match Islamic theology. He did the very thing he accused Christians of doing. But it is doubly ironic that in reinterpreting the biblical text, Ibn Taymiyya and many Muslims today are doing away with the very doctrine that allows them to worship a God who is great.

Muslims do not need to resort to such measures if their sincere goal is to believe in the one and only great God. If it is, then I would argue that they must believe in the Trinity for three reasons. First, the Bible (which a Muslim must believe is uncorrupted) teaches it. Second, the Trinity does not defy logic. And third, the Trinity proves God to be the Greatest Possible Being over and above a Unitarian conception of God.

THE WRITTEN REVELATION OF GOD'S GREATNESS

The efforts to interpret the Trinity out of the Bible have not been able to scale the great wall formed by the many passages that teach God's triunity. The Bible teaches that God has one nature or essence and three personhoods. God has one substance but three distinct personalities or centers of consciousness. While the biblical data supporting each aspect of the Trinity is legion, we need to consider only a few key passages to realize how important this is in the corpus of holy writ.

First, the Bible clearly teaches that there is only one God. From the Old Testament books of Moses, we get the famous Shema, the command to believe that God is one: "Hear, O Israel: The LORD our God, the LORD is one" (Deuteronomy 6:4). In Isaiah 45:5, God himself says, "I am the LORD, and there is no other, besides me there is no God." The New Testament writers—the same writers who affirm the Trinity—declare that there is only one God. James tells us, "You believe that God is one; you do well. Even the demons believe—and shudder!" (James 2:19).

But the Bible also teaches that three distinct persons—Father, Son, Holy Spirit—are simultaneously that same God. From beginning to end, we read in the Bible that the Father is God (Isaiah 64:8; Matthew 3:17), the Son is God (Psalm 110; John 8:58) and the Holy Spirit is God (Psalm 139:7-12; 2 Corinthians 3:17). Not only does the Bible teach that the Father, Son and Holy Spirit are God, but it also teaches that each of them is distinct from the other. As Saleeb and Geisler put it, "The Father and Son carried on conversations with each other. The Son prayed to the Father (John 17). The Father spoke from heaven about the Son at his baptism (Matt. 3:15-17)."[6] And Jesus specifically stated that when he departed from the disciples, "another [that is, separate] Helper"—the Holy Spirit—would come to them (John 14:16; 16:13). The Bible is filled with references to each person of the Trinity as separate yet equally God (see table 9.1).

From these passages, we can see that the case is overwhelming that the Bible teaches that God is one in nature and three in person. He has one divine essence and three divine but separate personalities. In fact, even in the Shema, the Hebrew creed uttered in the formative stages of the nation that would bring about the Messiah, we see glimpses of the Trinity. In English, the Shema is translated as "Hear, O Israel: The LORD our God, the LORD is one" (Deuteronomy 6:4). The Hebrew word translated as "God" in this passage is *Elohim*, which is literally a plural word for "gods." And the

Table 9.1

	FATHER	SON	HOLY SPIRIT
Is called God	Philippians 1:2	John 1:1,14; Colossians 2:9	Acts 5:3-4
Creator	Isaiah 44:24; 64:8	John 1:3; Colossians 1:15-17	Job 26:13; 33:4
Resurrects Jesus	1 Thessalonians 1:10	John 2:19; 10:17	Romans 8:11
Dwells in the believer	2 Corinthians 6:16	Colossians 1:27	John 14:17
Is everywhere at all times	1 Kings 8:27	Matthew 28:20	Psalm 139:7-10
Is all-knowing	1 John 3:20	John 16:30	1 Corinthians 2:10-11
Gives life	Genesis 2:7	John 1:3; 5:21	2 Corinthians 3:6
Is eternal	Psalm 90:2	Micah 5:1-2	Hebrews 9:14
Speaks	Matthew 3:17	Luke 5:20; 7:48	Acts 8:29; 11:12; 13:2
Is the Savior	1 Timothy 1:1; 2:3; 4:10	2 Timothy 1:10; Titus 1:4; 3:6	

Hebrew word translated as "one" is *ehad*, which can mean a singular unit but also can mean unification. In fact, *ehad* is used in the Old Testament to describe people from many nations coming together "as one" to fight against Joshua and the Israelites (Joshua 9:2). The Bible describes the union of Adam and Eve to become *ehad*—"one flesh" (Genesis 2:24).

In the entire context of Scripture, we see that the Bible teaches that God is one in his nature or essence, yet three in that he has three separate personages. So Muslims, who logically, theologically and historically cannot believe that the Scripture was corrupted, face the dilemma of having to reject the teachings of a book they cannot reject.

A MODEST GOAL

But Muslims ultimately do not have to sacrifice their sense of reason to see the reality of the Trinity. They can embrace the truth because it is taught in the Scripture, because it is consistent with logic and because it transcends human logic. This is a key distinction that must be kept in mind. A truth, like the Trinity, can exceed our logic without violating it. A concept can be transcendent in the sense that it is not illogical—it is not contradictory—but it is beyond our ability to fully understand.

Muslims and Christians share many such beliefs. They believe that God is a being without beginning and without end. There is nothing inherently contradictory about the belief in God's eternality, yet it is impossible for us to understand fully. How can we? We are finite beings, each of us with a beginning, living in a world where everything in the natural order has a beginning. So it would be impossible to comprehend God's eternality fully, though we might be able to apprehend it.

We can approach the Trinity in the same way, and so let us proceed by trying to achieve a modest goal at this point: to see only if the Trinity does not defy reason. Once we see that the Trinity is logically possible, we can see that it is theologically necessary if we are to believe that God is truly great.

In summarizing Scripture's teaching, the great theologian and church father Athanasius helped formulate a now famous creed: "We worship one God in Trinity, and Trinity in Unity; neither confounding the Persons; nor dividing the Substance." This formula helps us to understand, in conceptual terms, what the Trinity is and, almost as importantly, what it is not. It is important to start with what the Trinity is not, because it is so often the case that those who deny the Trinity, Muslims as well as non-Muslims, reject it based on an incorrect understanding of its basic concepts.

The Trinity is not the belief that God is one in his nature and three in his nature. That would be an obvious breach of the law of noncontradiction. Similarly, the Trinity is not the belief that God is one in his personhood and three in his personhood. That, too, is explicitly contradictory and nonsensical. In distinction to either of these ideas, the Trinity is the belief that God has one nature—one essence—and three personhoods, or three centers of consciousness. This would be contradictory only if something's "nature" is the same as its "person," because then the Trinity would teach that God is only one in one sense and also three in the same sense. But "nature" and "person" are distinct concepts, which keeps the Trinity from internal inconsistency.

Perhaps an illustration will help us unpack the nature/person distinction. Something's nature is its very basic or inherent characteristic. A nature is *what* something is. One can look at a rock and ask *what* it is. In its most basic nature, a rock is a nonliving or inorganic thing. But "personhood" is a far different thing. Personhood describes something's relational, volitional, intellectual and emotional qualities. Human beings have personhood because they relate to one another and to the world around them. They have a will, an intellect and emotions. But a human being also has a nature, a basic or inherent characteristic.

At a basic level, the nature of a human being is a living thing, or perhaps an organic thing. In contrast, a rock has a nature—it is a nonliving (or inorganic) thing—but it has no personhood. One can ask *what* a rock is, but one puts society's perception of sanity at risk if he sincerely asks *who* a rock is. But we can ask both questions of a human being. We can ask what a human being is and get an answer: a living thing. And we can ask who a human being is and get an answer: Abraham Lincoln, for example.

And so we see that nature and personhood are distinct concepts. And as distinct concepts, there is no law of logic that is violated— there is no contradiction—in claiming that God is one in his nature and three in his personhoods. This may transcend our reason, but it does not defy it. Just because we cannot fully comprehend how a single being can be tri-personal does not mean it is not possible.

Allow me to make one more observation: the more advanced the entity we are looking at, the more complex and differentiated it becomes. A rock is simple. It has only a nature. A plant has a higher nature and an animal has a higher nature still, plus something like volition. Human beings have an even higher nature and a full, complex personhood, complete with emotions, volition, intelligence and even a yearning to understand existence itself. And God, as the highest being, can easily have an unfathomably high nature and a complexity of personhoods.

May I suggest that we—Christians and Muslims—can find great comfort in the fact that the Trinity comports with our logic while at the same time exceeding it? C. S. Lewis put it well when he wrote, "If Christianity was something we were making up, of course we could make it easier. But it is not. We cannot compete, in simplicity, with people who are inventing religions. How could we? We are dealing with Fact. Of course anyone can be simple if he has no facts to bother about."[7]

Why should the very nature of God be so simple that we can easily grasp it? We are, after all, talking about the Greatest Possible Being, a being every Muslim theologian and philosopher would readily admit is unfathomable and even incomprehensible. It seems strange, then, that a Muslim would object to the Trinity on the basis of its theological complexity and philosophical difficulty.

Islam's history is marked by Muslims struggling with such difficulties only to conclude that some aspects of God are simply too mysterious for humanity to grasp fully. Influential Muslim thinkers even debated how to talk about God. For some, the issue was whether God was so grand, so wholly other, that human language outside the Qur'an could even be used to describe him. Others thought that positively asserting God's qualities in ways that we could understand ran the risk of anthropomorphizing him, of making him look and sound too much like us.

One proposed solution was to say that God is all-powerful, but even that ran afoul of differentiation, making him sound like humans. Humans are powerful, to some degree, and so to say that God is powerful suggests that we are like him or he is like us. This entire issue—that of God's total differentness from humanity (called *mukhalafa* in Arabic)—spawned a different way to talk about God. The school of thought that eventually prevailed talked of God in terms of negation. Muslims largely did not speak of what God is, but what he is not, to minimize the risk of limiting him.

So Muslims would say that God has no limitations, God is not finite, he has no peer, he is not affected by joy or sorrow and so on. But this did not fully solve the dilemma, because the Qur'an actually speaks positively about God. In the Ninety-Nine Beautiful Names, the Qur'an makes positive assertions about God's qualities: he is just, merciful, creator and so on. Thus human language has been used to describe God's qualities in a positive way. So Muslims resorted to saying that God's positive qualities are in no way similar to the qualities we find in creation. He is merciful, but we cannot look to human mercy as an analogy to try to understand God's mercy, for example. When one Muslim scholar was asked whether we can analogize God's attributes to human attributes, he responded that we cannot, because God is *la thani*—he is unique in every way.[8]

May I suggest that Muslims are on to something here, but only part of the way? Islam does not want to limit God, so it has its doctrine of God's utter differentness. If God is so far different from humanity that we cannot comprehend him, why would it be inherently blasphemous or against reason to assert that God is utterly different from us in terms of personhood and being? We exist as one in our nature and one in our personhood. If God is so wholly different from us, why should we expect him to exist in exactly the same way that we do? Shouldn't we expect him *not* to be just like us? Given the Muslim view of God's utter differentness, it is surprising that Islam makes God to exist in the same way we do. What would not be surprising is to find that God exists totally differently than we do. He is one in being, but three in personhood. He transcends our notions of existence, and because he is so much higher than us, this transcendence actually shows God to be great.

Muslims' affirmation of God's differentness practically screams out for the answer found in the Trinity. In fact, I would expect a Muslim to readily acknowledge that if God in his very nature were simple to understand because he resembles our single nature/single person existence, perhaps we invented him to be that way. In other words, if God in his very being looks just like us, then the chances are quite good that we created him in our image instead of the other way around. A Muslim would perish the thought. And so rather than bother us, the Trinity's grand yet logically consistent mystery provides us with the solace that we are on to something marvelous in our pursuit to worship the Greatest Possible Being.

At the risk of being indelicate, I must bring up some of the problems that come with conceiving of God as an absolute, undivided and singular deity. Duncan Black MacDonald points out that God would be an incoherent entity in such a case. He would be unknown to us and unknown even to himself. MacDonald makes the point that if we say God has knowledge, then he either has knowledge of something within himself or outside himself. If he has knowledge of something within himself, then he is differentiated after all, because his knowledge and the thing he knows about are not the same things. But if God is absolutely undifferentiated, then we cannot say that he has knowledge about himself. This, MacDonald concludes, would reduce God to a "bare, undefinable, unknowable unity."[9] Abdul Saleeb and Norman Geisler describe the problem of an undifferentiated, singular deity as preserving "a rigid unity in God but only at the expense of real personality. It clings to a rigid simplicity but only by sacrificing his relatability. In short, it leaves us with an empty and barren concept of deity."[10]

Muslims today do not think of God as an empty deity, but not because they have resolved the theological dilemma. Muslims have only passed by this problem. But it persists, based on orthodox Muslim theology, and has not sauntered away just because Muslims have placed their collective head in the sand. And yet the Trinity—the very doctrine that Muslims reject—resolves all of these problems. I like the way that W. H. T. "Temple" Gairdner asks the rhetorical question to get to the obvious answer: "Are we then going to apply to God the poorest, barest, and most abstract of the categories, unrelated Being, undifferentiated Unity, as if it were the sole possible and the highest one? Or also the richest, fullest and most significant?"[11]

Gairdner says that the fullest and most significant way to view God is as a trinity, because then God would be "living and real," and not "merely some abstract demand of thought."[12] The Trinity does not merely answer a philosophical quandary. It explains to us that God is living, vibrant and personal. His greatness comes not just from his coherence, but also from his purposefulness and relational essence. The Trinity provides us with a God who comports with our logic yet is sufficiently mysterious to satisfy our sense of devotion. He is knowable and known, yet his existence poses a grand mystery that stirs our minds, quickens our hearts and bends our knees.

REASON, REVELATION AND GOD'S GREATNESS

The Trinity is not just the logical formulation of a concept that *could be* true. I am convinced that it goes beyond the logically possible to the theologically necessary if we are to answer Islam's Grand Central Question about how we are to worship God in his greatness.

The Qur'an proclaims, "Allah! There is no god but He,-the [sic] Living, the Self-Subsisting, Eternal" (Sura 3:2). Muslim scholars tell us that God is unique and nothing resembles him in any respect. "He is One and The One. He is self-sustained, does not need anything but everything needs Him."[13] Now, on this last point, that God is self-sustaining and does not need anything, Christians and Muslims can agree. If God is the Greatest Possible Being, Allahu Akbar, then it must be the case that God does not depend on anything or anyone for his existence. But more than that, God must not depend on anything or anyone to be who he is.

Christians believe that God is a relational being. Every page of the Bible tells us that God is not only relational, but intensely so. He is relational in his very essence. More than that, love is the very essence of God's relational aspect, so much so that an unloving person cannot even know God. The apostle John writes, "Anyone who does not love does not know God, because *God is love*" (1 John 4:8, emphasis mine).

Despite Islam's assertions that God is unknowable, Muslims also believe, at least to some degree, that God is relational. The Qur'an calls God Al Wadud, which means that he is "full of loving kindness" (Sura 85:14). That loving kindness is conditional, of course, but nevertheless it is there. It is so important for Muslims to believe that God is loving and that his loving kindness is essential to his being, that Al Wadud is one of God's Ninety-Nine Beautiful Names. What all of this means, for both Christians and Muslims, is that love is a fundamental expression of God. All other relational expressions—mercy, forgiveness, compassion and even judgment—flow from God's most basic relational expression: love.

Atheists have leveled the charge that the concept of God as a perfect being, one who is independent of his creation and who has no needs, is logically incompatible with a God of perfect love. If God loves, then that implies a desire, and a desire implies a desire of fulfillment, so the argument goes. In response, William Hasker makes the excellent point that the triune God of the Bible is not susceptible to this kind of critique.

> In particular, the idea that God "needs" the world in order to fulfill his own life is sharply rejected by theism. God needs nothing outside himself, and so it is wrong to say (as is sometimes said even in orthodox Christian circles) that God "was lonely" and "needed our companionship" and therefore created us. God is, after all, according to Christianity, the Trinity of Father, Son and Holy Spirit. Is it to be supposed that their eternal companionship lacks something which could be made up by human beings?[14]

This point is important. The Trinity is not just a theological construct that Christians have come up with to make sense of the biblical description of God. The Bible tells us that God's triune existence shows him to be great. It shows him to be perfect. It shows him to be a God who eternally exists in relationship and so does not need to create humanity to fulfill any relational aspect of his personality. God's triune existence insulates him from seemingly logical attacks that might otherwise work in assailing other views about God—specifically Unitarian views—but not the biblical view.

Robert Wagenet expounds on Hasker's observation and applies it in a way that shows that God is not only compatible with perfect love, but also that his love is qualitatively perfect. Wagenet says,

> In our experience of love, it is frequently, if not always, tied up in the fulfillment of our own needs. A man falls in love with a woman in large part because he wants something from her (and she reciprocates for much the same reason). But love also carries with it a desire to give what is good to the beloved, and it is this desire to bless that defines God's love. A moment's reflection will show that an entirely self-contained person who has no desire to bless someone else may be perfect in some respects but certainly does not display perfect love. But God's

nature is not simply to possess his attributes to himself, but to pour out his attributes in love for the blessing of others. The nature of God as a union of three persons allows this perfect love to exist between Father, Son and Spirit as each blesses the other, so God does not need the creation in order to have something to love. However it gives God great joy to extend his love beyond the Trinity to others, for which purpose he created the universe. Thus God was not motivated by need in creating the universe, but by an abundant love. Clearly there is nothing incongruous about a perfect being, whose nature is exactly what it should be, acting in complete accord with that nature by doing that which brings him joy.[15]

It is critical that we understand the depth of what Wagenet is saying. As a Trinity, as a single Being existing with three separate centers of consciousness, God has never lacked anything in relationship. And yet he expresses his innate love outside of the trinitarian community to create us. This is what Wagenet calls God's "abundant love." God is love, as the Bible says, so when he creates us—with the purpose of giving us the opportunity to enjoy his companionship—he does so as a sheer expression of who he is. In other words, God's creation of humanity is loving, but it is more than that. It is gratuitously loving. God needs nothing from us. Our companionship does not supply a lack in the divine relationship he already has within himself. In creating us, God gets nothing out of it except the joy that follows from giving created beings a chance at divine bliss.

A Unitarian view of God cannot answer this challenge. Without a differentiated Godhead, how can God have eternal relationship within himself so that he does not need human beings to express relationship? Asked another way, if God is an absolute singularity of nature and person, who was God loving when there was no one in existence other than himself?

We don't just love in a vacuum. True love requires an object, after all. We love someone or something other than ourselves. But in Islam, God, as the only uncreated being, could not have loved or even related to anyone before he created angels and people. This means that God would have to depend on the existence of angels and humanity to love. He would have to depend on the existence of beings other than himself to be relational, to express a fundamental aspect of his very being. When there was no one but God, he lacked. Only when he created was his loving kindness able to be fulfilled. But Muslims cannot believe this to be true if they are to believe that God is self-subsistent, as the Qur'an says.

To deal with this problem, Unitarians have to maintain, yet reinterpret, trinitarian language that makes the relational connection between God's perfect self-existence and his interaction with the world.

> Unitarianism . . . seeks to carry over the emotional content of Christianity, after abandoning the metaphysical realities which make that emotion abidingly possible. The incarnate Word [according to Unitarians] is a metaphor, mythologized and misinterpreted, but it is still to declare to us the Father and to be the Light of the world. The Holy Ghost is a figurative expression, but it is still to be the abiding Comforter and the Lord and Giver of life.[16]

What sense of greatness, what awe can we possibly have, for a deity so abstract in description and so impossible to even talk about? The struggle is there; we want an emotional connection to God, which requires us to understand at least something about his relational aspect, yet we want to make his most relational qualities metaphorical and figurative expressions that lack real power or ability to inspire awe.

The Trinity—God in community—inspires a rationally and emotionally grounded awe. The depth of the very idea of a single being existing in the community of three distinct centers of consciousness is enough to inspire awe. But as a being in relationship, God stirs within us the wonder of understanding what true love actually is. Muslims view God as utterly transcendent—as wholly other and virtually incomprehensible. Even the attributes of God that we have in common, like relatability, love, mercy and justness, are completely different when applied to God. We might understand love in one way as humans, but according to Islam, God's love is completely different from ours and so is unintelligible. This prevents us from any sense of intimacy with God, and it prevents us from even approaching anything like knowledge of God's greatness.

Let's consider a Muslim comparison of human love with God's love provided by one of Islam's most prominent philosophers and theologians, Imam al-Ghazali. His views characterize the common Muslim belief about God, and so I quote him at length:

> That Allah does love his creatures is plain from diverse passages in the Qur'an and from many traditions. *"Love" is a word applied first to human relationships and secondly to Allah.* But when words are so transferred the meaning is always changed. They can never mean the same things in man and Allah. In man love is an inclination of the soul to something that suits it, that is lacking in it, and from the gaining of which it expects profit and pleasure. All that is impossible in Allah, the Perfect, the Unchanging, who can contemplate nothing but Himself and his own acts, as there is nothing else in existence. Love, then, in Allah means (1) the removal of the veil from the heart of the creature that he may see Allah; (2) the giving of power to the creature to draw near to Allah; and (3) Allah's willing this from all eternity. For Allah's love of a creature is from eternity, inasmuch as it is related to his eternal will, which requires that the creature in question should be given the power to follow the path to the action which draws away the veil. So there is no change in Allah, nor drawing near by

Allah, nor supply a lack in Allah. Those terms apply only to the creature. And the signs of Allah's love are the trials which come upon creatures. If anyone loves Allah and is sorely tried, he may know that Allah loves him and is drawing him near through these trials.[17]

In this, al-Ghazali is half right, which makes him all wrong. He is half right in that there is no supplying of a lack in God. But al-Ghazali does not provide us with a satisfactory explanation of how that can be. He says that God's love is shown in his external love for the creature. But does this really make any sense? How can God love a being who does not yet exist? He may know that the being will exist, but actual love requires an actual object. When we love, we give to others, but we also satisfy a need in ourselves. But if God is perfect, then love does not fulfill a need. To explain this from a Unitarian perspective, al-Ghazali asserts that love as applied to God is completely different from love as applied to humanity.

But how does this help, exactly? How can we even begin to acknowledge, let alone understand, God to be love or to be "full of loving kindness" if divine love is so completely foreign to us? There has to be something relatable, something we can understand about God's love; otherwise, why even talk about it? J. Windrow Sweetman asked the right rhetorical question: "Thus if the letter of the revelation [the Qur'an] is accepted and the content cannot be filled in by reference to the ordinary concepts by which thought is possible, then of what value is scripture or revelation except to use in ritual recitation?"[18]

In making the argument that God's qualities are totally different from what man understands, al-Ghazali goes wrong and deprives us of something valuable. He tells us that love is applied to humanity first and then to God. In the human context, love is a self-serving act in that while it gives to others, it also fulfills a lack in us. It is still love, but it is just the human version of love. And when applied to God, it is different. God's love *is* selfless and gratuitous, and it does not supply any lack in God, because there is no lack. It is still love, but just the divine version of it.

May I suggest that this is backward and even misleading? Love is not a relative concept that applies in one definitional sense to God and then in another sense to us. If God is the ultimate source of what is real, and if love is real, then God is the ultimate and fundamental source of love and relationship. That means that love does not *apply* differently to God. Rather, God is love—he defines it by his very nature. And love does not *apply differently* to us.

When God loves, he loves perfectly. He loves transcendently. In that sense, God and humanity *express* love differently. We express it with the taint of self-centeredness, in a way that fulfills a need in us. But God expresses it without need. He does not need to express love to fulfill something missing in him. Love is rooted in God because each person of the Trinity loves and relates to the others. God the Father loves God the Son. The Son loves the Father and the Holy Spirit, and God the Holy Spirit loves both the Son and the Father. And so God is eternally fulfilled. When he loves, he does so selflessly. When we love, it is an imperfect, sometimes even perverted, expression. But love is love. In fact, "God is love." He defines love. Circumstances do not.

The God who is great expresses love perfectly, and perfect love is selfless. It is others-centered. But how can love be perfectly others-centered if God is an absolute singularity, having one nature and one personhood? How can God express relational aspects of who he is independent of the existence of creation if he exists in such a way? It is quite impossible to see how.

The Trinity makes it possible. For God to have no lack in relationship, to have no lack of love or the expression of it, he must exist, from eternity, as a being in community. Historically, critics have seen the Trinity as a "problem" to solve—its mystery so difficult to grasp that some have labeled it incoherent. May I suggest, however, that the Trinity is not a problem, but a solution? If we strive to believe in a God who is perfect, who lacks nothing and needs no one to be who he is, we must look to the Trinity. The Trinity explains how God can love and not lack, how he can relate and not depend on others to relate. The Trinity solves the mystery of how to understand God's greatness.

ALMIGHTY BEAUTY IN THE DIVINE COMMUNITY

In view of all of this—the solution that the Trinity provides and how it leads us to embrace a God who is truly great—I am reminded of the words of a powerful hymn attributed to John Wesley. In "Come Thou Almighty King," he expresses the greatness of the triune nature of God:

> Come Thou Almighty King,
> help us Thy name to sing;
> Help us to praise:
> Father all glorious,
> o'er all victorious,
> Come and reign over us,
> Ancient of Days.

> Come, Thou Incarnate Word,
> gird on Thy mighty sword
> Our prayer attend:
> Come and Thy people bless,
> and give Thy word success—
> Spirit of holiness
> In us descend.

> Come, Holy Comforter,
> Thy sacred witness bear
> In this glad hour:
> Thou who almighty art,

Now rule in ev'ry heart,
And ne'er from us depart,
Spirit of pow'r.

To the great One in Three
eternal praises be,
Hence evermore:
his sov'reign majesty,
may we in glory see,
And to eternity love and adore.[19]

The Trinity does more than just give us a satisfactory answer to a philosophical and theological question. It tells us more than the fact that God needs no one to be loving or relational, because perhaps a more important question follows: if he does not need us to love and relate to, why did he create us at all?

The answer can be found in the very nature of the question. God gives because God is love. It is the very nature of love to give. He does not need us for relationship, but he creates us so that we can have the opportunity to have relationship with him. He does not need us to find fulfillment. He creates us so that we can have fulfillment in him. It is utterly gratuitous. He creates us for our gain, not for his. In this, God is glorified because his love is perfect; it is expressed without a hint of selfishness.

Although there are infinite ways to learn of God's greatness, another aspect of it will give us an even fuller picture. God's abundant, gratuitous love is expressed in the sheer act of creation. But the selflessness of his love is expressed in the greatest possible way through yet another divine act. Muslims can find rest in God's great independence and self-subsistence in the Trinity. And, ironically, Muslims can find the greatest possible expression of God's love in a doctrine their religion rejects: the incarnation of God in Christ. Let us explore this part of the picture of God's greatness.

GREATNESS INCARNATE

Jesus and the religious authorities of his day clashed quite often. Jesus' claims to divinity generated the most noise. John the apostle records a particularly noisy incident in which Jesus faces off with the Pharisees in the temple treasury. "I am the light world," he proclaimed. "Whoever follows me will not walk in darkness, but will have the light of life" (John 8:12). It's an audacious enough statement, claiming to be the "light of the world" who bestows life. The ubiquitous Pharisees pounce on his claim, chiding his testimony as self-serving.

The noise increases as Jesus gets bolder. "Unless you believe that *I am he*," Jesus says, "you will die in your sins" (v. 24, emphasis mine). "I am he" is *ego eimi* in Greek, which literally translates to "I am," meaning that Jesus identifies himself with the very name that God gave to himself when speaking to Moses in Exodus 3:14. As they begin to see the divine authority Jesus was claiming for himself, they ask him, *"Are you greater than our father Abraham, who died? And the prophets died! Who do you make yourself out to be?"* (John 8:53, emphasis mine).

The volume rises even higher with Jesus' response: "Your father

Abraham rejoiced that he would see my day. He saw it and was glad"
(v. 56). Finally, the Jews see where this is going. "You are not yet
fifty years old," they protest, "and you have seen Abraham?" (v. 57).
Jesus responds with a trumpet blast: "Truly, truly, I say to you, *before
Abraham was, I am*" (v. 58, emphasis mine).

His accusers are incensed. They pick up stones to kill him for
the blasphemy. They understand that Jesus is equating himself with
deity—and not just any deity, mind you. He claims to be the God
of Abraham, Isaac and Jacob. Jesus orchestrated the entire discussion at the temple treasury to crescendo to the point where he
appropriated the "I AM"—God's very name in Exodus 3:14—for
himself. Indeed, Jesus was claiming to be greater than Abraham. He
was claiming to be the incarnation of the Greatest Possible Being.

Muslims deny that Jesus ever claimed to be God. Show me one
place in the Bible where Jesus says, "I am God, worship me," they
protest. Those exact words do not exist in the ink of holy writ. But
humans don't get to dictate how Jesus formulates his claim to divinity. That is Jesus' prerogative. And in John 8:58 he clearly claims
to be more than just a god. He claims to be *the* God.

The common Muslim response is to reject Jesus' words in John
as fabricated corruptions. They argue that the earlier Gospels
record little to nothing about Jesus claiming divinity, but as more
Gospels were written, the writers put greater and greater claims on
Jesus' lips until he claims to be God in John's Gospel. A careful
reading of the Synoptic Gospels, from Mark to Luke, shows that
this is just not the case.

Others have detailed the biblical data demonstrating Jesus' deity,
and so I will not make an exhaustive case here.[1] Let us just consider
the Gospel of Mark, the first Gospel written. In chapter two, Jesus
claims to have the authority to forgive sins—the authority reserved
for God alone (Mark 2:1-12). Later in Mark's Gospel, he says that
he will later return as "the Son of Man coming in clouds with great
power and glory" (Mark 13:26), making a direct connection be-

tween himself and the divine Son of Man of Daniel 7. In the same Gospel (Mark 14:62), Jesus again claims to be that divine Son of Man as well as the One sharing authority with God, referenced in Psalm 110. So in the very first Gospel we see several accounts of Jesus' claim to divinity. There was no embellishment or exaggeration as the Gospels were written. And, as we have already seen, Muslims simply cannot claim that the Bible was corrupted with tales of Jesus' divinity if Muslims are still to believe in an all-powerful and trustworthy God.

But what are Muslims to make of the Qur'an's unequivocal rejection of Christ's divinity? The Qur'an specifically says in many passages that God has no son and is not incarnate in Christ:

> They say: "(Allah) Most Gracious has begotten a son!" Indeed ye have put forth a thing most monstrous! At it the skies are ready to burst, and the earth to split asunder, and the mountains to fall down in utter ruin, That they should invoke a son for (Allah) Most Gracious. For it is not [worthy of] the majesty of (Allah) Most Gracious that He should beget a son." (Sura 19:88-92)

> The Jews call 'Uzair [Ezra] the son of Allah, and the Christians call Christ the son of Allah. That is a saying from their mouth; (in this) they but imitate what the unbelievers of old used to say. Allah's curse be on them: how they are deluded away from the Truth! (Sura 9:30)

And should there be any doubt that the Qur'an utterly denies that Jesus is God, we need only look to Sura 5:17: "In blasphemy indeed are those that say that Allah is Christ the son of Mary. Say: 'Who then hath the least power against Allah, if his will were to destroy Christ the son of Mary, his mother, and all every-one that is on the earth?'"

The meaning is quite plain. According to the Qur'an, belief in the incarnation is "a thing most monstrous." And why? The context tells us. It is simply not worthy of God's majesty to have an incarnate son. But we must be careful here. Muslims revere Jesus not just as a prophet, but as a great prophet, a sinless, virgin-born person who performed great miracles. Yet he is not so great as to be God. And to think of God as incarnate, for Muslims, would be to impermissibly sully God's greatness. Kenneth Cragg notes that in the Muslim world, "there runs a great tenderness for Jesus, yet a sharp disassociation from his Christian dimensions. Islam registers a profound attraction [to Jesus] but condemns its Christian interpretation. Jesus is the theme at once of acknowledgement and disavowal. *Islam finds his nativity miraculous but his Incarnation impossible.*"[2]

But is it impossible? What is so impossible about it? Is it logically impossible? Does the impossibility stem from a fear that the incarnation lessens God's grandeur and sovereignty? If we properly understand what it means for God to be incarnate in Christ, barriers of logic fall away. And when we see the beauty and power of the incarnation, we can see that there is every reason to believe it as the expression of God's profound greatness.

INTUITING THE INCARNATION

As with the Trinity, objections to the incarnation of God in Jesus of Nazareth are based mainly on misconceptions. Again, understanding what the incarnation is not will help us to understand what it is. We should accept or reject the notion of God's incarnation based on the real thing, not a caricature or façade.

The classical understanding of the incarnation is that the second Person of the Trinity—God the Son—took on a human nature, and together those two natures were shared by one person, Jesus of Nazareth. It is critical that we come to terms with this, especially in light of what we've already seen: that *nature* is different from *personhood*. Belief in the incarnation is not belief that Jesus has only a divine nature, nor that he has only a human nature. Moreover, it is not the belief that Jesus is half-man and half-god, akin to mythological characters like Hercules. The incarnation is Jesus full humanity and full deity.

We must pause here, however, to make sure we understand this formulation, because it is easily given to misunderstanding. What it means to say that Jesus is fully human and fully God is that Jesus has 100 percent of the qualities of what it takes to be human and 100 percent of the qualities necessary to be God.

But, one might object, isn't this still a contradiction? Isn't it the case that being fully divine is to be infinite in knowledge, power and existence and to be fully human is to be finite in knowledge, power and existence? The answer, logically, is no, and theologian Thomas V. Morris helps us here. In *The Logic of God Incarnate*, Morris explains the difference between something's essential properties and its nonessential, or common, properties.[3] An essential property is, well, *essential* to what a particular being is. If an essential property is taken away, then that being is something else. Roundness is essential to being a ball, for example. Without roundness, something cannot be a ball; it is something else.

Omniscience, omnipotence and necessary existence are essential to being God. If we take any of these properties away, then we are not talking about God, but something else. But this does not mean that a *lack* of these properties is essential to humanness. To be sure, on a logical level, it is common for humans to lack omniscience, omnipotence and the like. But just because it is common for humans to lack these properties does not mean that it is essential that humans lack them. It is common for humans to have hair, but, as Morris puts it, "one can certainly be fully human, exemplify human nature while lacking this adornment."[4]

This helps us understand the distinction between Jesus' human nature and our humanness. Jesus is *fully* human while we are *merely* human. One is *fully* human if one has all the properties essential to being human. But "an individual is *merely* human [if he or she] has all the properties for being fully human (the component properties of human nature) *and also some limitation properties*."[5] Every human that we encounter is merely human—he or she has everything necessary to be human, plus he or she has the common human property of being limited in power, knowledge and existence.

But Jesus is not like every mere human we meet. He is fully human, but he doesn't have the common properties of limited existence, limited power or limited knowledge, and so he is not merely human. He has 100 percent of the properties necessary to be human. And without the nonessential limitations, he has 100 percent of the qualities necessary to be God, like an eternal existence, omniscience, omnipotence and the like. So there is nothing inherently contradictory in the idea of the incarnation, and, because there are no limitations in the incarnation, there is nothing in the idea of the incarnation that would limit God's greatness. If it is true that God incarnated himself in Jesus, God remains great, so Muslims need not fear going against their reverence for God.

But what of Jesus' apparent limitations throughout the Gospels? He gets tired, he hungers, he thirsts, he bleeds, he even dies. Are those not limitations showing that Jesus is merely human and that even if the incarnation is possible, it is not actual? Again, the answer is no, when we take into account two things. First, Jesus was physically human, with a human body. Absent intervention from his divine nature, his body would naturally get fatigued, experience hunger and die. But the divine nature persists and does not experience hunger or any lack.

Second, the Bible explains that when God the Son incarnated himself, he willingly "emptied Himself" to take on the form of a human servant (Philippians 2:5-11 NASB). He did not divest himself of divine attributes, because then he would not be able to display the divine power and authority we see in the Gospels—that is, God cannot stop being God. Rather, as Douglas Groothuis points out, he "temporarily suspended *the employment* of some of his divine attributes, but without ontologically *losing* these attributes."[6]

When my nine-year-old son and I wrestle, I suspend the full use of my strength, but I don't divest myself of it. And so when Jesus exhibits seeming limitations, it can easily be no more than the mere suppression of his power and knowledge. Is this difficult to understand comprehensively? Certainly. But is it impossible to understand meaningfully? Certainly not.

The point to see here is that Muslims need not fear that the incarnation detracts from God's utter majesty. But may I suggest something more? If we claim that it is impossible for God to become incarnate in a human being, does that not place an unwarranted limitation on God? If we shackle him because of what we don't fully comprehend, then perhaps we don't have such a high view of his greatness after all. Far be it from us to shackle God's power with the limitations of our full understanding. Every devout Muslim would (correctly) deny that God is limited to our ability to fully comprehend him. And so the next question to ask is this: if the incarnation does not limit God's greatness, does it demonstrate that greatness? Indeed it does.

THE GREATEST POSSIBLE REVELATION OF THE GREATEST POSSIBLE BEING

God has chosen to reveal himself to humanity at least to some degree. On this both Muslims and Christians can agree. But it is the degree to which God has revealed himself that is at issue. In Islam, God reveals himself in only a mitigated way. He reveals his will but only a glimpse of his personality. And even his will is revealed through mediators. Orthodox Islam teaches that God sent his message to the prophets of old through angels—specifically the archangel Gabriel. The messages—the revealed texts of the Torah, the Psalms, the Gospel and the Qur'an—were given to humans through an angel because God would not condescend to deliver the message directly. Such a thing would detract from his majesty. Al-Faruqi makes it quite clear how limited God's revelation is in Islam:

He does not reveal Himself to anyone in any way. God reveals only his will. Remember one of the prophets asked God to reveal Himself and God told him, "No, it is not possible for Me to reveal myself to anyone." . . . This is God's will and that is all we have, and we have it in perfection in the Qur'an. But Islam does not equate the Qur'an with the nature or essence of God. It is the Word of God, the Commandment of God, the Will of God. But God does not reveal Himself to anyone. Christians talk about the revelation of God Himself—by God of God—but that is a great difference between Christianity and Islam.[7]

Indeed, that is a great difference. The Bible tells us that God did not hold back from us the intimacy that comes with true self-disclosure. The author of Hebrews unfolds the story of God's revelation, from written code to the very revealed Word of God incarnate. "Long ago, at many times and in many ways, God spoke to our fathers by the prophets, but in these last days he has spoken to us by his Son, whom he appointed the heir of all things, through whom also he created the world" (Hebrews 1:1-2). These words illumine the precious New Testament theme that God's very Word was always meant to be revealed intimately.

John's Gospel opens by telling us that in the beginning "was the Word, and the Word was with God, and the Word was God" and that Word—God himself—became flesh and dwelt among us, full of grace and truth (John 1:1, 14). And Hebrews tells us that the Son through whom God speaks to us is "the radiance of the glory of God and the exact imprint of his nature" (Hebrews 1:3). How sweet is the intimacy of such a revelation? God has spoken to us not just of his will and not even just *of* his Son. No, God has spoken to us *by* his beloved Son, the very Son who is the radiance and glory of God. Majesty and tenderness, glory and warmth, all converge in the incarnate Word.

Think for a moment about how we disclose ourselves to those we care about. If someone is to understand us in the greatest possible way, do we just send that person letters, text messages or emails? Do phone calls suffice as the best possible revelation of another person? Not even a book, as long and as revealing as it might be of an author's thoughts, qualifies as a true self-disclosure. Can a relationship be anything but superficial if it subsists on nothing more than partial disclosures and mitigated communiqués?

Personal, direct interaction is the greatest way—arguably the only way—to reveal one's character and personality to another. Islam knows no such revelation; it has only words, brought to it by messengers other than God, concerning God's will. And while the gospel is given to us in the revealed text of the Bible, there is something intimately revealed as well. The Bible is the written revelation about the personal revelation. It is the revealed Word of God about God the Word.

Caution is in order here. I dare not say that God fully reveals himself to humanity. Our finite capacities (as mere humans) make a full understanding of God impossible, and Scripture makes the case as well (Moses could not see God's glory and live, says Exodus 33:20). But must God be chained by our limitations, narrowing his revelation to only his commands in a written text, but not more? Shouldn't it be the case that the Greatest Possible Being can find a way to make an intimate disclosure of himself to those he loves to the greatest extent possible? The incarnation, as described in the Bible and as each of us can personally experience, provides that way.

The gospel is an interlaced revelation. Throughout the written Word, we see God engaging human history through prophets, laws, angels and even directly. In the very beginning, he walked with Adam and Eve in the cool of the day (Genesis 3:8). He later visited with Abraham at the oaks of Mamre (Genesis 18:1-21). God manifested himself in the pillar of fire and the pillar of cloud that accompanied the Hebrews out of Egypt. And he wrestled with Jacob, giving him a redeemed identity (Genesis 32:24-30). God manifested himself to cut the original covenant with Abraham (Genesis 15:1-19). And God the Son, incarnate in Jesus, sat at a dinner table with his disciples and told them of the new covenant in his blood and body (Luke 22:14-20).

The interlacing revelation of the written Word and the incarnate Word shows us how God fought for us on battlefields, delivered laws from atop mountains and ate among us in a quiet room. We can know God in the beauty of a life lived in a person, Jesus of Nazareth—someone each one of us can relate to. The fact that God devised a way to make that kind of disclosure, despite our limitations, testifies to his great ingenuity and great affection.

THE CRUX OF GREATNESS

This new covenant is quite the stumbling block for Muslims. *If Jesus is the incarnation of God, how can God die on the cross?* And some Muslims would protest that regardless of the possibility of the incarnation, Jesus' death by humiliating crucifixion is unthinkable, because it is not befitting God's majesty. Hammudah Abdalati protests, "Is it consistent with God's Mercy and Wisdom [for us] to believe that Jesus was humiliated and murdered the way he is said to have been?"[8]

There are rather easy responses to both objections. In the Christian view, Jesus did not die *as God* or in his divine nature. That nature transcends his physical body and did not cease to exist just because Jesus' brain activity may have stopped for a time. Rather, Jesus physically died *as a man*. The physical death would not necessarily result in the death of the transcendent any more than the sudden loss of every Qur'an in the world would mean that the message itself would somehow cease to exist. More happened on the cross, to be sure, and we will address that shortly. Suffice it to say for now that God did not die, because, as a necessary being, he cannot die.

The second objection—that God would not allow one of his prophets to be killed—has always puzzled me, even when I was a Muslim. The Qur'an specifically acknowledges the fact that unbelieving Jews killed the prophets of old (for example, Sura 3:183). So, what makes Jesus' death at the hands of his enemies any more impossible?

These theological objections stem from the Qur'an's historical objection. The Qur'an denies, as a matter of history, that Jesus died by crucifixion:

> That they said (in boast), "We killed Christ Jesus the son of Mary, the Messenger of Allah,"—but they killed him not, or crucified him, but so it was made to appear to them, and those who differ therein are full of doubts, with no (certain) knowledge, but only conjecture to follow, for of a surety they killed him not: - Nay, [*sic*] Allah raised him up unto Himself; and Allah is Exalted in Power, Wise. (Sura 4:147-148)

According to the Qur'an, Jesus was neither crucified nor killed. But there must have been a cross, and there must have been someone on that cross, for it to be "made to appear to them." Muslim traditions about what actually did happen are quite varied. Wahab Bin Munabih first posited in the eighth century that an unnamed individual or a "simulacrum" was substituted for Jesus on the cross.[9] Since then, Muslims have advanced other candidates for Jesus' substitute, who were made to look like Jesus, from Simon of Cyrene to Judas Iscariot to a willing young follower who wanted to save Jesus the pain of death.

There are, of course, various problems that arise, especially for Muslims who cling to God's greatness. Historical problems are the most obvious. Based on the corpus of historical data, both Christian and non-Christian scholars agree that it was Jesus on that cross, crucified under Pontius Pilate. Even John Dominic Crossan, a liberal scholar and theologian of the Jesus Seminar, concedes this fact. "That he was crucified is as sure as anything historical can ever be."[10] To deny the crucifixion, one has to rely on theological bias and discard historical evidence.

But there is something more fundamentally troubling, isn't there? The Qur'an acknowledges that there was a cross, it seems to acknowledge that someone died there, and it even acknowledges that it was "made" to appear to others that it was Jesus. Strongly implied, of course, is that God made it seem like it was Jesus. Who else could have done so? But in light of the fact that every one of Jesus' disciples believed the crucified man to be the very one to whom they devoted three years of their lives, how could it be that God fooled not only Jesus' enemies but also his closest followers—those the Qur'an calls "inspired" and victorious to the day of resurrection? (See Suras 3:55; 5:111; 61:14.)

Given that the very basis of Christianity is Jesus' death on the cross—as the means of payment for sin—and his resurrection (which necessarily would follow his death), it follows that God would be responsible for starting the largest false religion in history. The disciples, after all, wrote and preached and gave their lives for the message that every person must believe in Jesus' substitutionary sacrifice and resurrection to be saved. Billions have died believing that message. But if it is false, then it is monstrously false.

I can think of no Muslim who would agree that a truly great God would be the author of such a malicious deception. That would turn Abdalati's own words on their head: Is it consistent with God's mercy and wisdom to believe that God lied to everyone about one of the most theologically important facts in history? Exactly how is God great in such a case? Allow me to sustain the fact that the crucifixion and resurrection did happen to Jesus, the incarnation of the second Person of the Trinity, not in derogation of his greatness, but in a display of it.

MISSION COMPOSSIBLE

Two of God's Ninety-Nine Beautiful Names in Islam are Al-Adl, "The Just," and Ar-Raheem, "The Merciful." As such, these attributes are fundamental to who God is. Thus, it follows that God, as the maximally perfect being, would be maximally just and maximally merciful. And because God is immutable, there can be no compromise in either his maximal justice or his maximal mercy. If there were, he would cease to be maximally perfect and thus he would cease to be great; he would cease to be Allahu Akbar. On this, Christianity and Islam agree.

But a problem arises based on another thing on which both Islam and Christianity agree. Under both systems, humanity is deserving of punishment for its sin. The Bible tells us that "there is none who does good, not even one" (Psalm 14:3) and that "all have sinned and fall short of the glory of God" (Romans 3:23). The Qur'an similarly characterizes humans as sinful and deserving of God's punishment: "If Allah were to punish men according to what they deserve, he would not leave on the back of the (earth) a single living creature" (Sura 35:45).

Is it not fascinating that, according to the Qur'an, humanity's sin is so pervasive that it pollutes the whole Earth, such that even lions, cockroaches and amoeba would be obliterated for it? In his theological treatise *Nahjul Balagha*, Imam Ali, the fourth *khalifa* (leader of the Muslims), wrote,

> O my Allah! Forgive me what Thou knowest about me more than I do. If I return (to the sins) Thou return to forgiveness. My Allah forgive me what I had promised to myself but Thou didst not find its fulfillment with me. My Allah forgive me that with what I sought nearness to thee with my tongue but my heart opposed and did not perform it. My Allah forgive me winkings of the eye, vile utterances, desires of the heart and errors of speech.[11]

Failed promises, winkings of the eye and errors of speech are affronts to a maximally holy God. All of us have been guilty of these and thus deserving of punishment and in need of mercy.

If God is maximally just, then he necessarily punishes sin. If God is maximally merciful, then he always wants to forgive it. But how can he do both without compromising either? One might say that God, as the Almighty, can just forgive sin as an exercise of sheer power. But this presents an incoherent view of omnipotence leading to logical absurdities, like saying that God has the power to create square circles or can cause himself to cease existing.

John R. W. Stott says that when we say that God can simply forgive sin, we rob him of his place as the holy Judge: "For us to argue 'we forgive each other unconditionally, let God do the same to us' betrays not sophistication but shallowness, since it overlooks the elementary fact that we are not God."[12] Thus, to think of God in these terms is to make him too much like us—to make God in our image, as it were. It is to make us more comfortable with the level of our own merit by lowering the level of God's. No, divine power must be thought of in terms of God's very nature to be coherent. God's nature is consistently just. To say that God can exercise raw power to forgive sins—to not act justly—is to posit a God who can defy himself. In other words, by exercising raw power to act contrary to his nature, God ceases to be himself. He ceases to be great.

The gospel—specifically the cross—flies in the face of our efforts to debase God and exalt ourselves. In committing sin, we incur an eternal debt to God. No penalty that we can endure in our temporal state can pay for that debt. Only a punishment that transcends time and a payment that comes from the eternal can right our wrongs. We are not capable of taking such a punishment or making such a payment without the cost of our very souls and eternal separation from God. What solution can there be then, if our sin is to be punished but God is to be merciful? The gospel, and the gospel alone, offers the solution.

We cannot help but see in the Bible's pages that God allows for atonement for sin through the shedding of blood. But that shed blood comes from a substitute, a proxy for God's wrath. This is a detail often overlooked, but in the very beginning, when Adam and Eve rebelled in the garden, they became ashamed of their nakedness in the midst of sin. They tried to cover themselves by sewing together fig leaves. But it took God's provision of clothes, in the form of animal skins, to hide their shame (Genesis 3:7, 21). In other words, to address the sin, blood had to be shed, because a serious payment—life—had to be made for a serious debt.

This continued through the sacrifices of Abel, Abraham and the Mosaic law. Psalm 49 tells us that a ransom is needed to redeem us: "But God will ransom my soul from the power of Sheol, for he will receive me" (v. 15). In the preceding verses, the psalmist tells us that "no man can ransom another, or give to God the price of his life, for the ransom of their life is costly and can never suffice" (vv. 7-8). A human soul is so valuable that the price for it is beyond our capacity. In other words, no human can pay a high enough ransom to redeem a soul. But a ransom must be paid. And only God can pay it. In fact, if God is both just and merciful, it seems that God must.

The Qur'an at least implicitly recognizes the need for a redemptive ransom. In Sura 37:102-107, we read a story of Abraham's willingness to sacrifice his (unnamed) son at God's command. As Abraham went to complete the act, God stopped him, telling him that it was all a trial and that Abraham had passed. But that was not the end. God did not just stop the sacrifice of Abraham's son. God provided an animal as a sacrificial substitute. In the words of the Qur'an, "and We ransomed him with a momentous sacrifice." Why the ransom for Abraham and his son? The answer is self-evident: because sin must be paid for, even the sin in the life of one with a sincere heart.

But the ransom provided by animals, lesser beings than us, can amount only to a temporary atonement. To effectuate the everlasting atonement, something more—*someone* more—is needed. An eternal ransom is necessary for eternal atonement. And on the cross of Christ, we find it.

God incarnate condescends to be on that cross and give himself as a ransom. Jesus tells us that he came "to give his life as a ransom for many" (Matthew 20:28). In that act—Jesus' death on the cross—God's maximal justice and maximal mercy are expressed without compromise. Justice demands that our sin is paid for, and Jesus died to pay for it. Mercy demands that our sin is forgiven, and Jesus died in our place for that too. This is what philosophers have called the *compossibility*—the harmonious and uncompromising existence of seemingly inharmonious things. As Baggett and Walls put it, God in Christ is "the greatest possible being who exemplifies all the great-making properties to the greatest maximal degree and to the greatest extent to which they're mutually consistent with one another; in other words, to the 'greatest compossible degree.'"[13]

But a question still remains: *How is the payment of an innocent person—Jesus—for what the guilty have done maximally just?* Perhaps an illustration that I have used elsewhere will help us understand the intricacy and profundity of the cross.[14] Every day we see justice meted out when one pays the debt owed by another. As a lawyer, I encounter this all the time in dealing with guarantors. The guarantor on a loan agrees to pay back money she did not borrow if the borrower cannot pay it back. Someone with bad credit, someone who has defaulted on other loans perhaps, will have a difficult time getting another loan given his financial history. But if someone with impeccable credit tells the lender that she will pay back the debt if the credit-challenged borrower defaults, then the lender just may make the loan after all.

Would it be unjust in such a situation to demand that the guarantor pay the loan when the borrower welshes? Of course not. The guarantor knew what she was getting into and willingly pays the price. Justice is served because the lender is made whole, yet there is an element of forgiveness because the borrower is no longer on the hook. There simply is no miscarriage of justice in having the innocent party pay if she is truly innocent and if she willingly agreed to it.

Something even greater happened on Calvary's hill and continues in the spiritual transaction that is the gospel. Jesus, as a person with a human nature and a divine nature, lived the perfect, sinless life. He had no debts of his own to pay. Thus, when we incur a debt to God, the debt of sin, Jesus is qualified to pay for it on our behalf. In fact, he is the only one qualified to do so. And sin is a debt, isn't it? A convicted criminal who serves his sentence is said to have "paid his debt to society." The Qur'an implies that sin is debt in saying that "those who earn sin will get due recompense for their 'earnings'" (Sura 6:120). And Jesus himself likens sin to a debt (Luke 7:41-50).

But the payment for that debt cannot be our performance of good deeds. How could it be? We are required to perform those deeds in the first place, so performing them cannot make up for what we have failed to do in the past. As the psalmist says, the price is too "costly" for our lives (Psalm 49:7-8). The payment is death—separation from God. Being unable to make that payment, we are in desperate need of a guarantor. And Jesus, as the Messiah, the Deliverer, the one who has no sins and needs to make no atonement for himself, can be our guarantor, having our debt transferred to him for payment (Hebrews 7:20-28). The Qur'an, after all, allows for sin to be transferred from one person to another (Sura 5:29).

Jesus willingly goes to the cross on our behalf, declaring, "I lay down my life that I may take it up again. No one takes it from me, but I lay it down of my own accord" (John 10:17-18). Laying down his life is the payment for our debt, which is why in his last moments on the cross, Jesus breathes out the words "It is finished" (John 19:30). The Gospel records his words in the Greek as *tete-*

lestai, which is a term used to signify the closing of a transaction, that a bill is paid in full.

But the believer in Christ does not walk away without consequence. The Son willingly pays the debt to the Father but gets something in return. He gets to dominate our lives, our very beings, should we embrace the payment he made for us. Part of what it means to embrace Christ's sacrifice is to understand that God will transform us and sanctify us through the indwelling of the Holy Spirit.

In this one amazing feat, God untwists the paradox of maximal justice and maximal mercy. Again Stott captures the essence so well:

> God overcame our evil by justifying us only because he first condemned it in Christ, and by redeeming us only because he first paid the ransom price. He did not overcome evil by refusing to punish it, but by accepting the punishment himself. At the cross human evil was both punished and overcome, and God's mercy and justice were both satisfied.[15]

As only the Greatest Possible Being can do, he takes what seems to be impossible and makes it possible.

HAIL TO THE VICTOR

Transformation is at the heart of what the cross is about. It turns a paradox into a solution. It changes death into life. It takes a debt owed and makes it a gift given. And it turns a seeming defeat into a victory. This is critical for Muslims, because they see the cross as an unthinkable defeat of the transcendent God at the hands of lowly creatures.

Consider Islam's claim about what happened at the cross. Jesus was rescued from the cross, according to Islam, by having someone substituted for him. In Muslim traditions, that substitute is unnamed, or he is Simon of Cyrene or Judas Iscariot. Ibn Kathir, one of Islam's most respected scholars, tells us that the Jewish authorities, seeking to kill Jesus, enlisted the help of the local authorities to arrest and crucify Jesus. As they came to the house in which Jesus was staying, Jesus asked one of his followers to be transformed into his likeness and die on the cross in his stead:

> "Who volunteers to be made to look like me, for which he will be my companion in Paradise?" A young man volunteered, but 'Isa thought that he was too young. He asked the question a second and third time, each time the young man volunteering, prompting 'Isa to say, "Well then, you will be that man." Allah made the young man look exactly like 'Isa, while a hole opened in the roof of the house, and 'Isa was made to sleep and ascended to heaven while asleep. . . .
>
> When 'Isa ascended, those who were in the house came out. When those surrounding the house saw the man who looked like 'Isa, they thought that he was 'Isa. So they took him at night, crucified him and placed a crown of thorns on his head.[16]

Regardless of who took Jesus' place, does that even remotely ring of victory? Or does it seem more like slinking away? The Islamic substitutionary theories are photo negatives of the reality. Where the Bible tells us that Jesus died on the cross in our place, Islam says that someone died on the cross in his.

What lacks in these theories (besides any historical evidence whatsoever) is divine power. Is it not more satisfying for God to conquer through the cross rather than scheme his way around it? God's power is displayed in his transformation of the ugly into the beautiful. In the movie *The Passion of the Christ*, there is an obscure line that left its mark on me. As Jesus proceeds on the Via Dolorosa, a bloody mess carrying his cross, he appears to be hugging it. One of the thieves about to be crucified with him mocks, "Why do you embrace your cross, you fool?"

Indeed, he did embrace it, because of what it meant for us. The payment Jesus wrought at the cross grants us eternal life. He turned the sinful act of nailing the innocent One to an instrument of torture on its head not by escaping from it, but by embracing it. Hiding from persecuting authority is not triumph; it is not might. Breaking its back is true triumph. The single greatest enemy of humanity is death, particularly the spiritual death that separates us from the Divine. In the greatest strategy of victory ever, God used sinful humanity to accomplish his goal of cleansing us of our sin. And in Jesus' resurrection, God arrays his power over death. Basking in the victory, Paul gloats, "O death, where is your victory? O death, where is your sting?" (1 Corinthians 15:55).

Can any other worldview claim that the living, though they will one day die, presently have victory over death and sin because of what God has done? Not even the worst execution the Romans could devise had power over the Lord of life. James Stewart, the Scottish writer, marvelously expressed God's victory and glory through the cross of Christ:

> The very triumphs of his foes . . . He used for their defeat. He compelled their dark achievements to serve his ends, not theirs. They nailed Him to the tree, not knowing that by that very act they were bringing the world to his feet. They gave Him a cross, not guessing that He would make it a throne. They flung Him outside the gates to die, not knowing that in that very moment they were lifting up all the gates of the universe, to let the King come in. They thought to root out his doctrines, not understanding that they were implanting imperishably in the hearts of men the very name they intended to destroy. They thought they had God with his back to the wall, pinned and helpless and defeated: they did not know that it was God Himself who had tracked them down. He did not conquer in spite of the dark mystery of evil. He conquered through it.[17]

God majestically took an instrument of death and transformed it into an instrument of life. And he did that because God is greater.

THE GREATEST POSSIBLE WAY

Nearly everyone would say that the fundamental ethic that under-girds all other ethical considerations is love—whether love of a romantic sort, a filial love for fellow humankind in general or love of neighbor. Our entire society is built on ethical rules and social structures that stem from the supreme and fundamental ethic of love. Without some form of love, there is no charity, no justice, no forgiveness and no relationships. Love is, in a very real sense, the greatest possible ethic.

The Bible specifically affirms this truth. In writing the famous "love chapter," Paul tells us that we can have the gift of prophecy, understanding and faith to move mountains, and it all means nothing without love (1 Corinthians 13:1-3). Love supports all other ethics and imbues our actions with meaning. The essence of love as a component of a good existence is expressed in the Bible's declaration that the one who creates our existence is, himself, love (1 John 4:8).

The Qur'an recognizes the fundamental importance of love in its proclamation that God is Al-Wadud, full of loving kindness. In their everyday lives, Muslims display how important love is to them. Fathers and mothers saturate their homes with love for their children, and they lavish generosity and hospitality on those who visit their homes. But the Islamic text tells us that God's love has its limits. His love is only for those who deserve it. Consider just a few examples of the Qur'an's description of God's love: "God does not love the ungrateful sinner" (Sura 2:276); "God does not love those who ignore his commands" (Sura 3:32); and "God does not love evil-doers" (Sura 3:57). And so while God is "full of loving kindness," ultimately that loving kindness is for only some of us.

And so a question arises: if God is the Greatest Possible Being, and love is the greatest ethic, where do we find love expressed in the greatest possible way?

The divine expression of love as the Qur'an describes it very much mirrors human expressions of love. We love those who love us; we love those who are lovable; and we lavish our affections and give of ourselves to those who love us. At best, we act lovingly toward strangers. But we do not love our enemies. We do not love the unlovable. Our love, in general terms, does not transcend the bounds of what is deserved. But the gospel tells us not just of God's love as an uncommon love, or even a great love, but as a uniquely great love. Luke preserves Jesus' startling teaching on what a true expression of love requires:

> If you love those who love you, what benefit is that to you? For even sinners love those who love them. And if you do good to those who do good to you, what benefit is that to you? For even sinners do the same. And if you lend to those from whom you expect to receive, what credit is that to you? Even sinners lend to sinners, to get back the same amount. But love your enemies, and do good, and lend, expecting nothing in return, and your reward will be great, and you will be sons of the Most High, for he is kind to the ungrateful and the evil. Be merciful, even as your Father is merciful. (Luke 6:32-36)

It is these kinds of teachings that have made Jesus the marvel of history, even for those who have rejected his claim to divinity yet have called him a good moral teacher (in fact, the paragon of a moral teacher). In this passage, Jesus is talking about unconditional love, especially for those who do not deserve it. He is telling us to express love in a way contrary to our human intuitions, to love the unlovable, to extend grace. But think for a moment about who is saying this to us. It is not a mere moralist or religious leader who utters these words, one who would like to put into practice what he preaches but sometimes misses the mark. No, in uttering these words, Jesus is telling us to mirror the very act of God's great love in the incarnation itself. In the brushstrokes of this passage we see the masterpiece of grace.

The incarnation's fundamental end is the cross. God the Son takes on human nature, lives among us and sacrifices himself for us. He makes the payment to God the Father on our behalf. The amount of self-giving in all of this is staggering. Is the incarnation, culminating in the cross, not the very epitome of what it means to love enemies? Is it not a grand expression of unconditional love? But a mere expression of unconditional love in and of itself is hardly compelling without context or purpose. And the purpose of Jesus giving his life is to rescue ours.

Before we continue, it is critical that we understand fully what happened at Calvary—what price was really paid and what sacrifice was really made—so we can understand the fullness and greatness of the love that the Gospels describe.

In the Garden of Gethsemane on the night of his arrest, Jesus was wracked by intense agony as his crucifixion grew near (Matthew 26:38; Mark 14:34). We read further that in his emotional anguish, Jesus cried out to God, "Abba, Father, all things are possible for you. Remove this cup from me. Yet not what I will, but what you will" (Mark 14:36). But what was so intense about the cross that caused Jesus to cry out to his Father and sweat blood? Although he asked if the Father could take away the "cup," he remained resolute in his mission to offer himself as a sacrifice for the sins of the world. Indeed, in his second prayer, Jesus said, "My Father, if this cannot pass unless I drink it, your will be done" (Matthew 26:42).

Jesus was not shrinking from the physical pain of the cross. Stott is right when he says that Jesus' indomitable physical and moral courage displayed during his ministry precludes such a possibility.[18] The Gospels record that as Peter tried to protect Jesus violently from those who seized him, Jesus ordered Peter to stand down and allow his arrest. "Shall I not drink the cup that the Father has given me?" he said to Peter (John 18:11). No, Jesus was agonized over a particular suffering that would befall him as he fulfilled the very purpose of his incarnation.

In coming to Earth and taking on a human nature, God gave of himself. The person of Jesus of Nazareth, a person with a human nature and the divine nature of God the Son, willingly died in our place. When Jesus was dying on the cross, he cried out something that some Muslims have found troubling. He said, *"Eloi, Eloi, lema sebachthani?"* meaning "My God, my God, why have you forsaken me?" (Mark 15:34). I have elsewhere addressed this question, but allow me to highlight something here.[19] In asking this question, Jesus was quoting the opening verse of Psalm 22, which begins with this question but ends with the proclamation that God has been victorious and a deliverer of his suffering servant. Nevertheless, there is something more about Jesus' question. He is pointing out, using Psalm 22, that in fact he is—at that moment—being forsaken by the Father. He had to be forsaken at that moment because he was taking our place, as forsaken sinners, on that cross.

But that meant more than any mere human can possibly imagine. There had never been even the remotest disruption in the relationship of the Godhead. But in that moment, when the Father turned his back on the Son and let him die that ignominious death, there was a momentary rupture in the relationship. There wasn't a severing of the relationship—that would be impossible within God. But there was a true forsakenness. As an earthly father might have to forsake the safety of his son if it meant saving the lives of others, so God the Father had to forsake his Son for our salvation. And if the anguish an earthly father feels over having to allow his son to be sacrificed, though finite, is terrible, then we can only ponder the exquisite and infinite agony of the forsakenness at the cross. There, in that act and at that moment, was an act of giving that we can never fully understand.

As we draw this part of our discussion to a close, let's consider something that we simply must grasp if we are ever to understand the heart of the incarnation and the cross as they display God's greatness. Growing up, I was taught to admire and emulate the self-giving of those who had gone before me. From my ancestors of old to my grandparents and parents, I was raised in a culture of sacrifice. Some gave up their dreams and others their lives to ensure a better future for their families, including me. Is there a culture on Earth that doesn't admire sacrifice? When we hear the story of a soldier who gave up his body to save his comrades, we feel the goose bumps and the tingles in awe of such selflessness. In fact, we see such acts as the ultimate expression of the greatest ethic we know of: love. Can we imagine a greater ethic than love? And can we imagine a greater expression of that ethic than one's self-sacrifice for those who love him? Self-sacrifice is the very hallmark of love.

But if that is the case, then shouldn't God be capable of such an expression of love? In fact, I will be so bold as to say that not only must God be capable of such an act, but God must express love this way. He is, after all, the Greatest Possible Being. Muslims and Christians agree on that very thing. But if that is the case, then he must act self-sacrificially. It simply follows that the Greatest Possible Being would express the greatest possible ethic in the greatest possible way: through self-sacrifice. And there is no other place in this world's theologies or its history where God has acted that way except at the cross of Christ.

But there is one more thing to consider. If God is the Greatest Possible Being, then his love and his expression of love cannot just be equal to ours—it must be greater. As humans, we sacrifice ourselves for others all the time. We give of our time or talent, our treasure and even our lives for those we love and for those who love us in return. And rarely we might sacrifice ourselves for a complete stranger.

But we do not sacrifice ourselves for the sake of those who hate us. We don't give of ourselves for our enemies. And there lies the great distinction between our expression of love and God's. The Trinity reveals God's love in creating us to be selfless and gratuitous in that he created us to have relationship with him without having to fulfill a lack in his own sense of relationship. But the incarnation and the cross demonstrate that his love is not just selfless, but self-lessly self-giving. Jesus did not die on the cross for those who loved him. No, he died for those who hated him.

I can vividly recall sitting at a table reading the fifth chapter of Romans as a Muslim, trying to understand the gospel. And as I came across Paul's words starting at verse 6, telling me that Christ died not for the strong in faith or the righteous, but for the "ungodly," I suddenly understood how amazing, pure and great God's love is. "God shows his love for us in that while we were still sinners, Christ died for us" (Romans 5:8). Does any other worldview know or speak of so great a love as that?

Al-Ghazali said that love as applied to God is different from love as applied to humanity. But he is wrong. Love is love. Love is, by definition, others-centered and self-giving. Our expressions, even our highest expressions, are but a shadow of the real thing. God's expression of love is the reality. This brings to mind C. S. Lewis's observation about the extent of God's true love compared to ours: "But the great thing to remember is that, though our feelings come and go, his love for us does not. It is not wearied by our sins, or our indifference; and, therefore, it is quite relentless in its determination that we shall be cured of those sins, at whatever cost to us, at whatever cost to Him."[20]

God's love is not different from our love. God's love is just truer, and so it is greater. The incarnation and the cross of Christ are the greatest possible demonstration of the greatest possible love from the Greatest Possible Being.

THE TRUE SUBMISSION OF A GRATEFUL HEART

The hymn writer Charles Gabriel captured the beauty of God's act in the incarnation and his self-sacrificial love on the cross, weaving the awe, beauty and greatness into our understanding of what God has done in expressing his greatness:

I stand amazed in the presence
of Jesus the Nazarene,
and wonder how He could love me,
a sinner condemned, unclean.

For me it was in the garden
He prayed, "Not My will, but Thine";
He had no tears for his own griefs
but sweat drops of blood for mine.

In pity angels beheld Him,
and came from the world of light
to comfort Him in the sorrows
He bore for my soul that night.

He took my sins and my sorrows;
He made them his very own;
He bore the burden to Calv'ry
and suffered and died alone.

When with the ransomed in glory
his face I at last shall see,
'twill be my joy thru the ages
to sing of his love for me.

How marvelous! How wonderful!
And my song shall ever be:
How marvelous! How wonderful
is my Savior's love for me![21]

For Muslims who have lived a life affirming that "God is greater," who have sought to understand and exemplify that, there is the gospel that tells us of a God who loves in the greatest possible way. Consider again the words of Imam Ali Ibn Abi Talib, one of the earliest Muslim leaders, in his book of sermons: "A group of people worshipped Allah out of desire for reward, surely this is the worship of traders. Another group worshipped Allah out of fear, this is the worship of slaves. Still another group worshipped Allah out of gratefulness, this is the worship of free men."[22] This was meant to describe a sincere Muslim. However, the believer who affirms God's greatness finds it in the God who is so great that he protects his self-revelation, which tells us of his great self-subsistence in the community of the Trinity, through which he incarnates himself on Earth to express the greatest possible ethic in the greatest possible way, his self-sacrifice. For Muslims' search, there is the treasure of the gospel.

A WORLDVIEW THAT VIEWS THE WHOLE WORLD

Science fiction author Samuel R. Delany once wrote that "endings, to be useful, must be inconclusive."[1] The reason is that, even though a work of fiction has a plot with a beginning, middle and end, there is still one thing that can never be dictated by the author: the impact on the reader. The reader is free to take the themes of the story and draw her own conclusions about how they apply to life.

I would argue that this kind of inconclusiveness is even more pronounced at the end of a nonfiction work like this one, which deals with questions of ultimate reality and provides answers that might cause us (or others) to change worldviews. We are challenged, provoked and ultimately left to decide the truth for ourselves. We can come to intellectual conclusions, but embracing those conclusions and shifting our worldview is an entirely different matter. And so in these ending pages, I will try to tie all of this together to offer the gospel as a comprehensive worldview that is worth embracing. How a person might react is not for me to write.

Our questions are as numerous as we are. I've learned very well from speaking engagements and personal encounters all over the world that there are no shortages of questions. But the Grand Central Questions—the questions around which all others orbit—are far fewer because we share them regardless of our backgrounds. What I've tried to demonstrate in the preceding pages is that the gospel answers the major worldviews' Grand Central Questions in ways that validate those questions while providing the true answers in the gospel.

The gospel affirms secular humanists' effort to understand the intrinsic value of each human being so that we can look to a brighter future. But that value can be found only in the transcendent God who places value in us. The gospel is the destination for humanists' search. Pantheists valiantly seek the path that meaningfully deals with suffering and pain, but the path that treats life and pain as illusions leads nowhere. The gospels' stark realism about the world's brutality, our role in it and the divine solution to our very real problem is where the path ends. And the gospel encourages Muslims' passion to worship God as the Greatest Possible Being. But the very doctrines that Muslims reject are the same doctrines that demonstrate God's greatness. That is a profound beauty of the gospel. It affirms the questions we all have, yet provides exclusive and wise answers in ways that touch the heart and stir the mind.

But I'm also convinced that the gospel does more than answer the major worldviews' Grand Central Questions. While each worldview has its own Grand Central Question, every person has one, unified Grand Central Question: *what does it all mean?* We are all looking for *the* answer. Perhaps we even capitalize the word, like so many bumper stickers I've seen that spout off platitudes like "Love is the Answer," "Tolerance is the Answer" or even "Jesus is the Answer."

In the movie *Forrest Gump,* as the title character runs across the United States (several times), he attracts quite a following. One man runs up alongside him and says that when he saw a news report about what Forrest was doing, a light went off in his head. He suddenly realized that Forest had "the Answer." It's ironic that Forrest supposedly had *the* answer while running back and forth along different roads. The oft-repeated, bumper-sticker-worthy cliché of the pluralist is "All roads lead up the mountain," suggesting that all the roads we pick to reach God are equally valid and reliable.

But I think this has reality a bit backward. Each worldview's Grand Central Question is itself a mountain standing in the path toward the ultimate destination. The fact that every worldview answers those questions so differently should tell us that they do not all get us over the mountains. Some roads can lead us right off a cliff. There are not many roads up the one mountain; there are many mountains along the one correct road to the ultimate destination. I'm firmly convinced that the gospel's answers to each of the Grand Central Questions we've addressed shows it to be the right road.

Allow me to offer one more signpost to assure us that we are headed in the right direction. The gospel's answer to one worldview's Grand Central Question provides the fulfillment of another worldview's Grand Central Question. Wrapped up in secular humanists' quest to understand the value of human life is the problem of pain and human suffering that pantheists try to answer. Wrapped up in pantheists' quest to try to understand ultimate reality and how we can address pain and suffering is Muslims' question of how to worship God as the source of ultimate justice and mercy. And wrapped up in Muslims' quest to exalt God as great is humanists' struggle to see the relationship between human value and ultimate reality beyond humanity. These questions intertwine with each other, showing that there is a connection every worldview shares.

Secular humanists want to affirm objective human value. Because we know something's value by what it costs, we can see that we have infinite value in God's eyes by what he paid for us at the cross. But that payment makes sense only if God is a triune being, a being that has one nature shared by three eternally distinct beings. The Son incarnates himself to live a perfect life and pay our penalty for sin to satisfy the Father's maximal justice and mercy simultaneously. And the Holy Spirit transforms us to reflect that sacrificial attitude toward others.

So when the gospel answers Muslims' Grand Central Question of God's greatness by pointing to the Trinity, the incarnation and the cross, it at the same time answers secular humanists' Grand Central Question. And when the gospel answers the Grand Central Question of secular humanists by showing us that God has allowed suffering to exist—in the sacrifice of his Son—for the salvation of humanity—the gospel simultaneously answers pantheists' Grand Central Question of how to address pain and suffering in a meaningful way.

I like to think that it is no accident that the word *crucifixion* has as its root the Latin word *crux*, which means the place where things converge or have a turning point. Jesus' crucifixion is the crux of history, theology and morality. It is the place where all our Grand Central Questions converge and all our doubts can have their turning point.

The cross tells humanists how much God values us by what he is willing to pay to redeem us. The cross is the instrument by which our suffering is dealt with, showing pantheists the true hope we have in resolving our pain. And the cross is the event in which the Greatest Possible Being expresses the greatest possible love in the greatest possible way in answer to Muslims' quest to worship the truly great God.

The answers to some of our questions are yet to be discovered. But the big questions, the Grand Central Questions, are answered by the gospel. That fact is why we can have such confidence that the gospel is not just true, it is comprehensively and coherently true. In his inimitable way, G. K. Chesterton describes what I'm talking

about when he says that "a man is not really convinced of a philosophic theory when he finds that something proves it. He is only
really convinced when he finds that everything proves it."[2] We don't
all need that level of proof, and I'm not suggesting that in this book
I've proven everything by the gospel. What I'm suggesting is that no
other worldview satisfies our hearts and minds like the gospel.

The answers are there to be had. But, yes, embracing them will
cost us something. The Bible records for us that Jacob, Abraham's
grandson, fled his home because he had incurred the wrath of his
older brother Esau after stealing his birthright. Some time later, Jacob
wanted to reconcile with Esau, but he feared his brother's wrath.

Before their reunion, Jacob wrestled the entire night with a manifestation of God (Genesis 32:22-32). Jacob refused to let go until
God blessed him. At that moment, God asked Jacob what his name
was. Of course, God knew Jacob's name, but long before that, Jacob
had pretended to be Esau to trick his blind father, Isaac, into giving
Jacob the eldest son's birthright. And so God confronted Jacob with
his true identity. And when Jacob confessed, God gave him a new
name, Israel, because Jacob had striven with God and men and
prevailed (v. 28). Jacob did not prevail against God. He prevailed
against the things that kept him from the truth. But his victory cost
him something. As they wrestled, God touched his hip so that he
limped the rest of his life.

That is something for all of us to consider as we try to find the
answers to our questions. We just might find the answers we are
looking for, but we may not want to accept the consequences of
making those answers integral to our lives. A secular humanist will
find objective human dignity in God, but his wound may be that
he must abandon secular humanism and embrace Christian humanism. This might result in the ridicule of his peers or an un-
wanted change in his associations. A pantheist who wants an
answer to suffering finds it in the God who suffers and transforms
suffering into glory. But her cost may be that she has to abandon

the belief in her own divinity or put her place in the community at risk. And a Muslim who wants to worship God as great finds, after wrestling with God, that God is truly great in the Trinity, the incarnation and the cross. But the price Muslims may face is that they must put away the familiar religious trappings of their tradition and may lose the closest relationships they have. No matter our background, our encounter with the truth just may leave us with a limp. The question for each of us is whether we are willing to walk that way to walk with God.

The answers to the Grand Central Questions are not inconclusive. But the answer to the personal question of whether we are willing to embrace those answers depends on each of us. That's what is inconclusive about this ending. If you are a believer in Christ, you have to ask yourself whether you are willing to engage with others in their struggles to find answers to the Grand Central Questions. If you are considering the credibility of the gospel, you must ask yourself whether you are willing to change everything if the gospel's answers to the Grand Central Questions speak to your heart and your mind. In either case, we must ask ourselves, *Does truth matter more than comfort?*

That is *the* Grand Central Question.

ACKNOWLEDGMENTS

In a bicycle race, everyone sees the cyclist climbing the hills, speeding down the descents and crossing the finish line. It looks like a one-person event, when it's nothing like that. Coaches, teammates, spouses and mechanics all make it possible for the cyclist to finish the race. That's what bringing a book to publication is like. My name is on the cover, but many, many names put time and effort into every page.

My heartfelt gratitude goes first and foremost to my wife and children. Nicole and I spent long nights talking about the ideas in this book and typing in the edits. My children waited patiently (as much as kids can) for me to finish each day so we could play "Spider-Man." My family's patience and understanding made this all possible. If true love is expressed through self-sacrifice, then their love for me is true indeed.

Marilyn Jelcin, a dear sister in the Lord, volunteered so much of her time cataloging my research and typing in my revisions. I cannot thank her enough for her service. Along those lines, Randy Pistor, a bright and budding apologist provided excellent feedback throughout the writing process as well as invaluable research that helped to make this the best it could be. Randy is a true asset to the kingdom.

Some of the sharpest minds I know helped me along the way and must be thanked. Mickey Badalamenti and Brian Wassom provided key insights into how to express a thought. Their abilities to see counterperspectives and counterarguments steered me in the right direction on many occasions. Nabeel Qureshi helped shape how I discussed Jesus' claims to divinity, and Scott Symington, who has forgotten more about the fine-tuning argument than I'll ever learn, contributed to my discussion of divine design. My conversations over coffee with Archie Hensley about Hinduism and Buddhism enhanced my understanding so that I could present what I believe to be a fair picture of pantheism.

Josh McDowell has been an incredible encouragement to me throughout this writing process and through my ministry in general. He and Dottie have nurtured and mentored Nicole so meaningfully, it makes saying thanks seem trivial.

Finally, my gratitude to God must be stated. If I were to write about all the answers he has given to all my questions, I suppose the whole world could not contain the books that could be written. We are all in this race together, but God is the One who gets the victory. It is an honor to be on his team.

NOTES

PROLOGUE: WHAT TRUTH COSTS—WHAT TRUTH IS WORTH

[1]Judith Viorst and Shelly Markham, *Love and Shrimp* (New York: Samuel French, 1993), p. 41.

[2]C. S. Lewis, *Surprised by Joy: The Shape of My Early Life*, rev. ed. (Boston: Houghton Mifflin Harcourt, 1995), p. 221.

[3]C. S. Lewis, *Mere Christianity*, HarperCollins ed. (San Francisco: HarperSanFrancisco, 2001), p. 32.

[4]Ravi K. Zacharias, *New Birth or Rebirth? Jesus Talks with Krishna* (Colorado Springs: Multnomah, 2008).

[5]Ravi K. Zacharias, *Why Jesus? Rediscovering His Truth in an Age of Mass Marketed Spirituality* (New York: Hachette Book Group, 2012), p. 55.

[6]Thomas Nagel, *The Last Word* (New York: Oxford University Press, 1997), p. 130, emphasis mine. Interestingly, Nagel has recently released a book in which he concedes to some degree the credibility of the evidence for a non-material cause of the universe. See Thomas Nagel, *Mind and Cosmos: Why the Materialist Neo-Darwinian Conception of Nature Is Almost Certainly False* (New York: Oxford University Press, 2012).

[7]Aldous Huxley, *Ends and Means* (London: Chatt & Windus, 1946), p. 310.

[8]Upton Sinclair, *I, Candidate for Governor: And How I Got Licked* (Berkeley: University of California Press, 1935), p. 109.

CHAPTER 1: GRAND CENTRAL QUESTIONS

[1]For an explanation of the arrangement of the names at the memorial, see "Learn How the Names Are Arranged," 9/11 Memorial, www.911memorial.org/learn-how-names-are-arranged.

[2]James W. Sire, *The Universe Next Door: A Basic Worldview Catalog*, 5th ed. (Downers Grove, IL: InterVarsity Press, 2009), p. 20.

[3]Coherentism is the view that a belief is justified if it makes sense in conjunction with other justified beliefs. But coherentism is not the only view about what justifies our beliefs. Foundationalism, for example, is the view

that some beliefs do not need to be justified based on other truth or other beliefs. In any event, coherence is essential for any system or belief to be valid. For more on coherentism and foundationalism, see James Porter Moreland and William Lane Craig, *Philosophical Foundations for a Christian Worldview* (Downers Grove, IL: InterVarsity Press, 2009).

[4]Ravi K. Zacharias, *Deliver Us from Evil* (Nashville: Thomas Nelson, 1998), p. 219.

[5]Interestingly, Sam Harris, the vociferous atheist and one of the so-called "Four Horsemen of the New Atheism," is trying to capture a secular meaning of the word *spiritual* to discuss "the deliberate efforts some people make to overcome their feeling of separateness" by inducing "non-ordinary states of consciousness." See "In Defense of 'Spiritual,'" Sam Harris's website, June 27, 2012, www.samharris.org/blog/itme/a-plea-for-spirituality/.

[6]Because the fundamental question of our origin is so closely linked, secular humanism has to answer that question as well.

[7]To some degree, Buddhism is a special case, because some forms are theistic while others are nontheistic. In later chapters, we will examine its differences and similarities and how they apply.

[8]Jerram Barrs, "Francis Schaeffer: The Man and His Message," *Reformation 21: The Online Magazine of the Alliance of Confessing Evangelicals,* November 2006.

CHAPTER 2: SECULAR HUMANISM—THE SECULAR SEARCH

[1]Quoted in Paul Kurtz, "Planetary Humanism," *Free Inquiry,* 24, no. 1 (Fall 1999), www.secularhumanism.org/index.php/articles/2573.

[2]British Humanist Association, "Non-Religious Beliefs," www.humanism.org.uk/humanism/humanism-today/non-religious-beliefs.

[3]Law No. 2004-228 of March 15, 2004, J.O., March 15, 2004, p. 5190, D.S.L. March 25, 2004, 12, 854.

[4]Ibid.

[5]Ibid.

[6]Ironically, the underground church in China is growing at an astounding pace, with an estimate of eighty million to one hundred million Christians in its ranks. This seems yet further proof of the two-thousand-year-old experience that the surest way to ensure the growth of Christianity is to try to stamp it out.

[7]The Humanist Resource Connection, "Transcript of Richard Dawkins' Speech from Reason Rally 2012," March 24, 2012, www.humanistresources.org/blog/transcript-richard-dawkins-speech-reason-rally-2012.

[8]Richard Dawkins, "Religion's Real Child Abuse," May 14, 2006, http://old.richarddawkins.net/articles/118.

[9]Sam Harris, *The End of Faith: Religion, Terror, and the Future of Reason* (New York: Norton, 2004), pp. 52-53.

[10]Atheists are not alone in the use of exaggerated rhetoric or hyperbole in conversations with those opposed to their views. In fact, debates among religious followers often devolve into name calling and *ad hominem* attacks. My point is simply that the common indictment coming from secularizers that the religious are always trying to "shove their beliefs down our throats" can easily be turned back against the accusers. In fact, in recent years, atheist and humanist groups have paid for billboard campaigns extolling atheism and denigrating religion. One such billboard campaign was run during the Christmas holiday season and showed a well-known picture of the "three wise men" following the Star of Bethlehem to Jesus' birthplace, and stated in large letters "You KNOW it's a myth. This season celebrate REASON." That billboard and others like it are obviously aimed at getting the religious to abandon their long-held beliefs in favor of atheistic "reason."

[11]Paul Kurtz, "A Secular Humanist Declaration" (issued by the Council for Secular Humanism, 1980), www.secularhumanism.org/index.php?section=main&page=declaration#introduction.

[12]David Bentley Hart has masterfully debunked the oft-repeated myth that there were even "Dark Ages" and that Christianity stifled human advancement. See David Bentley Hart, *Atheist Delusions: The Christian Revolution and Its Fashionable Enemies* (New Haven, CT: Yale University Press, 2009).

[13]Cited by James P. Eckman, *Exploring Church History* (Wheaton: Crossway Books, 2002), p. 72.

[14]See James W. Sire, *The Universe Next Door: A Basic Worldview Catalog*, 5th ed. (Downers Grove, IL: InterVarsity Press, 2009), p. 67.

[15]David Hume, *An Enquiry Concerning Human Understanding* (Minneapolis: Filiquarian, 2007), pp. 147, 149.

[16]Sam Harris, *The Moral Landscape: How Science Can Determine Human Values* (New York: Free Press, 2010).

[17]While we may be able to measure the benefits of certain actions scientifically and label them moral, the definition of what is moral remains, in its essence, a philosophical question that science has nothing to say about.

[18]Stephen Hawking and Leonard Mlodinow, *The Grand Design* (New York: Bantam, 2010), p. 5.

[19]Michael Polanyi, *Meaning* (Chicago: University of Chicago Press, 1975), p. 162.

[20]Kurtz, "A Secular Humanist Declaration."

[21]Paul Kurtz and Edwin H. Wilson, *Humanist Manifesto II* (Washington, DC: American Humanist Association, 1973), http://americanhumanist.org/Humanism/Humanist_Manifesto_II.

[22]Sire, *Universe Next Door*, p. 85.

[23]British Humanist Association, "Non-Religious Beliefs."

[24]British Humanist Association, "About Us: What Do We Want?" www.humanism.org.uk/about.

[25]*Humanist Manifesto II*, p. 17, emphasis mine.

[26]*Humanist Manifesto III* (Washington, DC: American Humanist Association, 2003), http://americanhumanist.org/humanism/humanist_manifesto_iii.

[27]Tom Flynn, "Secular Humanism Defined," Council for Secular Humanism, July 7, 2012, www.secularhumanism.org/index.php/13.

[28]Charles Taylor, *A Secular Age* (Cambridge, MA: Harvard University Press, 2007), p. 18.

CHAPTER 3: SAYING NOTHING AS LOUD AS WE CAN

[1]Stephen Jay Gould, quoted in David Friend, ed., *The Meaning of Life* (Boston: Little, Brown, 1991), p. 33, emphasis mine.

[2]Stephen Crane, "A Man Said to the Universe," in *The Poems of Stephen Crane, A Critical Edition*, ed. Joseph Katz (New York: Cooper Square Publishers, 1966), p. 102.

[3]James W. Sire, *The Universe Next Door: A Basic Worldview Catalog*, 5th ed. (Downers Grove, IL: InterVarsity Press, 2009), p. 112.

[4]See Lawrence M. Krauss, *A Universe from Nothing: Why There Is Something Rather Than Nothing* (New York: Free Press, 2012).

[5]Lawrence M. Krauss, "A Universe without Purpose," *Los Angeles Times*, April 1, 2012, http://articles.latimes.com/2012/apr/01/opinion/la-oe-krauss-cosmology-design-universe-20120401.

[6]Ibid.

[7]Ibid.

[8]Ibid.

[9]Ibid., emphasis mine.

[10]Lawrence Krauss, quoted by Richard Panek, "Out There," *New York Times*, March 11, 2007, www.nytimes.com/2007/03/11/magazine/11dark.t.html?_r=1.

[11]David Bentley Hart, *Atheist Delusions: The Christian Revolution and Its Fashionable Enemies* (New Haven, CT.: Yale University Press, 2009), p. 21.

[12]Richard Dawkins, *River out of Eden: A Darwinian View of Life* (New York:

HarperCollins, 1995), pp. 132-33.

[13]Richard Dawkins, "Growing Up in the Universe" (lecture, Royal Institution Christmas lectures, London, 1991), cited by John Lennox, "Challenges from Science," in *Beyond Opinion*, ed. Ravi Zacharias (Nashville: Thomas Nelson, 2007), p. 116.

[14]Richard Dawkins, *The God Delusion* (New York: Houghton Mifflin, 2006), p. 221.

[15]Raymond Smullyan, quoted in Friend, *Meaning of Life*, p. 194.

[16]Julian Baggini, "Yes, Life Without God Can Be Bleak. Atheism Is About Facing Up to That," *The Guardian*, March 9, 2012, www.theguardian.com/commentisfree/2012/mar/09/life-without-god-bleak-atheism.

[17]Ibid.

[18]Joel Marks, "An Amoral Manifesto I," *Philosophy Now* 80 (August/September 2010): 30.

[19]Michael Ruse, "Evolutionary Theory and Christian Ethics," in *The Darwinian Paradigm* (London: Routledge, 1989), pp. 22, 268-69.

[20]Dawkins, *River Out of Eden*, pp. 132-33.

[21]Guenter Lewy, *Why America Needs Religion* (Grand Rapids: Eerdmans, 1996), p. 146.

[22]Kai Nielsen, "Why Should I Be Moral?" *American Philosophical Quarterly* 21 (1984): 90.

[23]Allan Bloom, *The Closing of the American Mind* (New York: Simon & Schuster, 1987), p. 194.

[24]Dinesh D'Souza, *Life After Death: The Evidence* (Washington, DC: Regnery, 2009), p. 216.

[25]Frank Newport, Dan Witters and Sangeeta Agrawal, "In U.S., Very Religious Have Higher Wellbeing Across All Faiths," Gallup Wellbeing, February 16, 2012, www.gallup.com/poll/152732/Religious-Higher-Wellbeing-Across-Faiths.aspx.

[26]Ernest Nagel, "Naturalism Reconsidered," in *Logic Without Metaphysics and Other Essays in the Philosophy of Science* (New York: Free Press, 1956), p. 17

[27]Sam Harris, *The Moral Landscape: How Science Can Determine Human Values* (New York: Free Press, 2010), pp. 226-27, n 50.

[28]Ibid.

[29]Ibid.

[30]Ibid.

[31]Ibid. Harris dismisses this thought experiment as posing "no problem for our [human] ethics" because "there is no compelling reason to believe such beings exist" (ibid). Naturalist cosmologists who posit the existence of millions of life-sustaining planets might disagree. Nevertheless, this points out that even

Harris's views on morality, meaning, purpose and human value are essentially relative to the cognitive abilities of other creatures.

[32]G. K. Chesterton, *Orthodoxy* (New York: Doubleday, 2001), pp. 32-33.

[33]Bentley Hart, *Atheist Delusions*, p. 15.

[34]Baggini, "Yes, Life Without God Can Be Bleak."

[35]The retort has been that the institution of Christianity, once adopted by the Roman Empire, is guilty of the same horrors. For insightful rejoinders, see Bentley Hart, *Atheist Delusions*.

[36]Peter Singer, "Why It's Irrational to Risk Women's Lives for the Sake of the Unborn," *The Scotsman*, August 15, 2012, www.scotsman.com/the-scotsman /opinion/comment/analysis-why-it-s-irrational-to-risk-women-s-lives-for-the-sake-of-the-unborn-1-2467196.

[37]Ibid.

[38]Alberto Giubilini and Francesca Minerva, "After-Birth Abortion: Why Should the Baby Live?" *Journal of Medical Ethics* (March 2, 2012): 2.

[39]Ibid.

[40]Ibid., pp. 2-3.

[41]Ibid., p. 2.

CHAPTER 4: WILL THE REAL HUMANISM PLEASE STAND UP?

[1]John Templeton, *The Humble Approach: Scientists Discover God* (Philadelphia: Templeton Foundation, 1998), p. 19.

[2]Stephen Hawking and Roger Penrose, *The Nature of Space and Time*, The Isaac Newton Institute Series of Lectures (Princeton, NJ: Princeton University Press, 1996), p. 20, emphasis mine.

[3]For a fuller explanation of the *kalam* cosmological argument and the responses to it, see James Porter Moreland and William Lane Craig, *Philosophical Foundations for a Christian Worldview* (Downers Grove, IL: InterVarsity Press, 2009), pp. 468-80.

[4]Ibid., pp. 482-83.

[5]This summary is taken from William Lane Craig and Walter Sinnot-Armstrong, *God? A Debate Between a Christian and an Atheist* (New York: Oxford University Press, 2004), p. 9. Full citations to the sources for this information can be found in the notes on page 29 of that book.

[6]Stephen W. Hawking, *A Brief History of Time—From the Big Bang to Black Holes* (New York: Bantam Books, 1988), p. 125.

[7]Paul Davies, *God and the New Physics* (New York: Simon and Schuster, 1983), p. 189.

[8]Paul Davies, *Superforce: The Search for a Grand Unified Theory of Nature* (New York: Simon and Schuster, 1984), pp. 235-36, emphasis mine.

[9]Stephen Hawking and Leonard Mlodinow, *The Grand Design* (New York: Bantam, 2010), p. 164.

[10]See generally, Lawrence M. Krauss, *A Universe from Nothing: Why There Is Something Rather Than Nothing* (New York: Free Press, 2012).

[11]David Albert, "On the Origin of Everything," *New York Times Sunday Book Review*, March 23, 2012, www.nytimes.com/2012/03/25/books/review/a-universe-from-nothing-by-lawrence-m-krauss.html?_r=3&.

[12]Francis S. Collins, *The Language of God: A Scientist Presents Evidence for Belief* (New York: Free Press, 2006), pp. 1-2.

[13]See S. W. Fox, ed., *The Origin of Prebiotic Systems and of Their Molecular Matrices* (New York: Academic Press, 1965), pp. 309-15.

[14]Michael Polanyi, "Life's Irreducible Structure," *Science* 160 (1968): 1308-12.

[15]This is a very general summary of the competing naturalistic theories for the genesis of DNA. For a more detailed discussion and critique, see Stephen Meyer, *The Signature in the Cell: DNA and the Evidence for Intelligent Design* (New York: HarperCollins, 2009).

[16]The ENCODE Project Consortium, "An Integrated Encyclopedia of DNA Elements in the Human Genome," *Nature* 489 (September 6, 2012): 57-74.

[17]Michael Denton, *Evolution: A Theory in Crisis* (Bethesda, MD: Adler & Adler, 1986), p. 342.

[18]Francis Crick, *Life Itself* (New York: Simon and Schuster, 1981), p. 88.

[19]*Contact*, directed by Robert Zemeckis (Warner Bros., 1997).

[20]David Baggett and Jerry L. Walls, *Good God: The Theistic Foundations of Morality* (New York: Oxford University Press, 2011), p. 11.

[21]A well-known proponent of this solution is William Lane Craig in his many writings and debates. See, for example, Craig and Sinnot-Armstrong, *God?* pp. 19-20, 68-69. Others include Robert Adams, whom Craig refers to often.

[22]Paul Copan, *Is God a Moral Monster? Making Sense of the Old Testament God* (Grand Rapids: Baker Books, 2011), p. 211.

[23]Baggett and Walls, *Good God*, p. 186.

[24]David Bentley Hart, *Atheist Delusions: The Christian Revolution and Its Fashionable Enemies* (New Haven, CT: Yale University Press, 2009), pp. 167-68.

[25]Ibid., p. 171.

CHAPTER 5: PANTHEISM AND PAIN

[1]Swami Vivekananda, *The Complete Works of Swami Vivekananda*, 11th ed., 1962, http://en.wikisource.org/wiki/The_Complete_Works_of_Swami_Vivekananda.

[2]Ibid., emphasis added.

[3]See Mariasusai Dhavamony, *Classical Hinduism* (Rome: Gregorian University Press, 1982), p. 444, citing *Brhadaranyaka Upanishad* 3.4-5.

[4]See ibid., p. 442.

[5]Andrew Cohen and Ken Wilber, "The Guru and the Pandit: Andrew Cohen and Ken Wilber in Dialogue," *What Is Enlightenment?* Spring/Summer 2003, p. 86.

[6]James W. Sire, *The Universe Next Door: A Basic Worldview Catalog*, 5th ed. (Downers Grove, IL: InterVarsity Press, 2009), pp. 179-80.

[7]*Katha Upanishad* 3.11, quoted in Dhavamony, *Classical Hinduism*, p. 422.

[8]The Church of Scientology describes Jesus in much the same way as Hindus, Buddhists and Deepak Chopra, listing him among the spiritual revolutionaries who taught that our victory comes from the power of the spirit over the flesh. Jesus of Nazareth "brought new hope to man by preaching that life was not all men might hope for." "Though crucified, the hope that Christ brought to man did not die. Instead, his death became symbolic of the triumph of the spirit over the material body and so brought a new awareness of man's true nature." Church of Scientology International, *What Is Scientology?* (Los Angeles: Bridge Publications, 1992), pp. 34-38. It is difficult to imagine something sounding more like pantheism than that.

[9]Sire, *Universe Next Door*, p. 145.

[10]See Stephen A. Kent, "Scientology's Relationship with Eastern Religious Traditions," *Journal of Contemporary Religion* 11, no. 1 (1996): 21.

[11]Vivekananda, *Complete Works*.

[12]Eckhart Tolle, *The Power of Now: A Guide to Spiritual Enlightenment* (Novato, CA: New World Library, 1999), p. 224.

[13]Deepak Chopra, *The Seven Spiritual Laws of Success: A Practical Guide to the Fulfillment of Your Dreams* (San Rafael, CA: Amber-Allen Publishing, 1994), pp. iv-v, emphasis mine.

[14]Ravi K. Zacharias, *Why Jesus? Rediscovering His Truth in an Age of Mass Marketed Spirituality* (New York: Hachette Book Group, 2012), p. 13.

[15]Deepak Chopra, *The Third Jesus: The Christ We Cannot Ignore* (New York: Random House, 2009), p. 125.

[16]*Star Wars: Episode III—Revenge of the Sith*, directed by George Lucas (20th Century Fox, 2005).

[17]See *Bhagavad-Gita*, 18:50-53.

[18]See Sir Charles Eliot, *Hinduism and Buddhism, An Historical Sketch*, vol. 1 (public domain). This volume can be accessed in its entirety at www.gutenberg.org/files/15255/15255-h/15255-h.htm.

[19]Dhavamony, *Classical Hinduism*, p. 428.

[20]Ibid., p. 444.

[21]Geshe Kelsang Gyatso, *Modern Buddhism: The Path of Compassion and Wisdom*,

vol. 1, *Sutra* (Glen Spey, NY: Tharpa Publications, 2011), p. xi.

[22]See Vivekananda, *Complete Works.*

CHAPTER 6: ESCAPING THE ESCAPISM

[1]*The Complete C. S. Lewis Signature Classics* (San Francisco: HarperSanFrancisco, 2002), pp. 175-76.

[2]James Strong, *The Strongest Strong's Exhaustive Concordance of the Bible,* rev. ed., ed. John R. Kohlenberger and James A. Swanson (Grand Rapids: Zondervan, 2001).

[3]Mariasusai Dhavamony, *Classical Hinduism* (Rome: Gregorian University Press, 1982), p. 338, citing *Mahabharata* 12.332.44.

[4]Robert Pirsig, *Zen and the Art of Motorcycle Maintenance: An Inquiry into Values* (New York: Bantam, 1981), pp. 126-27.

[5]See Swami Vivekananda, *The Complete Works of Swami Vivekananda,* 11th ed., 1962, http://en.wikisource.org/wiki/The_Complete_Works_of_Swami_Vivekananda.

[6]Eckhart Tolle, *The Power of Now: A Guide to Spiritual Enlightenment* (Novato, CA: New World Library, 1999), pp. 223-25.

[7]C. S. Lewis, *The Problem of Pain* (New York: HarperCollins, 1996), p. 91.

[8]Tolle, *Power of Now,* p. 226.

[9]Dhavamony, *Classical Hinduism,* pp. 110-11, quoting S. Radhakrishnan, *The Philosophy of Rabindranath Tagore* (London, 1918), p. 15.

[10]James W. Sire, *The Universe Next Door: A Basic Worldview Catalog,* 5th ed. (Downers Grove, IL: InterVarsity Press, 2009), p. 157.

[11]Kenneth W. Osbeck, *Amazing Grace: 366 Inspiring Hymn Stories for Daily Devotions,* hymn 360 (Grand Rapids: Kregel, 1996).

CHAPTER 7: FROM WHENCE COMES GOD'S GREATNESS?

[1]While I firmly believe that the Muslim and Christian conceptions of God are quite different, I will use the words *Allah* and *God* in this section somewhat interchangeably. First, *Allah* is the Arabic word for *God* and is used in Arabic Bible translations and by native Arabic-speaking Christians to refer to Yahweh. Second, for our purposes, I am comparing Islam's view of the one and only Supreme Being to Christianity's view of the one and only Supreme Being. To repeatedly qualify the use of *Allah* and *God* would be distracting.

[2]A. J. Wensinck, "Takbir," *Encyclopaedia of Islam,* 2nd ed, Brill Online, 2012, http://referenceworks.brillonline.com/entries/encyclopaedia-of-islam-2/takbir-SIM_7330.

[3]Winfried Corduan, "A View from the Middle East: Islamic Theism," in James W. Sire, *The Universe Next Door: A Basic Worldview Catalog*, 5th ed. (Downers Grove, IL: InterVarsity Press, 2009), pp. 247-48.

[4]Alhaj A. D. Ajijola, *The Essence of Faith in Islam* (Lahore, Pakistan: Islamic Publications, 1978), p. 55.

[5]Muhammad Abdul Rauf, *Islam: Creed and Worship* (Washington, DC: The Islamic Center, 1974), pp. 2-3.

[6]Cited by Samuel M. Zwemer, *The Moslem Doctrine of God* (New York: American Tract Society, 1905), p. 31.

[7]Kenneth Cragg, *The Call of the Minaret* (New York: Oxford University Press, 1964), p. 39. See also Al-Bukhari, *The Translation of the Meanings of Sahih Al-Bukhari*, trans. Muhammad Muhsin Khan (Al-Medina: Islamic University), 6:493-95.

[8]Corduan, "View from the Middle East," pp. 248-49.

[9]Zwemer, *Moslem Doctrine of God*, p. 34.

[10]For a comprehensive list of the names, see *Tasbih Asma Allah al-Husna* by Muhammad al-Madani, cited in Arthur Jeffrey, *Islam: Muhammad and His Religion* (New York: Bobbs-Merrill Company, 1958), pp. 93-98.

[11]Fadlou Shehadi, *Ghazali's Unique Unknowable God* (Leiden: Brill, 1964), p. 37.

[12]Annemarie Schimmel and Abdoldjavad Falature, *We Believe in One God* (New York: Seabury Press, 1979), p. 85, quoted in Norman L. Geisler and Abdul Saleeb, *Answering Islam: The Crescent in Light of the Cross* (Grand Rapids: Baker Books, 2003), p. 30.

[13]Duncan Black MacDonald, "One Phase of the Doctrine of the Unity of God with Some Consequences," The Hartford Seminary Record, vol 20, no. 1 (Hartford, CT: Hartford Seminary Press, January 1910), p. 29.

[14]Kenneth Cragg, *Jesus and the Muslim: An Exploration* (Oxford: Oneworld Publications, 1999), p. 223.

[15]Corduan quoted in Sire, *Universe Next Door*, p. 247.

[16]Ibid., p. 248.

[17]This verse translated into English does not actually contain an Arabic equivalent of "trinity." Rather, the Qur'an literally says that it is blasphemy to say Allah is "a third of three."

[18]Ibid., p. 247.

[19]Hammudah Abdalati, *Islam in Focus* (Indianapolis: American Trust Publications, 1975), p. 5, quoted by Corduan in Sire, *Universe Next Door*, p. 250.

[20]Shabbir Akhtar, *A Faith for All Seasons* (Chicago: Ivan R. Dee, 1990), p. 180.

CHAPTER 8: GOD'S GREATNESS AND THE PRESERVATION OF THE GOSPEL

[1]This is a popular claim Muslims make, but it has serious challenges. On the historical development of the Qur'an, see Keith Small, *Textual Criticism and Qur'an Manuscripts* (Lanham, MD: Lexington Books, 2011). Interesting books by Muslim authors include Ali Dashti, *Twenty Three Years: A Study of the Prophetic Career of Mohammad*, trans. F. R. C. Bagley (Costa Mesa, CA: Mazda Publishers, 1991), and Mondher Sfar, *In Search of the Original Qur'an: The True History of the Revealed Text*, trans. Emilia Lamier (Amherst, NY: Prometheus Books, 2008).

[2]For excellent books on the reliability of the New Testament, see Paul Rhodes Eddy and Gregory Boyd, *The Jesus Legend: A Case for the Historical Reliability of the Synoptic Jesus Tradition* (Grand Rapids: Baker Academic, 2008); Andreas Kostenberger and Michael Kruger, *The Heresy of Orthodoxy: How Contemporary Culture's Fascination with Diversity Has Reshaped Our Understanding of Early Christianity* (Wheaton: Crossway, 2010); and Bruce Metzger, *The Text of the New Testament: Its Origin, Development, and Significance* (Oxford: Clarendon, 1987).

[3]Muhammad M. Pickthall, *The Glorious Qur'an: Arabic Text and English Rendering* (Des Plaines, IL: Library of Islam, 1994).

[4]Norman L. Geisler, *Baker Encyclopedia of Christian Apologetics* (Grand Rapids: Baker, 1999), pp. 527-28.

[5]Pickthall, *Glorious Qur'an*, emphasis mine.

[6]Ibid.

[7]Gordon Nickel, *Narratives of Tampering in the Earliest Commentaries on the Qur'an* (Leiden: Brill, 2011).

[8]Ibid., pp. 227-28.

[9]Mahmoud Ayoub, "Uzayr in the Qur'an and Muslim Tradition," in *Studies in Islamic and Judaic Traditions*, ed. W. M. Brinner and S. D. Ricks (Atlanta: Scholars Press, 1986), p. 5.

[10]Ibn Kathir on al-Bukhari, *Tafsir Ibn Kathir* (abridged), vol. 9, no. 614, ed. Shaykh Safiur Rahman al-Mubarakpuri, vol. 2 (London: Darusslam, 2003), p. 196, emphasis mine.

[11]Al-Qurtubi's commentary can be accessed in Arabic and English at http://quran.al-islam.com/Page.aspx?pageid=221&BookID=14&Page=1; emphasis mine. For an excellent article responding to the charge that Paul is the real founder of contemporary Christianity, see Sam Shamoun, "The Qur'an Affirms: Paul Passed on the True Gospel of Christ," Answering Islam, www.answering-islam.org/Shamoun/quran_affirms_paul.htm.

[12]For a specific case on this, see David Wenham, *Paul and Jesus: The True Story* (Grand Rapids: Eerdmans, 2002).

[13]N. T. Wright and A. N. Wilson, "Jesus or Paul: Who Founded Christianity?" debate, St. James Church, Piccadilly Circus, London, May 27, 1997.

[14]See Nickel, *Narratives of Tampering*, pp. 19-23.

CHAPTER 9: GOD'S TRIUNE GREATNESS

[1]Muhammad M. Pickthall, *The Glorious Qur'an: Arabic Text and English Rendering* (Des Plaines, IL: Library of Islam, 1994), emphasis mine.

[2]Ibid., emphasis mine.

[3]Ibid.

[4]Thomas F. Michel, ed. and trans., *A Muslim Theologian's Response to Christianity: Ibn Taymiyya's Al-Jawab Al-Sahih* (Delmar, NY: Caravan Books, 1985), p. 270.

[5]Ibid., pp. 261-62, 277.

[6]Norman L. Geisler and Abdul Saleeb, *Answering Islam: The Crescent in Light of the Cross* (Grand Rapids: Baker, 2002), pp. 271-72.

[7]C. S. Lewis, *Mere Christianity*, HarperCollins ed. (San Francisco: HarperSanFrancisco, 2001), p. 165.

[8]See J. Windrow Sweetman, *Islam and Christian Theology: A Study of the Interpretation of Theological Ideas in the Two Religions* (London: Lutterworth Press, 1947), p. 47.

[9]See Duncan Black MacDonald, "One Phase of the Doctrine of the Unity of God with Some Consequences," *The Hartford Seminary Record*, 20, no. 1 (Hartford, CT: Hartford Seminary Press, January 1910), pp. 25-26.

[10]Geisler and Saleeb, *Answering Islam*, p. 270.

[11]W. H. T. Gairdner, "God as Triune, Creator, Incarnate, Atoner: A Reply to Muhammadan Objections and an Essay in Philosophic Apology" (Madras, India: The Christian Literature Society for India, 1916), pp. 8-10.

[12]Ibid.

[13]Muhammad Abdul Rauf, *Islam: Creed and Worship* (Washington, DC: The Islamic Center, 1974), pp. 2-3.

[14]William Hasker, *Metaphysics: Constructing a World View* (Downers Grove, IL: InterVarsity Press, 1983), p. 115.

[15]Ralph C. Wagenet, "The Coherence of God: A Response to Theodore M. Drange," 2003, www.infidels.org/library/modern/ralph_wagenet/response_to_drange.html.

[16]MacDonald, "One Phase," p. 23.

[17]From Abu Hamid al-Ghazali's "The Book of Love for Allah and of the Longing for Him and of Friendly Intercourse with Him and Good Pleasure in Him," quoted by MacDonald, "One Phase," pp. 34-35, emphasis mine, and internal citations omitted.

[18]Sweetman, *Islam and Christian Theology*, p. 47.

[19]Kenneth W. Osbeck, *Amazing Grace: 366 Inspiring Hymn Stories for Daily Devotions*, hymn 360 (Grand Rapids: Kregel, 1996), "Come Thou Almighty King," hymn 161.

CHAPTER 10: GREATNESS INCARNATE

[1]For an excellent and detailed case for the Bible's affirmation of Jesus' deity, I recommend J. Ed Komoszewski and Robert Bowman, *Putting Jesus in His Place: The Case for the Deity of Christ* (Grand Rapids: Kregel, 2007).

[2]Kenneth Cragg, *Jesus and the Muslim: An Exploration* (Oxford: Oneworld Publications, 1999), p. 278, emphasis mine.

[3]Thomas V. Morris, *The Logic of God Incarnate* (Eugene, OR: Wipf and Stock, 2001), pp. 63-67.

[4]Ibid., p. 63.

[5]Ibid., p. 65, emphasis mine.

[6]Douglas Groothuis, *Christian Apologetics: A Comprehensive Case for Biblical Faith* (Downers Grove, IL: InterVarsity Press, 2011), p. 525.

[7]Ismail R. Al-Faruqi, *Christian Mission and Islamic Da'wah: Proceedings of the Chambesy Dialogue Consultation* (Leicester, UK: The Islamic Foundation, 1982), pp. 47-48.

[8]Hammudah Abdalati, *Islam in Focus* (Indianapolis: American Trust Publication, 1975), p. 160.

[9]Abdiyah Akbar Abdul-Haqq, *Sharing Your Faith with a Muslim* (Minneapolis: Bethany House, 1980), pp. 135-36, taken from F. F. Bruce, *Jesus and Christian Origins Outside the New Testament* (Grand Rapids: Eerdmans, 1974), p. 178.

[10]John Dominic Crossan, *Jesus: A Revolutionary Biography* (San Francisco: HarperCollins, 1991), p. 145.

[11]Ali Ibn Abi Talib, *Nahjul Balagha: Sermons, Letters, and Sayings of Imam Ali Ibn Abi Talib* (Elmhurst, N.Y: Tahrike Tarsile Qur'an, 1986), sermon 77.

[12]John R. W. Stott, *The Cross of Christ* (Downers Grove, IL: InterVarsity Press, 2006), p. 90.

[13]David Baggett and Jerry L. Walls, *Good God: The Theistic Foundations of Morality* (New York: Oxford University Press, 2011), pp. 51-52.

[14]See my article, 4TruthNet, "Jesus, Justification, and Justice: Answering Objections to the Justness of Jesus' Substitutionary Atonement," www.4truth .net/fourtruthpbworld.aspx?pageid=8589953013.

[15]Stott, *Cross of Christ*, p. 301.

[16]Ibn Kathir, *Tafsir of Ibn Kathir*, vol. 3 (New York: Darussalam, 2000), pp. 25-27.

[17]James Stewart, *The Strong Name* (Grand Rapids: Baker, 1972), p. 55.

[18]Stott, *Cross of Christ*, pp. 76-78.

[19]Abdu H. Murray, *Apocalypse Later: Why the Gospel of Peace Must Trump the Politics of Prophecy in the Middle East* (Grand Rapids: Kregel, 2009), p. 112-17.

[20]C. S. Lewis, *Mere Christianity*, HarperCollins ed. (San Francisco: HarperSan-Francisco, 2001), p. 133.

[21]Charles Hutchinson Gabriel, "My Savior's Love," 1905.

[22]Ali Ibn Abi Talib, *Nahjul Balagha*, p. 619.

EPILOGUE: A WORLDVIEW THAT VIEWS THE WHOLE WORLD

[1]Samuel R. Delany, *The Einstein Intersection* (Middletown, CT: Wesleyan University Press, 1998), p. 120.

[2]G. K. Chesterton, *Orthodoxy* (New York: Doubleday, 2001), p. 84.

Finding the Texbook You Need

The IVP Academic Textbook Selector
is an online tool for instantly finding the IVP books
suitable for over 250 courses across 24 disciplines.

www.ivpress.com/academic/textbookselector